S0-CXW-595

Guide to the Recommended

COUNTRY INNS

of New York, New Jersey, Pennsylvania, Delaware, Maryland, Washington, D.C., Virginia, and West Virginia

Guide to the Recommended

COUNTRY INNS

of New York, New Jersey, Pennsylvania, Delaware,
Maryland, Washington, D.C., Virginia,
and West Virginia

by Brenda Chapin
Illustrated by Olive Metcalf

The
Globe
Pequot
Press

Chester, Connecticut 06412

Text copyright © 1984 by Brenda Chapin
Illustrations copyright © 1984 by The Globe Pequot Press
All rights reserved.

No part of this work may be reproduced or transmitted
in any form by any means, electronic or mechanical,
including photocopying and recording, or by any information
storage or retrieval system without permission in
writing from the publisher.

Library of Congress Cataloging in Publication Data

Chapin, Brenda.
    Guide to the recommended country inns of New York, New Jersey, Pennsylvania, Delaware, Maryland, Washington, DC, Virginia, and West Virginia.

    Companion to: Guide to the recommended country inns of New England.
    Includes index.
    1. Hotels, taverns, etc.—Middle Atlantic States—Directories. 2. Hotels, taverns, etc.—Virginia—Directories. 3. Hotels, taverns, etc.—West Virginia—Directories. I. Guide to the recommended country inns of New England. II. Title.
TX907.C546   1985   647′.947501   84-27903
ISBN 0-87106-864-8 (pbk.)

Manufactured in the United States of America

Contents

*Dedicated to Charles T. Chapin
and my family*

How This Guide Is Arranged

The inns are listed by states, and alphabetically by towns within each state. The states are arranged in the following order: New York, New Jersey, Pennsylvania, Delaware—Maryland, Washington, D.C.—Virginia, and West Virginia. Before each state listing is a map and index, and on page 297 is a complete index of every inn in the book.

The abbreviations:

EP – European Plan—Room without meals.

EPB – European Plan—Room with full breakfast.

AP – American Plan—Room with all meals.

MAP – Modified American Plan— Room with breakfast and dinner.

BYOB – Bring Your Own Bottle.

B – Stands for Brenda. It means an additional personal comment.

The pointing fingers ☛ ☛ ☛ ☛ emphasize special features and highlights that I've encountered in each inn. While I've not actually rated the inns, the ☛ ☛ are thoughtfully and carefully inserted into the text.

There is no charge of any kind for an inn to be in this book. The inclusion of an inn is purely a personal decision on the part of the author. Please address any questions or comments to Brenda Chapin, The Globe Pequot Press, Box Q, Chester, CT 06412.

Caveats & Children

Rates: Inns may change their rates without notice. I have given the high-low figures to approximate the price range. They will give you a good indication of the prices to expect

Children: Children under age twelve aren't allowed unless stated. I have noted when children are especially welcome, or when an inn is a special family inn.

Pets: Pets aren't allowed unless stated.

Credit Cards: Visa and MasterCard are accepted unless otherwise specified in the rate section. Many inns accept other cards, too.

Reservations and Deposits: These are required with such regularity that they're not mentioned in each description. With exceptions, expect to pay a deposit or use a credit card to reserve a room.

Minimum Stay: A minimum stay of two nights on weekends

and three or more on holidays is required at some inns, as noted. If you're anticipating a vacation during busy seasons, plan ahead.

A Sound Night's Sleep: Rooms are often assigned on the basis of bed size. If you prefer a queen-sized, twin, or double bed, please ask before you make your reservations.

Televisions & Air Conditioning: Some inns have no television or air conditioning. If they are important to you, be sure to inquire in advance.

Vegetarians: The majority of inns serve meat, fish, and fowl, but within the text of the articles I've mentioned where a vegetarian dish is offered or special requests are considered.

Fly-ins: Where appropriate, I've mentioned the nearest airport for the convenience of private pilots.

Menus: Suggested menus may change.

A Few Words About Inns

One person perceives an inn as quaint while another calls it posh. I have tried to give some comparisons and my true feelings for the 136 inns in the book. I have personally visited every one, comparing, testing, and meeting with the innkeepers. Only the inns that offer both food and lodging are included in this book. If one of your favorites is missing, write me, and I'll gladly consider it for the Second Edition.

The intrigue of traveling the "inn-roads" of the Mid-Atlantic lies in discovering the remarkable diversity. I've found romantic mountain inns for couples nestled in the forest near a cascading falls, a refurbished country inn on the banks of the Hudson River where the swans swim gracefully outside the window, an elegant Victorian near the Atlantic, small-town historic Chesapeake Bay inns where famous entertainers continue the music traditions, ranch inns in the western valleys suited for the whole family, and quaint lake-district inns where cross-country skis hang before the wood-burning stove.

There are philosophers, soldiers, secretaries, international businessmen, farmers, and professional chefs who are drawn to the innkeeper's role. All ages, from the 82-year-old retired New York City art dealer to the 22-year-old woman from a Pennsylvania village who began her own restaurant during high school, have gravitated to this way of life bringing with them a broad range of experiences.

Innkeepers are a special breed—perhaps more eclectic than any other group. Most are extremely curious about people and adept conversationalists as well as downright friendly, kindly souls.

Inns go beyond breaking the monotony of standardized look-alike lodging and providing a heartwarming setting. They are retreats where we go to regroup, to grow and plan, to relax and do nothing. I know of one inn where a surgeon sequestered himself the night before a very difficult operation, and others where movies, books, and song lyrics have been written. "On the Waterfront" was written in the Black Bass Hotel, "There's a Small Hotel" was written in Colligan's Stockton Inn, and Thomas Wolfe grew up in the small inn-like guest house that his mother ran.

Inns are often the scene for weddings, and a place where couples sequester for romantic anniversaries and for that "first" weekend without the children. They are also a tradition with families and friends who gather annually for holidays and summer or winter vacations. I've run into family reunions where an entire clan has reserved a small inn for a few days. Business travelers, the innkeepers tell me, are on the rise, and many inns offer a special rate to singles.

Some inns have always been inns. Many began along the old stagecoach lines like the New York to Philadelphia run that spawned the confluence of inns along the Delaware River in the New Hope area of Pennsylvania. Waterfront inns such as the Maryland Inn and the Robert Morris Inn grew up in America's early port towns. Inns began in the wilderness and were the birthplace of towns like the Asa Ransom, the Wayside Inn, the Red Fox Tavern, and the Beekman Arms. Others were family summer homes such as the Overlook Inn where relatives and friends gathered in such numbers that eventually they decided to invite the public, too.

New or old, inns are more than palatable food and cozy lodging, they are an "inn experience."

I go to an inn, if not physically, then mentally to relax and leave the world behind. Hope to meet you at a favorite inn.

Brenda

Numbers on map refer to towns numbered
on index on opposite page

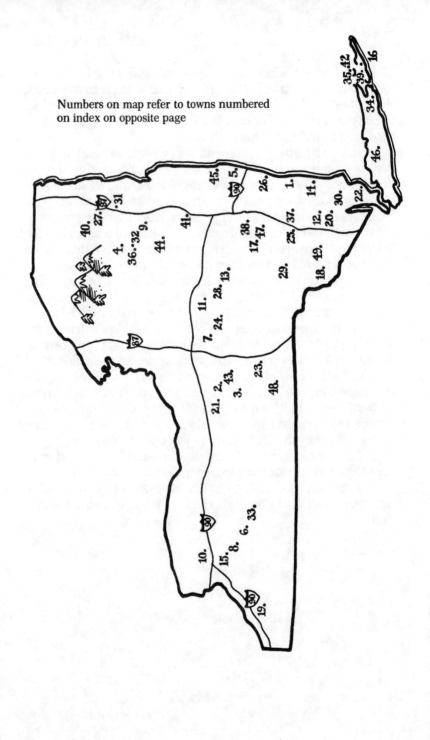

New York

Olive Metcalf

Troutbeck
Amenia, New York
12501

Innkeepers: James Flaherty and Robert Skibsted
Telephone: 914-373-8581
Rooms: 28, most with private baths.
Rates: Friday through Sunday, $475 to $680 per couple, AP, includes all spirits. Children under 1 and over 12 allowed.
Open: Midweek open to executive groups. Weekends open as a country inn. Breakfast, lunch, dinner, alcoholic beverages.
Facilities & Activities: Swimming pool, tennis courts, walled gardens, 422 acres, hiking, cross-country skiing, brook and creek, audio-visual equipment. Vanderbilt Mansion, Roosevelt Home, antiquing. Jim Flaherty maps out individualized tours.

Remember the Mad Hatter's hat in *Alice in Wonderland*? It's here. It is made from burgundy leather and is trimmed with a wide black band. Appropriately, it sits atop a magnificent hall table at Troutbeck.

Innkeeper James Flaherty is an American and at the same time a British country gentleman. With a slight bow and a warm smile he welcomes you to the ☞ exquisite manor he oversees. Without hesitation James proffers you a drink from an English teacart and politely welcomes you to discreetly appraise the harmonious surroundings. He adroitly choreographs your weekend or lets you indulge yourself in the silence of the surroundings. Whether it's for romance, the enjoyment of the great outdoors, a rousing weekend of sports and activities, or relaxation by the pool, everything is enhanced by fine dining.

The chefs are Paul and Elisabeth Milner Bernal, a pair whose talents tempt the guests to ☞ gourmandize themselves. Chef Paul might prepare swordfish Normande, baked with apples that float on sour cream and calvados. The extravagant desserts of Chef Elisabeth range from lemon-cranberry mousse to pumpkin praline mousse, or mocha dacquoise. Leave the calorie counter at home.

New Year's Eve, a black tie event, is informally known as the "weekend of excess." But every weekend could be called that.

☞ The rooms are distinguished. Jim has a talent for design and pattern. The parlours are enticing in their beauty. An unhappy thought isn't conceivable at Troutbeck.

You walk across the ☞ stream to the Century Farmhouse. Depending on whether you turn right or left from the central lobby, you're in the 240-year-old farmhouse or the more contemporary addition that blends stylistically with the old. Every room has a writing desk and a good reading lamp. The manor has an excellent library of 13,000 books. Alarm clocks are to remind you of cocktail hour.

Florence, Prince, and Montana admit you to the inn. They might bark when you arrive, but once you step over the threshold you've made three friends for life.

How to get there: Directions given with brochure request. Fly-in, Bradley Airport, Hartford, Connecticut.

☒

B: *The week's work fades away here and life returns to thoughts of leisure.*

Olive Metcalf

Springside Inn
Auburn, New York
13021

Innkeeper: William C. Dove
Telephone: 315-252-7247
Rooms: 8, 5 with private bath.
Rates: $45, double occupancy; $32 single; continental breakfast included. Request weekend fling rate. Children welcome.
Open: Closes Christmas Day and January. Dinner, bar.
Facilities & Activities: Hiking, cross-country skiing, sailing, fishing, golfing, tennis, antique shops, Seward House, Cayuga Museum of History & Art, Agricultural Museum, and winery tours. Across the road is Owasco Lake, access elsewhere.

Broadway comes to Springside Inn guests on July and August evenings. You might call ahead and inquire about the ☞ show. Comedies and musicals are favorites.

Or perhaps you prefer a quiet dinner in the dining rooms. The inn can accommodate parties large and small, intimate or expansive.

This is a second-generation family-owned inn that serves ☞ delightful foods. In the guest book I found the following: "Excellent, as usual," "exquisite," "awesome," "superb," "worthy of the raves," and "Great, I ate too much."

You can dwell on the food at an inn like the Springside. I do like their dish for those who can't decide. The combination platter is a trio of prime rib, Alaskan king crab legs, and clams casino. Sunday family dinner is a tradition that includes an array of meats and vegetables and the house cheese souffle. On Saturday evenings a pianist plays while you eat.

The lodgings are countryish, antique filled, and have pretty print curtains on several windows. The wood floors are painted black. The inn grounds are relaxing with their stately pines and the freshwater spring. Five acres behind the inn are yours to roam.

Cayuga Indians once came to the natural spring that flows in front of the inn. Later, a boy's school called Springside was built here. In 1941 it came into the Miller family. William C. Dove is a descendant.

Auburn is a town of handsome neighborhoods located on Owasco, the smallest of the Finger Lakes. Sailing on Owasco by morning, bicycling around it by afternoon, and an evening of dining and a good musical—that's what vacations are for.

How to get there: From the intersection of Routes 20 and 38 in Auburn, take Route 38 South for 3 miles. Continue past the circle at the high school, and the inn is in a short distance on the right.

🍸

I can't get your cheese souffle out of my mind. Would it be possible for you to share the recipe?—Ann Gawman, Waterloo, Ontario

olive Metcalf

Aurora Inn
Aurora, New York
13026

Innkeeper: Cindy Ladd
Telephone: 315-364-8842
Rooms: 17, 7 with private bath; 2 suites.
Rates: $25 to $65, double or single occupancy; $50 to $65, suite;
    continental breakfast included. Children welcome.
Open: April through Thanksgiving. Lunch, dinner, bar.
Facilities & Activities: On Cayuga Lake. Facilities of Wells College
    available: swimming, boating, fishing, tennis, paddle tennis,
    and golf. Ithaca, 30 minutes.

Aurora is a ☛ tranquil and pretty village. The Aurora
Inn dates from 1833, stagecoach days. It's very casual and
relaxed and has a ☛ lovely waterfront view.

Aurora's historians say the Cayuga Indians called this
settlement Village of the Constant Dawn because the eastern
ridge prolongs the sunset. They also called it Peachtown and
nurtured large peach orchards for many years.

Blended into the hillside of the town is a four-year liberal
arts women's college founded by Henry Wells of Wells Fargo
fame. The Aurora Inn was bequeathed to the college in 1943.
As a guest you may use the facilities of the college, which in-

clude a nine-hole golf course designed by Robert Trent Jones, boating facilities, tennis courts, and the lake dock.

You enter the inn down a long hallway with murals on its ceiling. To the left is the large parlour, to the right the library where continental breakfast is served. Follow the hallway to the restaurant and bar, which provide a panoramic view of Cayuga Lake. A gristmill ruin lies below.

For luncheon I ordered a fresh quiche abundantly filled with morsels of baby shrimp. The breads were fresh, hot, yeast rolls that went just right with a tossed green salad. I was wisely advised to try the chocolate chestnut pot de crème. I wonder if another exists that tastes so heavenly. Another dessert deserves equal accolades; the Oreo chestnut cream mud pie, an irresistible ice cream pie. One of the favorites served at these tables is the duckling glazed with raspberries and pears. How do collegians stay slim living near the Aurora Inn?

You can ask for a room with a water view, but with the lake so close it need not be a priority. Several rooms have been remodeled with plush mauve carpeting, and the others have nice, old-fashioned pine floors.

How to get there: From Route 20 take Route 90 south to Aurora. The inn is red brick and on the right in the village.

B: *Next door to the inn is the charming stone bank. Look carefully for the hand-painted windows. If you don't see them, go inside and ask.*

The Hedges
Blue Mountain Lake, New York
12812

Innkeeper: R. J. Van Yperen
Telephone: 518-352-7325
Rooms: 10, all with private bath; one suite; 8 cottages.
Rates: $45 to $55, per person; $18, per child up to age 14; MAP.
  Weekly rates $2 less per person per day. 10-percent gratuity
  suggested. No credit cards.
Open: Late June through early October. Breakfast, dinner. No alco-
  holic beverages in lounges or dining room.
Facilities & Activities: Swimming, canoeing, and fishing in Blue
  Mountain Lake. Tennis court, volleyball, horseshoes, Ping-
  Pong, hiking. Adirondack Museum a 5-minute drive. Family
  inn.

The Hedges is the former ☛ "Adirondack Camp" of
Colonel Hiriam Duryea on the shores of ☛ Blue Mountain
Lake. It's surrounded by tall trees, has striking views, and
the summer activities are convenient and satisfying to all
ages.

The Colonel was a demanding builder. In the tradition
of the "Great Camps" the construction is superb. The bark
exterior of the main lodge is a lovely texture. In the stone

20

house near the main lodge the woodwork shines. The new wallpaper selections in brown and gold prints enhance its perfection. The innkeepers care for their treasured "Camp" and have a good eye for decorating that's consistent with the style. The lodge and stone house are stunning for their beauty.

There's a nice little library and a busy Ping-Pong room, and big comfortable Adirondack-style furniture everywhere for enjoying the lake views. In the library sits a rustic music stand made by a guest. Music is a spontaneous evening event. If the guests are in the mood they sing and play the piano. The woodland animals probably enjoy it.

Meals are served at your reserved table in the dining room. One entree with vegetables, homemade breads, and salads is the fare. Saturday nights it's buffet style. Between 9:00 and 11:00 P.M. the hot chocolate and coffee appear with cookies, cakes, and fresh pastries for a nighttime snack.

You're not roughing it here. You have daily maid service and although the activities aren't organized, there's plenty to do. I think an afternoon of lake fun ranks high on the list of priorities. You can sit on the porch in big Adirondack chairs and revel in the view.

How to get there: From I-87 take Route 8 west. At Weavertown take Route 28 north to Blue Mountain Lake. At junction of Routes 28 N, 30, and 28 proceed one mile west on Route 28 to the Hedges Road. The inn is on the right hidden in the trees.

B: *Summertime, when it's hot in the city, a lakeside inn is the place to be.*

Olive Metcalf

Hemlock Hall
Blue Mountain Lake, New York
12812

Innkeepers: Mr. and Mrs. Robert Webb
Telephone: 518-352-7706
Rooms: 23, includes cottages.
Rates: $73 to $98, double occupancy, MAP. 12% gratuity. Children
   welcome. Request special rates for children aged 2 to 8. No
   credit cards.
Open: May 15 to October 15. Breakfast, dinner. Spirits not allowed.
Facilities & Activities: Short walk to lake, sunfish sailboats, canoes,
   rowboats, swimming, fishing, play equipment for children,
   Ping-Pong, badminton, recreation room, Adirondack Mountain
   Museum, Adirondack Lakes Center for the Arts with crafts and
   other classes, and 60 miles of hiking trails.

You enter, struck by the beauty of the ☞ woods that
compose this small and friendly lakeside mountain inn.
You're standing on shiny yellow birch floors that Robert
Webb strips and coats annually. The small pine dining room
looks into the trees and upon the mountain brook. The union
of the three common rooms is a granite fireplace with separate hearths in each room.
   The innkeepers are busy behind the scenes, but ring a

bell and they drop their tasks and greet you warmly. Young Bryan might appear with his Dad.

If you've selected a room in the inn it could be upstairs in the suite with its own private screened porch and view of Blue Mountain Lake. The rooms have the original marble sinks. You also can stay in the cottages, which are really petite pine chalets in the woods. Several have a lake view. Many have fireplaces. Robert has stacked firewood for the guests to use.

Meals are a special affair. Everyone arrives from all directions and meets one another around family-style helpings of New England corned beef on Thursdays, fish and ham on Fridays, turkey on Saturdays, roast beef on Sundays, lamb on Mondays, roast pork on Tuesdays, and chicken on Wednesdays. Breakfasts are large with hot and cold dishes. There's enough to feed Paul Bunyan, were he known to these parts.

A wide porch surrounds half the inn and lot of chairs make this a wonderful place for listening to the mountain birds sing. The nearby Mountain Museum is worthy of a long visit. If you return for an afternoon swim you walk through the trees down to the inn's beach. Rowboats and sailboats await your use at dockside.

The inn is a mile back in the woods from the main road. It's a quiet snuggery.

How to get there: From I-90 take Exit 31 at Utica and follow Route 12 North toward Alder Creek. Go north on Route 28 to Blue Mountain Lake. At the intersection of Routes 28 and 30, take Route 28 North for ¾ mile. Turn left at the inn's sign.

B: *I doubt if the innkeeper wastes a moment of his day, but ask him a question and you think he has all the time in the world.*

olive Metcalf

The Inn at Shaker Mill Farm
Canaan, New York
12029

Innkeeper: Ingram Paperny
Telephone: 518-794-9345
Rooms: 20, all with private bath.
Rates: Full weekend is $130 per person, $150 summer season. (Includes two breakfasts, two lunches, and two dinners, afternoon tea, beverages, and snacks.) Call for MAP, EPB, and midweek rates.
Open: All year. Wine served. BYOB.
Facilities & Activities: Pond for swimming, hiking loop, and a stream. Inn on 55 acres. Two Shaker museums, Tanglewood, Williamstown Theater Festival, downhill and cross-country skiing, antiquing, walking, and dreaming.

Ingram Paperny lives here with Toby, the golden retriever. Guests arrive every week and fill the inn, eating good food, socializing, and meeting Ingram. You come for ☛ journeys, on skis, on foot, and of the mind. To explore others. Maybe to chart a new path or to refine a previously properly chosen one. To clear the mind.

24

The setting is beautiful. The inn is a Shaker gristmill that dates to 1824. Ingram, the carpenter, has transformed it into his inn. The rooms are white walled, simple, have pegs for hanging your clothes, and a slate etching. There are no decorations or bric-a-brac.

The meals are a moving feast. You begin upstairs with a variety of hors d'oeuvres. Then you go to the dining room where hot towels lie at the side of your setting. Dinner is buffet style, with a choice of meats and fish and always plenty of vegetables. For desserts Ingram likes fruits in pies or more exotic recipes.

For lunch there's hot soup and homemade breads. There's always plenty to eat and hot teas with fruits or cakes on the sideboard.

The Inn at Shaker Mill has been called rustic, Shaker, and Danish primitive, but it shouldn't be. It's Papernistic. Ingram resembles a monk in appearance; in personality it would take years to fathom the man. He's quick to make a friend, an art at which he excels. This artistry pervades the inn and he creates the circumstances for a "community of strangers" that flourishes here weekly.

The inn is a study in contrasts. You enter through a casual swinging door, as if all may enter, climb a white-walled staircase to a windowless room, the inn's center. The albums turn, the fire burns in the round fireplace. Step into the next room and large picture windows connect you to the trees and stream. All is sunlight, stone, wood, and friendliness.

How to get there: From the Taconic Parkway take Route 295 East. Turn north at Route 22 and past Berkshire Farm you'll see the small wooden sign for the inn on the right, down Cherry Lane.

The Inn at Shaker Mill Farm is Ingram Paperny. His facile wit and nurturance attract a host of the most interesting and diversified guests. The meals are excellent from northern Italian cooking last summer to the sushi and misotaki of this winter's cuisine. . . .
Renee A. Mendez, New Rochelle, New York

Glen Iris Inn
Letchworth State Park
Castile, New York
14427

Innkeepers: Peter, Cora, and Paula Pizzutelli
Telephone: 716-493-2622. Write during winter months.
Rooms: 18, all with private bath; 3 suites.
Rates: $35, double occupancy, $45 to $49, suites, EP. Children
    welcome. (Specify inn or motel room.)
Open: Easter or earlier through first Sunday of November. Break-
    fast, lunch, dinner, alcoholic beverages.
Facilities & Activities: 14,350 acres of state park. Swimming pool,
    hiking, park museum, and seasonal park events.

    The Seneca Indians believed the Middle Falls of the
Genesee River "made the sun stop at midday," that's how
powerfully beautiful they are. Within view of these falls William Pryor Letchworth built his home in 1859. Today it's an
inn encompassed within 14,350 acres of ☞ a lush state park.
The park has a fascinating history of Indians, a pioneer cap-
tive, bravery, industry, and Mr. Letchworth himself.
    You drive through gently rolling farmlands to reach
Letchworth Park, but you must peer down a 400-foot gorge to

see the river valley below. Through meandering forests you reach the Glen named Iris for the colors that mist over the falls. The waters roar an impressive 107 feet down to the gorge bottom. The setting is exquisite.

The ☞ fall-view suites are very popular. The other rooms are petitely comfortable. Seven rooms are "motel" rooms.

There are ☞ lithophanes around the doorway entrance. They are lovely black and white images that transmit light. To the right is the Victorian parlour. Opposite is the gift shop. The library has a river view. One dining room has a wall of windows looking out to the multiple shades of green of the lawn and trees, There's a reflecting pool outside the dining room window. The house was built to reflect its image here. Mr. Letchworth chose his site well.

Guests may come down to the dining room for a large breakfast before they set off to explore the park. If you choose the smallest dining room you're actually eating where the philanthropist himself ate. When you return to dinner, you'll find such entrees as boneless chicken stuffed with fresh spinach, mushroom, rice, and pine nuts, and tender slices of milk-fed veal sautéed in lemon butter. The pastries are baked right here and are delightful.

Cora and Peter have been joined by their daughter, Paula, in the inn. Together they do a wonderful job as inn-keepers.

An ☞ elegant high-span train bridge passes above the falls. Twenty trains cross it daily. Cora said the post cards in the gift shop are accurate views of the Middle Falls. But only by going there do you experience the wonder of their beauty.

How to get there: From I-390 take Exit Route 20-A West to Route 39 West. South of Castile follow signs to Letchworth State Park and Inn. After park entrance follow signs.

B: *An inn in the middle of a State Park overlooking a waterfall is the best of all possible worldly places.*

Olive Metcalf

The Brae Loch Inn
Cazenovia, New York
13035

Innkeeper: H. Grey Barr
Telephone: 315-655-3431
Rooms: 12, all with private bath.
Rates: $58 to $125, double occupancy; $48 and up, single; continental breakfast included. Children welcome; under age 6 free.
Open: All year. Dining room closes Christmas Eve and Christmas Day. Dinner, Sunday brunch, bar.
Facilities & Activities: Golf privileges for guests. Robert Burns birthday celebration late January. Horseback riding, cross-country skiing, hiking, canoeing, Lorenzo House, August antique auto show and quilt show, carriage driving competition in July.

You enter the inn on a rich plaid carpeting. Wander into the ☞ Wee Gift House. Kilts, tams, wool sweaters, and wooden golf clubs from St. Andrews are a pleasure to touch and see. Suzanne Barr Longo, the innkeeper's daughter, has wonderful taste and stocks the shop well. This is a ☞ bonny Scottish inn where the staff wear kilts.

At the base of the stairs is a beautiful table carved with a Robert Burns' quote. Suzanne says Robert Burns' birthday is celebrated to the tune of 🖝 bagpipers and drummers. What a delightful tradition in this second- and third-generation inn.

Dinner is the thing here. First you go to the Victorian lounge downstairs where the appetizer buffet tantalizes with a broad assortment of breads, fresh greens, vegetables, and relishes. Dinner offerings are tender spring lamb chops with mint jelly, Finnan Haddie, a filet of Scottish haddock steamed in cream with thinly sliced onion, puff pastry steak pie, generous cuts of sirloin or ham, and more. Children's portions are served. The "Scottish Thistle" is purple and white and appropriately served in a thistle-shaped glass. Try the ice cream pie made with strawberries and topped with an oozing hot fudge for a summertime dessert. That's hedonism.

The 🖝 four rooms with fireplaces are the oldest. They are special beauties. The Queen Elizabeth has Biblical verses on the tiles surrounding the fireplace and a long window seat where you can curl up and read. The bed has a lovely canopy. In the Princess Diana Room the white eyelet canopy is so pretty it will make brides blush. The Robert Burns Room has striking plaid curtains. Other rooms are pine paneled and comfortably furnished.

The inn is across the street from a park and Cazenovia Lake and is in walking distance from the Lorenzo Mansion. Cazenovia is a pleasant little college town. Just the right setting for a night's stay in a Scottish inn.

How to get there: From I-81 take Exit Route 20 East to Cazenovia. The inn is located at the ninety-degree turn where Route 20 merges with Main Street across from the park. It's painted brown and is on the left. Fly in, Canastota Airport.

🥛

B: *The innkeeper wears the tartans of other clans as well as his own to share the experience. How thoughtful.*

Olive Metcalf

Lincklaen House
Cazenovia, New York
13035

Innkeeper: Helen Tobin
Telephone: 315-655-3461
Rooms: 21, all with private bath; 4 suites.
Rates: $45 to $80, double or single occupancy; $80 to $110, suite;
  EP. Children and pets welcome. Two- or three-night minimum
  stay on college and holiday weekends. Checks preferred.
Open: All year. Breakfast, lunch, dinner, tavern.
Facilities & Activities: Swimming, fishing, sailing, water-skiing on
  Cazenovia Lake, tennis, horseback riding, and cross-country
  skiing. Chittenengo Falls. Winter Festival early February, July
  Fourth parade, August quilt and antique auto show, Lorenzo
  House.

John Lincklaen founded the town of Cazenovia. He
named the town for his boss. ☛ Lorenzo House is the historic residence of Lincklaen overlooking Cazenovia Lake that
is now open to the public.

The Lincklaen House, which was named for John
Lincklaen but not built by him, was constructed in 1835 with
bricks made locally. It made a grand stagecoach stop. The ☛
East Room lobby is stellar. The ceilings are very high and the

woodwork is painted white. It's light and cheerful. Williams-burg is the theme here. Groupings of chairs, couches, and tables invite you to sit and relax. A smaller lobby has a game of chess ready.

In the dining room you can sit before the fireplace and munch on hot savory popovers that precede the meal. The cheese souffle is light and the ☞ coffee toffee pie, which may not be on the menu every day, is velvety smooth and refreshing.

During summer, lunch is served on the outdoor patio, which is surrounded with potted flowers. Then take a stroll about town and down to the lake or take a drive through the rolling countryside.

In the Seven Stone Steps Bar on wintery evenings, Fred Palmer, a local banjo and guitar player, entertains. On the walls are local scenes painted by an artist. They are lovely cold weather images of sleighs and horses that take you back in time. Every inch of the table is carved with initials. Some whittlers had the audacity to try and carve their initials over the old ones. Above the bar it says, "Enjoy thy drink."

The rooms are pleasantly updated and several have been beautifully stenciled by a local artist. They have tiny portable televisions and are very tidy. The hallways are large and impressive.

In 1985 the inn celebrates ☞ 150 years of continuous operation. Helen Tobin adds, "We never close. I believe an inn should be open to travelers twenty-four hours a day." Her pleasant staff helps, of course.

How to get there: From I-81 take Route 20 to Cazenovia. The inn is located on the town's main street, 79 Albany Street.

☿

B: Christmas Brunch at the Lincklaen House is a delightful local custom.

Olive Metcalf

The Butternut Inn
Chaffee, New York
14030

Innkeepers: Keith and Arletta Slocum
Telephone: 716-496-8987
Rooms: 3, all with private bath.
Rates: $45, double occupancy, EPB. MAP available. Children welcome.
Open: Closes January and reopens Valentine's Day. Closes Mondays and Tuesdays. Breakfast, lunch Wednesday through Friday, dinner, bar.
Facilities & Activities: Downhill and cross-country skiing, snowmobiling, hiking, boating, fishing, swimming, golfing, Winter Wonderfest, antiquing and country auctions, Letchworth State Park, and Rorycroft shops in East Aurora.

  This is a genial inn in farm country. You're likely to meet every member of the Slocum family during a visit to the inn. You'll like them right off. Butternut trees to the north cut the winds and provide tasty meats for homemade cakes, besides giving the inn its name.
  Arletta is the head innkeeper, but every Slocum has a hand in the inn's smooth operation. Arletta prepares the ☛ dessert menu, which is a glorious compilation of earthly de-

lights. Keith tends bar and prepares the delicious soups. Son, Chef Ken, prepares the popular entrees; Eric is a college student, handyman, and waiter; and daughter Denise is a full-time mother and waitress.

Arletta has decorated the guest rooms with comfortable antiques and well-chosen reproductions. How fresh and cheery they are, and clean, too. This farmhouse was extremely well constructed during the 1930s. There's steam-radiator heat, which means a sound sleep.

There is much to do here. Nearby are rolling hills for cross-country skiing, two alpine ski centers, and the spectacular Letchworth State Park that is worthy of a day's visit. On your return, you can relax in the lounge area where there is a small fireplace and buggy seats to sit on with early American magazines to read.

The Strawberry Porch with a southern exposure is another nice place to be during an afternoon. The tablecloths and napkins are strawberry prints. Two more petite dining rooms are very inviting.

You'll find the daily menu on the chalkboard posted outside. The food is scrumptious. My fresh ☞ perch baked over spinach was nutritious and delicious. The spicy ginger muffins were delicate and light. There are five types of salad dressings. The curry dressing was my favorite.

In the morning coffee arrives in a silver pot and a cold glass of champagne accompanies your hearty breakfast. You'll probably linger longer than you expected.

How to get there: From Springville take Route 39 East to Route 16, and go north toward Chaffee. The inn is on the left at the intersection of Route 16 and Genesee Road.

❦

B: *A lounge reserved for the guests is a signal the innkeepers have your comfort at heart.*

olive Metcalf

The Balsam House
Chestertown, New York
12817

Innkeeper: Frank Ellis
Telephone: 518-494-4431 or 494-2828
Rooms: 20 all with private bath; one suite.
Rates: $85, double occupancy on weekends; $65 midweek; EP.
    $135, double occupancy on weekends; $108 midweek; MAP.
    Children welcome.
Open: Closes first two weeks in November and April. Breakfast,
    dinner. Lunch can be arranged. Bar.
Facilities & Activities: On Friends Lake. Swimming, canoeing, sail-
    ing, fishing, barge cruise, ice skating, and bicycling from inn.
    Cross-country skiing, downhill skiing at Gore Mountain, snow-
    mobiling, hayrides, sleigh rides, hiking, hot-air ballooning, an-
    tiquing, visit to garnet mine, and Lake George Winter
    Carnival.

Before the initial taping of the Bob Newhart television
show about a country inn in Vermont, the star, Mary Framm,
spent a fall week at the Balsam House doing what you might
do and collecting ideas for the show. She jogged, canoed,
went horseback riding, took a boat trip on Lake George, and
spent a morning ballooning. The Balsam House provides an

☛ activity sheet before you go. You check your interests and they help coordinate your vacation. That's a sporting idea.

Frank Ellis has put heart, soul, and beauty back into a 19th-century inn. It is beautifully restored in a pretty setting, and decorated with a ☛ palette of vivid colors. You'll probably go home and repaint your house.

In the parlours the purple walls contrast artistically with the oriental carpets, the lace lampshades, and lovely fabrics. One parlour closes off and you can select a movie tape to enjoy in private. The hallways are pale peacock blue. Some rooms are in fresh peach colors with antiques and modern twists for comfort. One suite is two story; you climb to the bedroom on a winding stairwell.

On a summer evening you can smell the ☛ pine trees that surround the inn. Sit on the patio off the bar and watch your steak being grilled while you sip an apéritif. There's often jazz in the bar, which is painted a striking green and red. You also can go for an evening barge ride and enjoy your drink on Friends Lake with new or old friends.

We sat in the sunny atrium and plotted the next day's activities in these lovely mountains. The dinner menu is in French and the variety is divine. Translated you'll find sweetbreads sautéed in lemon butter with capers and shallots served with spaetzle, half-crisp duckling with an aromatic sauce of red wine and truffles served with saffron rice—how interestingly scrumptious.

We found stories and "finds" posted on a wall that were discovered during the inn's restoration. Frank has a respect for the past as well as for our comfort in the present.

How to get there: From I-87 take Exit Route 9 North toward Warrensburg. Go 4 miles to Route 28 and proceed on Route 28 for 3 miles to Potterbrook Road and turn right. The Balsam House is in 4 miles on the left side of the road.

B: *Frank is from Mobile, Alabama. He's a successful businessman who lets his romantic nature flourish in a lovely lakeside inn.*

Olive Metcalf

Asa Ransom House
Clarence, New York
14031

Innkeepers: Bob and Judy Lenz
Telephone: 716-759-2315
Rooms: 4, all with private bath.
Rates: $60 to $65, double occupancy; $45, single; EPB. Children
welcome. No credit cards. No smoking in rooms.
Open: Closes January 2 to 31, Christmas, occasional holy days, and
every Friday and Saturday. Lunch on Wednesdays, and dinner
Sunday through Thursday. Taproom.
Facilities & Activities: Wine tastings. Niagara Falls is 40 minutes
away, Genesee Country Village, Art Park in Buffalo, opera in
Lancaster, Kodak tours in Rochester, antiquing, golf, sports
and winery tours.

On Main Street in Clarence you turn in at the red railing for some really fine food and a ☛ handsome inn named
for Asa Ransom, the founder. You'll marvel at the size of
Asa's original inn that warmed travelers around the hearth.
The little taproom is wood from ceiling to floor. It must have
been very reassuring after a few days in the wilderness. It
still is.

The library, with a cozy fireplace, is just the right size

for reading or visiting. An unfinished jigsaw puzzle awaits your attention, or you may have a casual browse through the gift shop off the library. Your frame of mind can't be other than 🖝 relaxed and receptive in this warm inn.

Upstairs the rooms are furnished stylishly in Early American. One has marvelous American eagles stenciled around the ceiling. Each room has good reading lamps.

The area is rich with activities. Bob gives firsthand advice on cultural events and wineries. Fall through spring he holds occasional wine tastings presented by local wineries.

On the menu the wines are rated from 0 to 7 for dryness to sweetness. Very helpful. But before dinner you might try one of the taproom's special drinks, like the rum and coconut.

Dinner is delicious. There's a smoking and non-smoking dining room. Take your time with the menu. Children read theirs from the apron of a Raggedy Ann doll or the sail of a boat. Judy came up with that innovation. The soup arrives in a hot bucket and is ladled out to suit your appetite. Then walnut spice muffins and breads arrive with three flavors of butter, unsalted, apple, and honey. I had the 🖝 goulash and dumplings, which were served with a mouthwatering sauce seasoned just right. There also are vegetarian selections. When I had leisurely finished that course, the divinely rich walnut pie came with real home-brewed coffee in a silver pot.

You can request tapes of radio shows to listen to in your room. The Shadow, Fibber Magee and Molly, and others.

How to get there: From I-290 take Exit Route 5 West to Clarence. The inn is on the right in the city limits one block before the park. Fly-in, Buffalo International Airport.

B: *When you see the inn, you're not surprised to find out that Judy has an art background.*

olive Metcalf

The Clinton House
Clinton, New York
13323

Innkeeper: Robert Hazelton
Telephone: 315-853-5555
Rooms: 4, all with private bath.
Rates: $40 to $45, double occupancy, includes coffee and juice in
  the morning. Children welcome.
Open: Closes for Christmas. Lunch, dinner, bar.
Facilities & Activities: Jazz Wednesday evenings by known musi-
  cians. Hamilton College, golf, tennis, Kirkland Art Center, fac-
  tory outlets in Utica, one hour from Adirondacks.

☛ Jazz on Wednesdays. You might keep that in mind
before you visit Clinton.

On the pretty town square in the college town of Hamilton is the Clinton House. The university crowd comes
here—the professors, not the students. The rooms are pleasant, each different, and the food is excellent.

There isn't really a lobby, but the bar is the relaxing
kind, and in the rooms are chairs and often hassocks. The
Madison room has pineapple wallpaper, wooden floors, and a
huge mirror in the bathroom. How nice. Some rooms have
carpeting; one has a handsome fireplace. I chatted with a

young professor who was lecturing at the university. She agreed it's comfortable lodging.

The inn was built in 1826 as a private home. It had a reputation for gracious hospitality. After World War II it became the Alexander Hamilton Inn which explains the AH in the grill work at the entrance. After a fire in 1976 it was restored and became the Clinton House.

This is a veal house. The portions are large and the succulent veal Alfredo is covered with scallions, artichoke hearts, and crabmeat. Before dinner you're served fresh vegetables with onion dip and fresh hot bread with garlic butter. Even the fresh salads had scrumptious dressings. I don't like to admit this, but I couldn't resist dessert. The chocolate pie was superb. Precede this with a New York State wine and you're glad that you have a room in the inn.

This town is a great place for a stroll. A town dog came along to keep me company. We circled the town square and he went home to supper.

How to get there: From I-81 exit onto Route 12 North to Route 12 B to Clinton. The Clinton House is at the east end of the town park near the fire station.

B: *If you like factory outlets, you'll love Utica. There are historical sights here as well.*

Olive Metcalf

Hudson House
Cold Spring, New York
10516

Innkeeper: Mary Pat Bevis
Telephone: 914-265-9355
Rooms: 14, all with private bath; one suite.
Rates: $70, double occupancy; $60, single; $110, suite; continental
    breakfast included. Children welcome.
Open: Closes January, but call. Lunch, dinner, bar.
Facilities & Activities: Bicycle rental on premises. Sailing cruises
    on the Hudson aboard 32-foot Mariner, ice skating, swimming,
    boating, hiking, golfing, fishing, Vanderbilt Mansion, Roose-
    velt Estate, antique shops, wineries, Boscobel Mansion, West
    Point.

    The key to your room is attached to a ☞ heart-shaped
pillow that fits perfectly into the palm of your hand. On the
walls hang merry patchwork quilts of sheep, cows, and a very
fat black cat perched on a large hassock. To find the hassock
you go into the Half Moon Bar, which looks more like a living
room than a bar. Near the fireplace sits an unusual player
piano. You can relax on the couch and listen to tunes from
the early 1900s. Backyard animals parade across a shelf near
the ceiling. It's the ☞ homiest bar I've ever seen.

Hudson House is a restored historic inn, formerly known as the Hudson View Inn. It's painted mocha. Several rooms have small balconies. You can sit and enjoy the river, the mountains, West Point, and the village cupola across the street. At dawn you can walk the river bank and feed the swans. You might be up that early because you're eager for the continental breakfast, a hearty assortment of muffins, Danish pastries, breads, and raspberry preserves. A day in the area should include antiquing in the town, which you can walk in an afternoon, and a cruise on the Hudson River.

In the river-view dining rooms a large paisley print is reversed in the curtains. Don't ignore the cream of mushroom soup. Almost as you're seated, a hot loaf of molasses bread arrives. Taste the grilled shrimp that comes with a tangy barbecue sauce. Mmmm. . . . the food is good here.

In the rooms the wallpaper patterns are reversed in the curtain fabrics and some of the lamps are French water bottles. The towels are one-hundred-percent cotton and thick. Period guest rooms are available.

In the entryway hangs a piece of prose called "Everywhere Town." I extracted this quote: "You know you live in a small town when you don't have to signal your turn because everyone knows where you're going."

I can size up a town by its inn. This one is antique-filled, classy, has a sense of humor, and loves good food.

How to get there: From the Taconic Parkway take Route 301 West to Cold Spring. Follow Main Street to the deadend at the railroad. Turn left and immediately right over bridge. Go right again and left, which resumes on Main Street. The inn is at the end of the street on the river's edge. (Railroad splits Main Street.)

❊

B: "Half Moon" was the ship Henry Hudson sailed up the Hudson in search of China. Search out the Half Moon Bar in the Hudson House and you'll search no further.

olive Metcalf

The Cooper Inn
Cooperstown, New York
13326

Innkeeper: Robert Holiday
Telephone: 607-547-2567
Rooms: 20, 15 with private bath.
Rates: Spring/Fall: $66 to $70, double occupancy; $50, single; July
    to Labor Day: $70 to $75, double occupancy; $55, single; conti-
    nental breakfast included. Four original inn rooms by special
    request. Children welcome. Golf packages.
Open: May through October. Call. Breakfast, lunch, dinner, bar.
Facilities & Activities: Full privileges at the Otesaga Hotel: Heated
    swimming pool, 18-hole golf course, tennis, children's play
    area. Baseball Hall of Fame, James Fenimore Cooper House,
    Farm Museum, boating, sailing, canoeing on Otsego Lake,
    hiking, biking, and touring the back roads.

   The Cooper Inn is on lovely grounds in downtown Cooperstown. Dating from 1812, it is stately and surrounded by
flowers and a high iron fence. A few blocks away on the ☛
shores of Otsego Lake is the Otesaga Hotel, which owns the
little inn.
   ☛ Four rooms remain from the original inn. They are
large and simply elegant with very high ceilings. The other

rooms are an addition and nice for families sharing adjacent rooms. They have wooden sea chests for storing extra blankets.

Oil paintings and early American scenes decorate the inn. Three downstairs lounges are big and comfortable. One has a television if it's a rainy day. Like many New York inns, there is air conditioning. More often the guests open the screened windows and enjoy the natural evening breezes. A pretty brook runs behind the inn.

From here it's only a short walk to the Baseball Hall of Fame and Doubleday Field. All the bubblegum cards evoked wonderful memories for my husband. He swears he could smell the gum. He loved it.

By six o'clock everyone changes from sporting clothes into dressier things for dinner at the Otesaga Hotel. You look forward to a different menu every night. It's cyclical and changes every fourteen days. The menu appropriately includes several American classics and continental fare. I like the variety of choices. Everything from prime rib, a broiled steak, seafood, to a cold meat platter and a golden brown omelette for dinner. You can even order cookies for dessert occasionally, which is almost a novelty but still an American tradition.

You might want to carry a copy of *The Deerslayer* by James Fenimore Cooper to read by the side of ☛ Otsego Lake. He called this lake "Glimmerglass" in the book.

How to get there: From I-88, exit onto Route 28 and go north to Cooperstown. Proceed through the intersection of Routes 80 and 28 on Chestnut Street to the light. The inn is across the street.

🍺

B: *Cooperstown is a lovely town.*

Olive Metcalf

The Hickory Grove Inn
Cooperstown, New York
13326

Innkeepers: Jim and Polly Renckens
Telephone: 607-547-8100
Rooms: 4, all with private bath (3 baths are across the hall from
their room).
Rates: $38, double occupancy, continental breakfast included.
Children welcome.
Open: March 30 to October 31; November depends on weather.
Dinner, bar.
Facilities & Activities: Lake access across the road. National Base-
ball Hall of Fame, James Fenimore Cooper House, Farm Mu-
seum, tour on Lake Otsego, biking, hiking, swimming,
cross-country skiing, Utica factory outlets, beautiful back
roads, and antiquing.

Hickory Grove is one of those inns where you'd love to
be stranded during a winter snowstorm. The companionship
is topnotch. Jim and Polly are innkeepers with a fresh down-
to-earthness who do everything in their inn. Their three children help by sharing their toys with young travelers.
Last year Jim and Polly raised the roof in one dining
room and found a craftsman to restore the rosetta pattern

around the ceiling. In the 🖝 bar hangs a collection of signs from the area. Remember "Burma Shave"? A player piano with a stack of music rolls sits against the wall.

Ask to see the "bell." To call guests to dinner from the lake a bronze bell was rung. Over fifteen years ago a neighbor stole the bell because a previous owner used it to crack bottles. It was getting badly marred. After Jim had Hickory Grove open for three years the neighbor returned the bell to a deserving innkeeper who appreciated history. What a lovely story. Jim just naturally collects oral histories from his neighbors and learns more all the time.

One guest room has beautiful oak furniture and a feather tick. Everyone doubts its comfort at first, then loves it. Another room has the original wood floor and a cozy blue quilt with matching blue print wallpaper. Every room has antiques. Sometimes the rooms have nightshirts that say Hickory Grove. Sometimes the nightshirts walk away in the night. An upstairs room with a television is reserved for a 🖝 guest lounge. Thoughtful touch.

You can see the lake from the porch-dining room. Jim and Polly precede every meal with fresh relish and 🖝 apple muffins. There is one recipe that's a secret. It's the shrimp tempura. The menu has a special section for children and grownups with small appetites. You may order seven selections with child-size prices and portions. Friends and family can order their own private smorgasbord of fried chicken, shrimp, and barbecued ribs. After that there's a smorgasbord of things to do. It's a marvelous area.

How to get there: From I-88 take Route 28 North to Cooperstown. Take Route 80 out of town toward the museums. The inn is 6 miles north, on the left.

☗

B: *There's a big front porch with one of the longest pews ever seen outside a church and a nice wooden swing.*

Olive Metcalf

Old Drovers Inn
Dover Plains, New York
12522

Innkeeper: Charles Wilbur
Telephone: 914-832-9311
Rooms: 3, all with private bath.
Rates: Rooms from $90, double occupancy, EP.
Open: Closes last three weeks of December. Restaurant closes Tuesday and Wednesday. Lunch, dinner, bar.
Facilities & Activities: Antiquing, Hyde Park, Berkshire Music Festival 1½ hours.

The tavern fireplace is the central structure supporting the Old Drovers Inn. Around this the inn has settled over 235 years. The main floor rises and falls as a very old building will.

New England cowboys, or cattle drovers, developed their appetites driving their herds to the New York market. They stopped at inns along the way; among them was the Old Drovers Inn.

The inn hasn't changed a great deal in the past few years. There are overstuffed chairs and couches. Years ago books were selected for the library and they are still here.

It's a very settled inn on a country road with trees for neighbors and a seasonal antique shop across the road.

The mural in the Federal Room where guests have breakfast is bright greens and pinks. It's an artist's vision of nearby country scenes.

The linens and towels are in a large glass-doored hall closet ready for inspection. There are down comforters on the beds during winter time. In the largest bedroom, which is painted a bright yellow, is a very old, irregularly shaped, working fireplace. Many of the colors in the inn are bright solid hues, deep pinks, greens, and yellows.

☞ The restaurant is an important part of this inn. The chef has been here for four years. She carries on the traditions of the Old Drovers. Browned turkey hash is one of those traditions. So is the cheddar soup. You can request a copy of the recipes. The menu is a big blackboard that hangs from the old rafters. The dining room surrounds the tavern's fireplace and enormous hurricane lamps sit on the tables.

You might order a rum and pull up to the bar before dinner. Just like the old drovers might have on a gentle spring night during cattle-drive season.

How to get there: From I-84 take Route 22 North toward Dover Plains. Three miles south of town will be a sign for the inn. Turn right at the sign and continue to deadend; the inn is on the right. Inn guests drive to south parking lot and enter through the main floor stone walk.

B: *The* ☞ *Key lime pie is delicious. Not too sweet and not too sour. It's just right.*

Olive Metcalf

The Roycroft Inn
East Aurora, New York
14052

Innkeeper: Edythe Turgeon
Telephone: 716-652-9030
Rooms: 15, 10 with private bath; 7 suites.
Rates: $35 to $55, double occupancy; $32 to $40, single; continental
    breakfast included. Request ski packages. Children welcome.
Open: All year. Lunch, dinner, Sunday brunch, bar.
Facilities & Activities: Eleven buildings on Roycroft Campus on
    National Register of Historic Places, campus tours, Roycroft
    Convention in June, occasional guest speakers, crafts shops,
    antique shops, summer theater, swimming pool, Farmers Mar-
    ket on Saturdays, Millard Fillmore House.

The Roycroft is more than an inn. Founded in 1895 by
Elbert Hubbard, millionaire, philanthropist, and eccentric, it
is a ☞ landmark in the arts and crafts movement. It represents a philosophy and a way of life. Its symbol is the hand,
head, and heart.

The Roycroft Inn provided lodging, work space, and a
stimulating environment for the craftsmen and famous
guests who were drawn together by Hubbard to produce fine
quality books, manuscripts, furniture, metals, and philoso-

phy. Edythe, an experienced restaurateur, became inspired through Hubbard's descendants to restore the inn. It's a project she views as ever-continuing. She wears an elegant Roycroft bracelet made by a contemporary silversmith, one of twenty or more in the area's craft guild who carry on the traditions of fine craftsmanship.

It's an unusual inn. I found it fascinating. On the door is carved: "We awaken in others the same attitude of mind we hold towards them." In the hallway is geometric wallpaper composed from the Roycroft dish pattern that's still used today. The furniture is geometric "mission style" with Morris chairs in some rooms. The Ruskin Room is preserved as an informal museum that depicts life here in Hubbard's day. The dining room looks over the Japanese garden. The lounge is large with murals painted by Alain Fournier that circle the room. Pictured are the eight wonders of the world, the eighth being Elbert Hubbard, explained his great-granddaughter. "He wasn't a modest man," she says.

On the menu are several appetizers. The Working Man's Soup is a crock of blackbean soup topped with scallions and baked with a thick layer of New York cheese. The more elegant main courses list Lobster Fournier, a blend of lobster and spinach mousseline.

East Aurora is just the right size for a small town. There's a Five and Dime, theater, music in the parks, farmers markets, a swimming pool, and quality activities that make a stay a pleasurable series of small interconnected events. You can leave the car and explore life afoot again.

How to get there: From I-90 take Route 400 East to East Aurora. Follow Route 20A West to South Grove Street, turn left, and the inn is in one block on the left at 40 South Grove Street. Fly-in, Buffalo International Airport.

Even if you don't save room for dessert try a couple bites of the pumpkin walnut pie!—Cynthia Adele Gray, Forest Hills, New York

olive Metcalf

Hedges House
East Hampton, New York
11937

Innkeepers: Ken Baker and Richard Spencer
Telephone: 516-324-7100
Rooms: 11, all with private bath.
Rates: Available upon request by writing the inn at 74 James Lane.
Open: Closes February 1 through March 15. Open weekends from
   March 15 through Memorial Day, and Labor Day through Jan-
   uary; lunch and dinner served. Lunch and dinner served
   Tuesday through Sunday from Memorial Day to labor Day.
   Taproom.
Facilities & Activities: Beach, bicycling, ice skating, antiquing,
   shopping, tennis, boating, swimming, museums, fall foliage.

   At the entry to the village, tucked behind the pond and
ensconced in the trees, is the mocha-colored Hedges House.
It's bordered by a white picket fence and flowers skirt the
pathways. Open the door, and a little bell that is suspended
from a green velvet bow will ring. That ring is followed by a
meeting with innkeeper and restaurateur, Ken Baker.
   Ken's pulse beats with the inn. He's rarely away. He
lives here, and he makes the inn a "home in the Hamptons"
for his guests.

Built in 1774, the inn's light pine floors, small informal taproom, and more formal living room have a New England flavor. Outside the ☞ slate patio is shaded by magnificent old trees.

The rooms are light and sunny. I like the white-walled contrast with deep lush curtains and the ☞ designer linens. It might be a fluffy, flouncy white eyelet, or a soft peach-toned Laura Ashley. In the Strawberry Room the kelly green carpet contrasts with the gigantic ceramic strawberry atop the chest of drawers.

For total privacy you can request the rooms with the raised fireplaces and a romantic table for two at dinner. Ken reads his guests' desires with an intuitive friendliness. "Some guests wouldn't think of coming in summer," says Ken. They love the quiet times, ice skating on the village pond across the road, a walk along the isolated beach, and coming back in for a warm grog by the fire.

The innkeepers say the menu isn't influenced by their Beverly Hills restaurant, En Brochette, but I wondered. For lunch I had a scrumptious ☞ advocado omelette, beautifully garnished with fresh summer fruits. My companion was delighted with a light summery salad of curried chicken. The evenings are delicious here, with such offerings as steamed lobster, shrimp scampi, jalapeno beef "en brochette," and American paella. Sunday evenings are an ☞ international buffet that requires reservations.

Breakfast occurs around a long pine table before the fireplace in the front dining room where you never know who you might meet.

How to get there: From 1-495 exit onto Route 27 and go east to the first stop light and deadend. The Hedges is opposite. Circle around the Village Pond to reach the inn. Fly-in, East Hampton Airport.

B: *Thanksgiving and Christmas dinners have all the trimmings. Guests arrive for the holidays as well as Hamptonians who wouldn't think of turkey at home.*

olive Metcalf

The Maidstone Arms
East Hampton, New York
11937

Innkeepers: Rita and Gary Reiswig
Telephone: 516-324-5006
Rooms: 16, all with private bath; 2 cottages.
Rates: $70 to $165, double occupancy, continental breakfast included. Credit cards accepted for lodging, not in dining room. Three-day minimum stay on summer weekends, 4-day minimum on holidays. Children allowed.
Open: Inn open year round. Restaurant closes January and February; and Tuesdays July through September; Mondays and Tuesdays May, June, October, and November, Mondays, Tuesdays and Wednesdays March, April, and December. Dinner, tavern.
Facilities & Activities: Sunbathing, boating, windsurfing, swimming, biking, tennis, museums, shopping, antiquing, ice skating.

Wear your summer whites. You'll look stunning seated in the white wicker-filled sun porch. The wicker is covered with a dreamy pastel fabric and in one corner hangs a painting of a large cow in a pasture. By winter the fire is burning and across the street is the village pond, ideal for ice skating.

Whatever the season the day starts right at the Maidstone Arms, with a fresh piping-hot cup of roasted coffee. Try the orange spice and raisin muffins. *Gourmet* has published the recipe and they're delicious.

Rita aptly refers to the guest rooms as "froufrou." It's a tasteful froufrou with antiques and white frilly cotton curtains, strawberry curtains, or dotted swiss curtains and contemporary stylish prints for the bedding. One of the suites has a skylight, another room a handsome antique set. In my room was a black Windsor chair with a handmade pillow that matched the handmade quilt spread across the white iron and brass bed.

I like the pace here. There are the comings and goings of guests but it's not busy, busy. On a summer afternoon the inn might even be temporarily deserted with everyone off to the beach or strolling downtown for some fun shopping. Around evening everyone returns to shower and dress for dinner.

The dining room is in the skilled hands of Morris and Nancy Weintraub. There's a vegetable selection for vegetarians; the asparagus vinaigrette has a light, savory dressing. Traditional ☞ roast Long Island duckling is served with orange sauce and wild rice, and ☞ poached sea bass is permeated with a lobster sauce. The food is superb with a French influence.

After a day of exploring the Hamptons or relaxing on the beach, you find yourself relishing your evening return to the Maidstone Arms.

How to get there: From Route 495 East, exit onto Route 27 East into East Hampton. The inn is on the left at 207 Main Street, shortly after the left turn after the light. Fly-in, East Hampton Airport.

B: *East Hampton was originally called Maidstone for the settlers who arrived here in the early 1600s from Maidstone, England.*

Olive Metcalf

The Palm at the Huntting Inn

East Hampton, New York
11937

Innkeeper: Linda Calder
Telephone: 516-324-0410
Rooms: 26, all with private bath.
Rates: Provided upon request. EP. Children allowed. No accommodations for infants.
Open: Late April to early November. Cold buffet breakfast, dinner, tavern.
Facilities & Activities: Beach, tennis privileges, golf, charter fishing, boating, swimming, windsurfing, bicycling, horseback riding, shopping, Guild Hall Theater, museums.

The warm woody tones of the oak wainscotting reflect the evening lights. Little Tiffany lamps and unusual ornate lamps highlight small oak tables in front of plush green sofas. Oak mirrors, no two alike, hang on the wall opposite the oak bar. You might order wine that has been aged in oak barrels and settle into an oak booth to savor its flavor.

"There are nine Palm Restaurants across the country," explains the raven-haired innkeeper, Linda Calder, "all interconnected through family. The first opened in 1920 in New York City. Our chef married into the family." Another family member decorated the tavern and dining room. Linda decorated the individual rooms, which she is constantly redecorating as if they weren't already perfect. Several have chintz on the walls, wicker, antiques, and fresh flowers in the hallways. They are 🖝 soothing stylish rooms. Linda adds her cheerfulness to these already bright surroundings.

A white picket fence encircles the inn. Follow the path under the trees out to the 🖝 English garden. In summertime the butterflies bounce between the flowers. There's a profusion of hollyhocks, baby's-breath, daisies, and lilies. If you arrive in the cool of the early morning while the dew is on the grass you can pull up a cushiony lawn chair and settle back. But the day hours are for the beach. Ask Linda for a beach pass.

Toward evening, the candles are lit downstairs. Maybe you've plans to walk up the street for a movie after dinner. You're starved after a long walk on the beach and an invigorating day of sun and sand between the toes. You're glad you skipped lunch.

Say, the Palm, and it stimulates images of 🖝 large thick cuts of steak and four-or-five-pound lobsters along with handsome portions of fresh salads, potatoes, clams casino, shrimp cocktail, and fresh pastas. Think hearty servings and you're in the right ball park.

How to get there: From Route 495 East follow Route 27 into East Hampton to where it merges with Main Street. The inn is at 94 Main Street on the right-hand side past the Presbyterian Church and Guild Hall Theater. Watch for the white picket fence. East Hampton Airport, fly-in.

B: *The Home Sweet Home Museum is up the street. The song was written by the lyricist while away from this little house in East Hampton.*

55

Olive Metcalf

1770 *House*
East Hampton, New York
11937

Innkeepers: Miriam and Sidney Perle
Telephone: 516-324-1770
Rooms: 10, all with private bath.
Rates: Provided upon request. July, August, and holiday weekends,
    4-day minimum; 2-day minimum other weekends.
Open: All year. Restaurant open every day but Thursdays from July
    4th through Labor Day. Open Friday and Saturday rest of year.
    Thanksgiving and New Year's dinners served.
Facilities & Activities: Beach, bike riding, boating, swimming, ice
    skating, museums, Theater Guild Hall, downtown Hampton a
    short walk.

   100% charm. 100% antiques. 100% delicious = 1770
House.
   Miriam's amber eyes flash warmly when she talks about
food. She recalls family occasions that were food extravagan-
zas. Sometimes her father would bring home the most in-
credible lobsters. Among the dishes she serves on antique
china is an occasional ☛ fresh lobster with an aromatic
mustard vinaigrette sauce on the side or a gray sole stuffed
with thick lumps of crabmeat.

The inn is a most unusual place. "A timely inn." Everywhere you look are visuals. Clocks, ornate French grandfathers, beautifully carved American timepieces, mantel clocks, and decorative clocks that merge into a soft tick-tocking in the dining room.

The original post office of East Hampton forms one part of the small inn office. Miriam and Sid share their love of antiques. Each guest room in the inn is uniquely decorated. Three more sumptuous and spacious guest rooms are in the innkeepers' own home, a short walk from the inn. One room looks out to the ornate gardens where you can have coffee in the morning under the bougainvillea and admire the Greek and Italian sculptures.

Dinnertime. Knowing Miriam's French culinary training you might select a filet mignon with a perfectly blended Sauce Diane, or knowing her love of New Orleans cuisine it might be a shrimp and chicken gumbo filled with tender jumbo shrimp and boned breast of chicken. The fresh herbs are grown outside the kitchen door.

For dessert her assistant, her daughter, might serve a raspberry mousse sprinkled with fresh rosebuds, a macadamia nut pie, or a chocolate amaretto rave that's been well named. The desserts are as expertly prepared as everything else. Miriam is a perfectionist who entertains more than cooks as if her best friends are coming to dinner.

How to get there: From Route 495 exit onto Route 27 into East Hampton. The inn is past the Village Pond on the left-hand side at 143 Main Street. East Hampton Airport, fly-in.

☒

The evening's atmosphere is set by the clocks, candlelight, and classical music softly played in the background. The 1770 House serves an ecstasy of tastes.—Nedra G. Boelts, Washington, D.C.

Olive Metcalf

The Redcoat's Return
Elka Park, New York
12427

Innkeepers: Tom and Peggy Wright
Telephone: 518-589-6379
Rooms: 14, 7 with private bath.
Rates: $65 to $70, double occupancy; $45 to $55, single; EPB. Two-
night minimum on holiday and high-season weekends.
Open: Closes April 1 to May 25 and November 1 to November 15.
Restaurant closes Thursdays. Dinner, picnic lunch can be ar-
ranged, bar.
Facilities & Activities: Downhill skiing at Hunter Mountain, cross-
country skiing, hiking on adjacent Catskill Game Preserve,
horseback riding, golfing, tennis. Trips to Woodstock, Frederick Church Mansion, and antiquing.

Front and center on the bar rests a brass sign: "On this
site in 1877 nothing happened."
Three dogs and a fat golden-haired cat named Quilty
call this home and make it their duty to be on hand for a
group greeting with a lot of tail wagging. Out front hangs a
double-sided portrait of an English gent and lady, the
friendly innkeepers, Tom and Peggy Wright.
On a winter night you can 🖝 visit with Peggy in the

bar, and later have dinner near the woodburning stove. Over the stove hangs a gigantic moose head. Many people don't know how to properly care for a moose head, but Tom does. Twice a year he rubs Vaseline into it. Above the bar are paintings of sporting dogs, and on the walls of the dining room are the Redcoat's, Tom's, souvenirs. There's a scarf his father saved from a world prizefight posted along with the story.

Peggy wallpapered every room in the inn, except two that Tom helped with. They are country patterns and in my petite room were Wyeth prints. She has a lovely kitchen cupboard in one of the small dining rooms. In another is a large fern terrarium. Peggy is an energetic lady, and between the two of them they are a down-to-earth balance of ☞ fun and hospitality.

Tom has been around the world a few times as chef on several Cunard line ships including the Queen Mary. His ☞ steak and kidney pie is juicy and tender and the crust on the apple pie thin and light. The hearty servings of two fresh vegetables that come with the entree are beautifully seasoned.

At breakfast the tiny menu has a socket plug with a smiling face on it. I felt rejuvenated after a plateful of Tom's French toast.

The inn is in a flat country valley surrounded by ☞ mountains. In the springtime you step out the door for a peaceful wildflower hike. There's good skiing and Woodstock isn't far.

How to get there: From I-87 exit onto Route 23-A West to Tannersville. Turn left at the traffic light in Tannersville and follow the winding road to the Police Recreation sign. Turn left and continue. Turn right at the sign for the inn. Total mileage from Tannersville is 6.4 kilometers.

♟

B: *Peggy handed me the key to my room and said, "You won't need this but take it anyway." You feel safe and cozy here.*

Olive Metcalf

Inn at Lake Joseph
Forestburgh, New York
12777

Innkeepers: Ivan Weinger and Monique Jirard
Telephone: 914-796-1202
Rooms: 8, 5 with private bath.
Rates: From $49, per person, double occupancy, MAP and after-
noon tea. Two-day minimum on weekends.
Open: All year. Breakfast and dinner for guests.
Facilities & Activities: Lake Joseph, inflatable 8-foot raft, rowboat,
fishing, ice skating. Hiking, cross-country skiing, lawn games,
2 bicycles available for rental. Antiquing and summer theater
nearby.

This inn is a Country Victorian mansion with weathered
shingles for siding and an elegant cupola above the entrance.
Located in a clearing in the woods, it's a beauty that dates
from the 1880s. This was home to Cardinal Hays who occasionally hosted Cardinal Spellman.

There are three living rooms and a formal dining room.
Three windowseats stretch across one wall of each living
room. You look out to the expansive lawn that stops at the
woods.

If it's winter the fireplace has a big fire burning. There's a cup of hot tea in your hand and yummy cakes and cookies are on the coffee table. If it's summer you're thirstily drinking iced tea or a freshly minted lemonade and biting into a spice cookie still warm from the oven, and you'll probably be seated on the screened porch. You also can eat dinner on the porch, in the formal dining room with the exquisitely ornate chandelier, or very casually around the wooden table in the kitchen.

Monique prepares chef's choice. Diet restrictions are discussed prior to arrival. If it's summer she picks fresh vegetables and herbs from the garden outside the kitchen door. Among her favorite entrees are chicken cordon bleu, veal marsala, Rock Cornish hen, and elaborate vegetable casseroles. Desserts include Black Forest cake, apple pie, or profiteroles among others. She bakes all the breads: among her tastiest is a whole wheat that's woven with ribbons of flavorful cinnamon.

The rooms are individually and 🖝 tastefully decorated by Ivan. Every one is sunny and quiet, as you'd expect in a grand old mansion. The bathrooms are tiled and huge. The woodwork trim around the doors is a handsome detail.

Ivan says when an innkeeper can no longer remember each guest by his first name, that's when an inn has grown too large.

How to get there: From I-84 take Route 97 West at Port Jervis. Turn north on Route 42 to Forestburgh. Go through the blinking light and on the right is a Farmers Market; turn right up the hill. The inn is in one mile on the right-hand side.

🌾

B: *You can have temporal peace in this lovely setting.*

olive Metcalf

The White Inn
Fredonia, New York
14063

Innkeepers: David Palmer and David Bryant
Telephone: 716-672-2103
Rooms: 21, all with private bath.
Rates: $49 to $69, double occupancy, continental breakfast included. Two-night minimum stay on college weekends. Children welcome.
Open: All year. Lunch, dinner, tavern.
Facilities & Activities: Chautauqua 30 minutes, winery tours, Lake Erie 3 miles. Antiquing, boating, downhill skiing, cross-country skiing, golfing, fishing, cultural activities at college during school year.

Two very tall maple trees mark the entrance to the inn. They cast a long shadow in the snow. They were planted in 1821 by Squire White who first named the inn. The deed says if the trees are ever destroyed or removed by unnatural causes the property reverts back to the living White descendants. "We want nothing to happen to our trees," say the innkeepers. I believe their aesthetic interests are foremost.

Out front hangs a Duncan Hines sign. It belongs here. For those of you who don't remember, Duncan Hines went around the country finding good places to eat and sent a brochure to his friends. His name became the stamp of approval. Hines would still approve.

The inn has been freshly restored by two former academics-turned-innkeepers. Each has a Ph.D. in philosophy. David Palmer is the congenial official greeter, while David Bryant is the congenial behind-the-scenes-restoration expert. The 🖝 rooms are a delicious blend of quality antiques. Some have Jenny Lind reproductions. The designer wallpapers, curtains, and carpets are stylishly coordinated by art historian, Nancy Palmer. In one room a cherry wood bedroom suite is strikingly handsome. In another, the elegant living room suite will make you desirous of staying the season. Spic and span, clean and quiet, and sunny. What pleasant rooms these are.

Pass through the lobby to the unusual slate top bar. Here's an amiable gathering place. Above the fireplace hangs the White family coat of arms. You're an hour from Buffalo here and Buffalo wing tips (chicken wings, not shoes) are served with a special hot sauce.

Ask the headwaiter to help you make a dinner selection. You might have the sea scallops bathed lightly in Pernod, or the rognon de veau served with tender mushrooms. To keep in mind the region, there's duckling served with local Fredonia grapes. A basket of 🖝 fresh homemade yeast rolls provides a tasty counterpoint. The chef was a member of the U.S. Culinary Olympics in 1984, and his cooking shows he's an award winner.

The area is 🖝 beautiful with its vineyards and gently rolling farmlands. There's a marvelous antique barn in nearby Stockton. Then you catch the ferry across Lake Chautauqua in time to catch an evening concert.

How to get there: Take Route 17 East from I-90, then take Route 20 North to Fredonia. The inn is in town on the left side of East Main Street. It's white brick.

B: *Innkeepers are certainly a diverse and interesting crowd.*

Bird and Bottle Inn
Garrison, New York
10524

Innkeeper: Ira Boyar
Telephone: 914-424-3000
Rooms: 2, both with private bath; 2 suites.
Rates: $155 to $180, double occupancy, MAP. $95 to $120, double
occupancy, EPB, Sunday through Thursday. Two-night mini-
mum on weekends.
Open: Closes Christmas Day, and from November 1 to May 1 closes
Mondays and Tuesdays. Lunch, dinner, bar.
Facilities & Activities: Five acres and a brook. Boscobel Restora-
tion, West Point, mansion tours, Tarrytown, Roosevelt Estate,
Vanderbilt Mansion, nature preserve, and variety of sports.

No, the guests at the Bird and Bottle Inn did not eat the
large flocks of wild pheasants that lived in the inn's meadow.
But yes, the inn does serve a scrumptious pheasant, roasted a
golden brown and napped with a Madeira wine sauce. The
"bird" is a stuffed pheasant who sits in the window near "the
bottle." Frankly, no one can remember how they came to be
paired. Probably by someone of good sense.

The inn was a resting place for the horses and the folks
on the New York to Albany stagecoach run beginning in

1761. It served as a farm for several years and in 1940 was restored to its original purpose. The Map Room is the oldest part of the inn. I like the plain English title for the bar: the Drinking Room.

Be sure to sign the guest book in the foyer. You might sign next to well-known socialites, judges, or New York producers.

Tall men occasionally duck when they climb the narrow hallways to the rooms, and high-heeled women find the floors of meandering levels. These irregularities add to this charming inn. The bedrooms are intimate with four-poster and queen-size canopied beds and working fireplaces. Each room is 🖝 tastefully decorated.

Since the rooms are Modified American Plan you may want to eat out for lunch. But it's hard to resist a pewter tankard of ale and a fresh chicken and tarragon sandwich made on homemade bread. Your ale is free when you order lunch. In the summertime you'll lunch beside Indian Brook and still have time to tour Boscobel or go down to Rip Van Winkle country.

At dinner the pâté is an aromatic blend of ground pork and veal and is made on the premises. The smoked trout with horseradish cream sounds heavenly. The Bird and Bottle chicken is served with my favorite stuffing, oyster. Before you leave, ask the chef to make an extra loaf of pumpkin bread so you can take it home.

How to get there: From Taconic Parkway, go north to Route 202, and then go left 3 miles to Bear Mountain Parkway to Route 9. Go north 8 miles on Route 9 to the sign, turn right, and off the road is the inn. Fly-in, Dutchess County Airport.

B: *In 1982 the movie, "Kiss Me Goodbye," starring Sally Fields, James Caan, and Jeff Bridges, was filmed here.*

olive Metcalf

The Inn at Belhurst Castle
Geneva, New York
14456

Innkeepers: Robert J. and Nancy Golden
Telephone: 315-781-0201
Rooms: 10, all with privte bath; 2 suites.
Rates: May through October, $65 to $175; November through April, $55 to $100; double occupancy; continental breakfast included. Children welcome.
Open: Closes Christmas Day. Breakfast, lunch, dinner, Sunday brunch, bar.
Facilities & Activities: Dock on Seneca Lake in front of inn. Boating, fishing, water-skiing, sailing. Hiking. Public golf course nearby, winery tours, skiing 1 hour, Corning Museum 45 minutes, Watkins Glen 45 minutes.

New York State has lovely inns and among the gems is the Inn at Belhurst Castle. It offers ☞ grand elegance, privacy, and a view of beautiful ☞ Seneca Lake.

The inn was built in 1810 by an expansive millionaire. During the 1930s "Red" Dwyer, a local legend, transformed it into a gambling casino. It became a luxurious inn under the guidance of the present owners, Nancy and Robert

66

Golden. Each of the rooms is named for Belhurst owners, past and present.

On the way to your room you may want to see the wine spigot ensconced in marble in the hallway. It's serve yourself for guests. You may even have a 2 a.m. glass.

The fireplaces throughout the inn, including those in the guest rooms, are masterpieces of craftsmanship. One is surrounded by mosaics. Others are simply lavish marble. The woodwork gleams; it is polished to a permanent sheen. The rooms are like this, too. And they have views of the graceful grounds or lake.

A daily luncheon buffet is served in season. The meat loaf bathed with creamy sauce was superb. Next came veal baked in cheese and tomatoes, salads, breads, and a table of luscious desserts. The chocolate sour cream cake and fresh hot coffee were made to order. The dinner menu is more sophisticated and thoughtfully offers a vegetarian specialty.

One oddity is the bust of Henry Clay, a former owner, that sits on the lawn. It has never rested on a pedestal. It looks surrealistic, as if he's standing in the ground. The grounds are a dreamy picture. Ducks float on the lake. There's beauty everywhere for aesthetes to appreciate.

Several wineries are within driving distance. You can tour and taste by day and wine and dine by night.

How to get there: From I-90 take Route 14 South to Geneva. Continue south. The inn is on the left, the lake side, of Route 14 on the outskirts of Geneva.

B: *Staying at the Belhurst is like going to your rich uncle's for the weekend. You know, the one who's the connoisseur.*

67

olive Metcalf

Greenville Arms
Greenville, New York
12083

Innkeepers: The Stevens Family
Telephone: 518-966-5219
Rooms: 20, 14 with private bath.
Rates: $45 to $55, per person, double occupancy; $55 to $60, single;
    MAP. Two-night minimum on holidays. Children allowed.
Open: Mid-April to mid-November. Breakfast and dinner for house
    guests. BYOB in your room. No credit cards.
Facilities & Activities: Swimming pool. Near Catskill Mountains.
    Painting workshops May through October, Monday through
    Friday.

    Built by William Vanderbilt in 1899, this inn has eleven
bedrooms, and dining and living rooms. The carriage house,
with nine more rooms, is located in the rear. The rooms in
the inn are furnished with handsome antiques, and plush
carpeting softens your footsteps through the hallways.
    The house has the feeling that you are staying with your
great-aunt, the one who's very proper and likes everything in
its place. It has always been well cared for. It is clean and
pretty. The woodwork throughout the house is 🖝 exquisite.
In the entryway are ornate lattice pieces above the doorways.

Built-in cabinets with leaded windows are in the dining room and are filled with china. There's a grand old bookcase in one of the sitting rooms, and the parlour is very cozy. Delicate white lace curtains frame the windows everywhere.

Greenville is a small town. During the summer and fall it becomes filled with painters who come to work outdoors and take occasional naps by the lovely swimming pool. You can enroll in a ☞ painting course under some fine teachers.

The meals are ☞ all-American and prepared by Barbara Stevens. She doesn't use a microwave because this isn't a restaurant, and she serves only to house guests. Barbara has the touch for baking and prepares all the breads and desserts in her well-equipped kitchen. A summery lemon sour cream pie, a fresh raspberry cream cheese pie, and a chocolate cake filled with a delicious cream and chocolate filling are among her specialties.

"We are lucky," explains Laura Stevens, "the fish market delivers daily as does the butcher shop." One entree is served each evening along with fresh soups and vegetables. Among the dishes Barbara prepares are a ham and yam casserole with chopped walnuts; roast turkey, mashed potatoes, and peas served with Moravian orange rolls; baked fresh haddock; and chicken breast with a seasoned cream cheese filling. Meals are served around a long table and are a genial highlight. What a pleasant way to enjoy your evening after a day of lounging by the pool or exploring the beautiful countryside.

How to get there: From I-87 exit onto Route 23 West to Cairo. 90 north on Route 32 to Greenville. The inn is in town. It's a white house with a big front porch on the left side of Route 32.

B: *The swimming pool behind the inn is most inviting.*

olive Metcalf

Benn Conger Inn
Groton, New York
13073

Innkeeper: Margaret J. Oaksford
Telephone: 607-898-3282
Rooms: 2, with shared bath; 2 suites with private bath.
Rates: $45 to $65, double occupancy; $60 to $75, suite EPB. Well-behaved children allowed, but no infants. In May and October, two-night minimum on weekends.
Open: All year. Call about Christmas. Breakfast and dinner served to house guests. BYOB.
Facilities & Activities: Swimming club in Ithaca available for guests' use. Golf, hiking, cross-country skiing, downhill skiing, wineries, and antiques.

Coming to the Benn Conger is like visiting a good friend who owns the largest private mansion in a small town. It's friendly, warm, and very comfortable. It's just the right style for the president of a large American company, and that's who Benn Conger happens to have been. President of the Smith Corona Corporation.

The innkeeper is a delightful woman who has a fascinating sideline. She's the librarian at the Cornell School of Hotel Administration. We fell into a discussion of 100-year-old

menus and food and life before fast foods. She knows marvelous things about food, food lovers, and food books. When
you're not discussing good food you can spend the rest of
your time eating.

The inn is a Georgian-style mansion, located on a high
promontory. You can find your way around the five acres that
extend out from the back door. Dutch Schultz lived here,
using the mansion as a hideaway. Now you can hide away
without even needing an excuse.

You enter under a high portico into a large foyer.
There's a small elegant sun porch in the front of the house. A
large living room is to the right followed by an equally large,
formal dining room. For dinner you don't pin down the innkeeper to any set menu. As a professional cook she charms
the chicken, beef, or fish into delicious symphonies: roasts,
crisply baked chicken or heavenly creamed versions, and fish
filets with sauces. It's all in the style of the Eastern United
States. This is chef's whimsy served with complimentary
wine.

The rooms are spacious, especially if you stay in the
Groton Suite, Dutch's room. The house was built long ago for
luxury. The furnishings are a blend of antiques and other
comfortable pieces. Electric blankets are available.

Breakfast is a hearty affair served in the ☛ bright conservatory in the back of the house where three Palladian
windows open out to the woods. It crossed my mind while I
was sitting here: "So this is how he lived, a leader of corpo-
rate America and United States Senator, graciously and in a
☛ home of quality."

How to get there: From Ithaca take Route 366 to Freeville, and then
go north on Route 38 to Groton. At the junction with Route 222
turn left or west on West Cortland Street.

Olive Metcalf

Colgate Inn
Hamilton, New York
13346

Innkeeper: Thomas Gilpatrick
Telephone: 315-824-2300
Rooms: 41, all with private bath; one suite.
Rates: $48 to $54 double occupancy; $40, single; $100, suite; continental breakfast included. Children welcome; under age five free.
Open: All year. Lunch, dinner, bar.
Facilities & Activities: Golf privileges on Seven Oaks Golf Course. Guests may use university pool, gym, and tennis facilities during specified hours. American Village on Lake Moraine, Farmers Market on Saturdays, May through October, Christmas caroling on the green.

The Colgate Inn nourishes educators, young scholars and their parents, and guests to the area. The present inn dates from 1925, but an inn has stood here since 1800.

The inn is stone and white wood with square pillars. It faces the triangular village green, which is the site of the local Farmers Market every Saturday from May through October.

The rooms are furnished with stenciled Hitchcock

chairs and dressers with American eagle knobs. The prints are a variety of early Americana. The lamps are ceramic books, appropriate since Colgate University is nearby and professors and alumni make this a busy scene with school-related functions. Everything is clean, modern, and spacious.

The lobby is immense. The staircase is lovely. It climbs past large windows to the rooms. To the left is the Salmagundi (meaning potpourri or medley) dining room. Its wooden floors and walls are a dark brown hue. The prim lady that hangs on the wall as you enter the dining room casts a stern eye on the scene. I never let portraits interfere with my dining.

After an active day, come here for a thick cut of roast prime rib followed by a big piece of apple pie and American coffee. The chef also has ☞ delightful surprises on the menu, such as iced gazpacho and lobster à la menagerie.

You may use the ☞ school's facilities when you stay at the inn. This includes the Robert Trent Jones-designed eighteen-hole golf course. You'll want to walk through the pretty town. Hamilton was the site of the Great Chocolate Crash of September 27, 1955. A train derailed, sending several cars up a side track. Two rail cars were filled with chocolate bars. Every child in Hamilton learned about the crash by the next morning and unloaded the spilled contents without charge to the shipper.

The early Hamiltonians were primarily Baptists. They were very education oriented, and from their efforts to educate young Baptists for the ministry, Colgate University was born. The campus rises with the hillside on the south side of town.

How to get there: From Route 20 take Route 46 South 4 miles to Hamilton. Route 46 becomes Route 12 B after 2 miles. The inn is the large building on your left that faces the town square to the south.

⧖

B: *A college-town inn in the fall exudes a special vibrancy.*

Olive Metcalf

The Depuy Canal House and The Brodhead House
High Falls, New York
12440

Innkeeper: John Novi
Telephone: 914-687-7700
Rooms: 3, with one shared bath.
Rates: $58, double occupancy, continental breakfast included.
Open: Inn open all year, but may close in March. Call. Restaurant
   open Thursday through Sunday, and closes Christmas Day.
   Checks preferred.
Facilities & Activities: Culinary Institute of America, Vanderbilt
   Mansion, Roosevelt Estate, parks, cross-country skiing, anti-
   quing, hiking, boating, and eating.

Chef John Novi leads his guests on an 🖝 eatable journey down gustatory lane at the Depuy Canal House. It's filled
with visual surprises and palatable sensations. He instills ex-
citement and artistry into the food.

From the second floor balcony John has built a special
viewing spot. You look down into the 🖝 magnificent kitchen
and watch him in action with his bevy of helpers. It looks like
an artist's studio. Enormous copper pots dangle from the raf-

74

ters, home-canned tomatoes, pickles, and onion marmalades line the shelves. This is a kitchen where the unusual is usual.

I can't read a Novi menu without developing a huge appetite. You find fresh eel smoked over mesquite; triangles of phyllo fat with ricotta and mozzarella, ham and salami, and eggs and picorrino cheese; boneless breast of veal filled with fresh corned beef with a dollop of Dijon mayonnaise. These are only a few of the appetizers. Tiffany of the Sea is lobster, scallops, tilefish, and mussels steamed in a sauce of cream, saffron, leeks, and white wine, served with black mushrooms and Japanese-style noodles. Novi ignores international food boundaries. I even like the way he writes, "Eight course dinner: Forty Bucks."

John began ☞ restoring the Depuy Canal House at a youthful 22. It's friendly, like he is. In one room is his ginger bottle collection. In the bar are two photographs of his ☞ paintings and an original. He's not just an artist in the kitchen. His paintings are wonderful country farm scenes of special places.

The rooms are in the Brodhead House, just across the street. You could take old-time photographs in these Victorian settings. The stenciling is a recent touch. Parasols sit against the wall in one room.

On the first floor of the Brodhead House is a restaurant run by Chef John Cotton. He served an externship from the Culinary Institute in Novi's restaurant. A recent guest gave me a raving account of the soups and fish. He smokes red snapper over mesquite, then serves it with a bold Yucatán sauce.

With two superb restaurants on hand, you can't go wrong here.

How to get there: From Route 209 take Route 213 East to High Falls. The Depuy Canal House is on the right and the Brodhead House is opposite in the yellow brick house.

B: *Eight months after Innkeeper Novi opened his restaurant he received* ☞ *four stars from Craig Claiborne.*

Olive Metcalf

L'Hostellerie Bressane
Hillsdale, New York
12529

Innkeepers: Jean Morel and Madeleine Morel
Telephone: 518-325-3412
Rooms: 6, 2 with private bath.
Rates: $55 to $85, double occupancy, EP. No credit cards.
Open: Closes February and March in 1986 and March and April in
1985. Closes Mondays and Tuesdays, and just Mondays in July
and August. Dinner, wine cellar, alcoholic beverages.
Facilities & Activities: Tanglewood, 30 minutes. Skiing at Great
Barrington and Jiminy Peak, Berkshire Playhouse, Sharon
Playhouse, antiquing, sports of all four seasons. Adult inn.

If a twinkly eyed dark-haired man wearing a white tunic
answers the door, it is Chef Morel. Even his name is a food, a
delectable mushroom. It's with food on your mind that you
arrive at this 🖝 classic French four-star inn and restaurant
that overlooks the crossroads in the hamlet of Hillsdale.

In the tradition of the great chefs of France, Chef
Morel's grandmother was a great cook, and a Cordon Bleu
graduate. At the age of 14 Jean Morel arrived in New York
with a letter of introduction. He spoke no English. Today his

culinary degrees and awards fill a lengthy paragraph and his best introduction is his menu.

To unravel the 🖙 secrets of Chef Morel's kitchen you can spend four days taking a cooking class. "I'm not far out on nouvelle cuisine," says Chef Morel. "You can call me 🖙 'light classic.' " Be assured that all is absolutely fresh. The "amiable" innkeeper oversees the inn with a relaxed good nature, but he's a tough man when it comes to the raw foods that enter his domain.

Only sixty-four seats compose the small dining rooms, so the attention to detail is "de rigueur." When a grand china plate arrives it might be filled with the freshest of sole filet stuffed with moist and tender scallops, or rack of lamb for two dripping with juices, or tender chicken breast ordained with fresh crayfish and cream.

Chef Morel prepares one of my absolute favorites for desserts, a feathery light crepe filled with a savory sweet hazelnut cream. For those traditionalists there are the classic French desserts, the mousse, the caramel custard, the cheeses, and, of course, pastries that defy the imagination.

A rich burgundy carpet in the hallway opens to 🖙 clean, comfortable rooms furnished with carefully chosen colonial reproductions. Several have raised imported Mexican tiles in the bathrooms, and two have Palladian-style windows. The fresh linens promise a sound night's sleep.

As I left Chef Morel asked naturally, "Is there anything else I can get for you?" Then the telephone rang. It was another gourmet on a quest soon to be fulfilled. Perhaps it was you.

How to get there: From I-684 North from New York City, take Route 22 North to Hillsdale. The inn is located on the northwest side of the intersection of Routes 22 and 23.

B: *On the menu is the quote: "La critique est aisee..L'art est difficile."*

olive Metcalf

The Bark Eater Lodge
Keene, New York
12942

Innkeepers: Joe Pete Wilson and Harley McDevitt
Telephone: 518-576-2221
Rooms: 13, all with shared baths; one cottage.
Rates: From $26, per person, double occupancy, EPB. Children
    welcome, lower rates. Weekly rates available. 8 percent service
    charge. Two-night minimum stay on weekends. No credit
    cards.
Open: Closes in April. Call. Breakfast, lunch, dinner, BYOB.
Facilities & Activities: Cross-country and downhill skiing, hiking,
    swimming, Lake Placid, fishing, canoeing, golfing, tennis,
    horseback riding, ice skating. Inn to inn ski touring can be ar-
    ranged.

    This 150-year-old farmhouse inn is a ☞ mountain har-
bor of friendliness. Skiers by the winter fire, hikers on the
summer porch, and fine food the year around. "You wouldn't
believe the foods that come from that stove," said a guest
who pointed at the plain old stove. But the scent of herbs told
me Harley is someone who devotes time and talent to fine
cuisine. I saw baby Katie smile when we discussed desserts,

78

the pumpkin cheese pies, the maple cream parfaits, and the pots de crème.

If you want professional cooking tips you ask Harley. For professional ski tips there is no one more qualified than Joe Pete Wilson. He's an Olympic skiing competitor who also has competed nationally in the biathlon, cross-country skiing, and bobsled. He's written a book on cross-country skiing. And he's got a great sense of humor to boot.

Joe Pete's parents took summer guests here. It was a stagecoach stop before that. Now it's a year-round inn, with a two-acre pond for swimming, 200 acres for hiking and skiing, and at hay baling time you can pitch in and give a hand or go off to the mountains for some fine fishing.

If your visit coincides with that of the Outward Bound Hurricane Island school you're in for some brave tales. They come here before they leave and stop again on their way home.

The furniture is a diverse collection of family pieces; among them are antiques old and new. There are mountain views from the windows. It's a place where you can feel comfortable moving down the hallways in your pajamas. If you want more privacy you might take the log cottage that's a short drive away. A new carriage house with four private baths is under construction.

Dinner is in front of the fireplace and served with plenty of wine. Bring your repertoire of life's stories and you'll create a few new ones to tell next year.

How to get there: Take Exit 73 from I-87 and go north to Keene toward Lake Placid. One mile past Keene bear right on Alstead Hill Road at the inn sign. The inn is in ½-mile, on the right, adjacent to the barn.

This is our fifth visit to The Barkeater. The food has always been prepared in an outstanding manner.—The Anonymous Gourmet

Olive Metcalf

The Horned Dorset Inn
Leonardsville, New York
13364

Telephone: 315-855-7898
Innkeepers: A host of innkeepers
Rooms: 2 rooms and 2 suites, all with private bath.
Rates: $60, double or single occupancy; $85, double occupancy, suite; $110 for four occupying suite; continental breakfast included.
Open: From January to May 1st restaurant and inn close two days a week. Call each season. Dinner, cocktail lounge for guests. No credit cards.
Facilities & Activities: Hiking or cross-country skiing through 100-acre apple orchard at hilltop. Cooperstown, New York, with Baseball Hall of Fame, James Fenimore Cooper House, and Farm Museum, is 30 minutes away.

The Horned Dorset is named for the beautiful Dorset sheep. This elegant inn is an aesthete's retreat and never advertised. Inside awaits ☞ gourmet dining, classical music, sophisticated surroundings, and a lovely time. It's an outstanding inn in the middle of an unlikely setting in the hamlet of Leonardsville.

Between them the four innkeepers have several advanced literary degrees. They were former educators and in the antiquarian book business. Fifteen-thousand books are still in the attic awaiting space.

You enter under an ornate church chandelier, three impressive Palladian windows give southern exposure, and a marble fireplace and travertine marble staircase are to the left. You ascend to a small library, which is the cocktail lounge. The three dining rooms are elegant. One has a wall lined with walnut bookshelves. A harpsichord sits waiting for its weekend player. A beautiful spray of flowers scents the air.

The rooms are next door, in the white Federal house with the high picket fence. In its parlor is a piano and a glass-covered coffee table filled with curling medals and magazines. My husband loved the old *Life* magazines. One of the innkeepers says they gave so many away as gifts that they finally decided to keep these for the guests.

Upstairs two angels sit in the hallway. It's a heavenly inn. Down comforters on the beds; the sheets turned down before you retire; and the antiques are well-chosen quality pieces. Each room has a table. Fresh fruit and a crystal pitcher filled with icewater sits on a silver tray. The next morning your continental breakfast is placed here. Again on a silver tray, the coffee in a silver pot, the croissants flaky and hot, the raspberry jam homemade. One room and one suite have pretty, working fireplaces. ☛ What a romantic place.

Chef Don Lentz, innkeeper, prepares the classic French cuisine. The ☛ tournedos châteaubriand melt in your mouth. The rice is flavored with pine nuts. The ☛ chocolate bombe is delectable. Kingsley Warren, innkeeper, knows wines and even several New York vintners. Bruce Warren, innkeeper, serves your meal. Harold Davies, innkeeper, directs you toward the hilltop to watch the setting sun from the apple orchard.

How to get there: From Route 20 go 4 miles south on Route 8 to Leonardsville. The inn is on the east side of the road. Fly-in, Utica Airport.

olive Metcalf

Lanza's Country Inn
Livingston Manor, New York
12758

Innkeepers: Dick and Yolanda Lanza
Telephone: 914-439-5070
Rooms: 6, all with private bath
Rates: $58, double occupancy; $44, single; EPB and taxes and gratuities included. Three-night minimum on some major holiday weekends.
Open: Inn closes two weeks before Christmas. Restaurant open daily in July and August, but closes Wednesdays rest of year. Lunch, dinner, taproom.
Facilities & Activities: Fly-fishing on the Beaverkill and Willowemoc rivers, horseback riding, swimming, boating, hiking, biking, golfing, woodland trails for cross-country skiing, 4 covered bridges, triple-arch stone bridge, and Roebling suspension bridge.

Roscoe, New York, is a haven for American fly-fishing. This is the southern Catskills and the valleys are wide, long, and beautiful. You'll find crystal clear streams and ponds for this "quiet sport."

Fly-fishing is a year-round sport. From October through March the no-kill areas are open for those with barb-less hooks who aren't satiated with the April to September fishing season.

The inn is on a mountaintop. It is shingled wood exterior with a side deck nearing completion. You enter from the side to a small lounge area that focuses around a woodburning stove. The rooms are attractively decorated by Yolanda, and 🖝 two have canopy beds. In one room is a family-heirloom quilt made by Yolanda's grandmother. Such a treasure it is.

Lanza family portraits and mementos line the upstairs hallway. You see the Lanza history told through photographs, diplomas, awards, and birth certificates.

A potential new family member is always given a trial run at the inn, joke Yolanda and Dick. They come right into the kitchen and pitch in or out they go. This is a family-chef-run inn and several recipes have come through close relatives.

Yolanda and Dick invite guests to use their pond or hike the nearby acreages. They know all about fishing. Visitors call ahead to discover the conditions. Get the Lanzas to direct you to the local ponds and the swinging bridge.

The food here is delicious. Although far from the sea, the inn's 🖝 shrimp scampi is a delightful meal. It comes with a fresh loaf of hot bread. The lasagna is a family recipe. The menu is extensive, which tells you food lovers live here. In season Yolanda makes fresh fruit pies and the walnut pie is tempting to your sweet tooth.

Yolanda often uses her fresh breads for picnic lunches, along with thick slices of cheese, fresh fruit, and a slice of homemade pie. Whether you're a hiker, biker, fisherman, or simply a picnicker out to explore the local sights, Dick and Yolanda will get you off to a good start.

How to get there: Take Exit 96 from Route 17 to Livingston Manor. Continue through town toward Shandelee; the inn is on the left-hand side in Shandelee. Sullivan County International Airport, fly-in.

Olive Metcalf

Kittle House Inn
Mt. Kisco, New York
10549

Innkeepers: Richard C. and John C. Crabtree
Telephone: 914-666-8044
Rooms: 12, all with private bath.
Rates: $60, double occupancy; $54, single occupancy; continental
   breakfast included.
Open: Closes Christmas Day. Lunch, dinner, Sunday brunch, bar.
Facilities & Activities: Piano player Wednesday through Saturday
   evenings. Dancing. Beautiful countryside.

Don't come expecting an old inn, nor a brand new one.
In 1925 the inn was built around the remnants of an old barn
that formed part of Ivy Hill Farm. Strawberries, raspberries,
and blackberries were ushered from here to the city markets.
Now when the chef finds fresh fruits like these he'll make
fresh tarts.

☛ The mahogany bar is 150 years old and is a richly
hued beauty. Mostly this is a modern inn with contemporary
furnishings except for the magnificent bar. One of the guest
rooms has a four-poster white bed. All the beds have modern
quilts that look old-timey. The hallways look as if you're
climbing to your room in a comfortable farmhouse.

The piano player comes Wednesday through Saturday evenings. He plays melodies that will tug at your heartstrings. He must know hundreds. There's a space near the piano before the fireplace where you can dance should the urge strike.

Decorations festoon the inn on holidays. On St. Patrick's Eve Richard Crabtree sports green. It highlights his red hair.

Chef Stefano De Pietro prepares an eclectic blend of French country, north Italian, and classic American dishes. His homemade country 🖝 veal pâté is made with pistachios. On any single night you might choose between Yankee pot roast, fettucine Alfredo, or chicken oriental. The cheesecake is a classic here and you'll find zabaglione, a light Italian custard.

While you savor your meal you can look out at the country club golf course. The view is lovely. So is the patio below in the spring and summer.

How to get there: From Route 684 going north to Mt. Kisco, exit onto Route 172. Turn left at the end of the exit. Continue 1½ miles to hilltop and turn left at Kittle Road. The inn is in ½ block on the left, nestled into the hillside of a family neighborhood.

ប

B: One dining room is called Blackie's Room. Years ago Blackie, the dog, slept here and permanently named the room.

olive Metcalf

Elk Lake Lodge
North Hudson, New York
12855

Innkeeper: Peter Sanders
Telephone: 518-532-7616
Rooms: 6, all with private bath; 7 cottages.
Rates: $54 to $80, per person, AP. Two-day minimum on weekends.
  Children welcome; inquire about rates. No credit cards.
Open: Early May to the Sunday before Thanksgiving. Breakfast,
  lunch, dinner. BYOB.
Facilities & Activities: 12,000 acre private forest preserve on Elk
  Lake and nearby Clear Pond. Canoes, rowboats, swimming,
  fishing, hiking, mountain climbing, bird watching, and animal
  watching.

   She turned to look once again at Elk Lake. Mrs. Sally
Sanders has lived on the shores of this stunning beauty for
thirty years. "I look a dozen times a day," she said, "and it's
different every time. It's something you never grow tired of."
   It's a ☛ wilderness lake to behold, and Elk Lake Lodge
is the only dwelling group on it. From the dining room windows you see the peaks of Boreas, Au Sable, Nippletop, Dix,
and Macomb opposite the lake. Tree-filled islands beckon for
an afternoon of canoeing exploration.

86

As you travel the five-mile stretch of dirt road leading to the lodge, you pass Clear Pond, a 200-foot-deep glacial clear-water pond. The term "great outdoors" bears significance here.

The lodge is covered with weathered shingles. You enter a "great camp" style ☛ common room where the log beams glisten and the fire burns in the great stone fireplace. Sally recovered the Stickler design furniture in dark brown leather. In the corner is an "aesthetic rustic" bark corner hutch. Animal skins hang on the walls near a fishing basket.

The meals at Elk Lodge are all-American. Betty Heber has been the backbone of the kitchen for eighteen years. One whiff of her hot luncheon casseroles, chili, and chicken à la king, and you'll stay close to the inn for lunch. Dinner might be pork chops, pot roast, beef stroganoff, or chicken in every imaginable style. Desserts range from homemade pies to cheesecake to ice cream.

The rooms in the inn are small, pine paneled, and are floored in clean linoleums. The cottages are similar but larger, and some have fireplaces. They are more private, and the Hadley Cottage has a patio with an unobstructed view of the lake.

One family began coming to Elk Lake Lodge long ago. First it was just the two of them. The next year they brought the baby. The following year they brought the toddler and a new baby. Now it's a family tradition and all seven of them look forward to their wilderness outing on this ☛ 12,000-acre private preserve.

How to get there: From I-87 take Exit 29 or Route 9 West toward Newcomb. In 4 miles turn right at the lodge sign and follow the dirt road to the lodge.

Olive Metcalf

Garnet Hill Lodge
North River, New York
12856

Innkeepers: George and Mary Heim
Telephone: 518-251-2821
Rooms: 26 in 4 buildings, 20 with private bath.
Rates: $34 to $46, per person, double occupancy; add $10, single;
MAP. Children 10 and under, $18, in room with parents. Two-
night minimum on weekends, 3 nights on holiday weekends.
Open: Closes late May to mid-June. Breakfast, lunch, dinner, bar.
Facilities & Activities: Located on Thirteenth Lake. Cross-country
ski center, rafting, hiking, swimming, canoeing, fishing, tennis
courts. Downhill skiing at Gore Mountain, tour garnet mine,
Adirondack Museum, boat cruises, caving, bird watching, scenic plane rides, Telemark skiing clinics.

This is a gem of an inn. In fact, there are gems everywhere. Garnets sparkle from the 🖝 exquisite fireplace in the
Manor House, and minuscule garnets gleam from the gravel
as you walk between the buildings that compose Garnet Hill.
Indoors and out this inn is a pleasure. 🖝 Cross-country
skiers follow the trails that lace through the mountains. You
can ski from the top of Gore Mountain to Garnet Hill, all ten
miles. The day I arrived there was a nighttime ski trip across

88

the frozen and snow-covered Thirteenth Lake. What an experience! The moonlight and the stars over the lake and then back to the lodge for hot mulled wine.

April and May is white-water rafting season on the nearby Hudson River Gorge. Mary gets up early to fix breakfast for the rafters. During summer you can walk the mile to Thirteenth Lake and swim or go boating. There's a hike to a nearby abandoned garnet mine. George has prepared a good year-round map for hiking and skiing.

The Log House dates from 1936. The rooms here are the smallest of all and beautifully paneled in a rich pine. A short distance away is the Birches, with large rooms and private baths. The Manor House has seven rooms and four baths, which are rustic beauties with spectacular views. All choices are good ones. The Ski Haus has a loft, so ideal for families.

There's a beautiful mountaintop view from the lodge picture window. Picnic tables fill the room and the logs that form the walls are as sturdy as the day the lodge was built.

Mary is the chef. She is famed for her Saturday night smorgasbords during skiing and rafting seasons. Come with a big appetite. She always has plenty of vegetables, various homemade breads, and a selection of several entrees such as roast beef, poached salmon, and shellfish. She's a prolific cook.

George is an avuncular innkeeper with a subtle sense of humor. He also has a lot of overshoes. He'd loaned out every last pair to guests and was wearing his street shoes through the snow the day we arrived.

How to get there: From I-87 exit onto Route 9 North. After Warrensburg take Route 28 West to North River. From Weverton it's 11.5 miles to the left turn onto 13th Lake Road and the inn's sign. Follow this road 5 miles to the inn.

❦

B: *An Adirondack mountain inn is one of life's rewards.*

olive Metcalf

The Genesee Falls Inn
Portageville, New York
14536

Innkeepers: Ed and Lea Brosche
Telephone: 716-493-2484
Rooms: 12, 10 with private bath.
Rates: $18 to $33, double occupancy, EP. Children welcome.
Open: Closes from Thanksgiving to February. Call for exact dates.
   Breakfast on weekends, lunch and dinner every day but Tuesday. Bar.
Facilities & Activities: ☛ Letchworth State Park, canoeing, wineries, Genesee Country Village, antiquing, steam railroad runs during summer in Arcade, and golf.

   In the lobby of the Genesee Falls Inn sits a row of jars filled with Mrs. Davis's Cinnamon Syrup. Mrs. Davis no longer brews this concoction. Lea Brosche now is the chef and parfait expert; she still uses the ☛ original syrup recipe that oozes temptingly over summertime ice creams. They are a favorite among guests at the Genesee Falls.
   Ed Brosche, former teacher of math and science, turned innkeeper with Lea six years ago. Together they nurture their inn.
   The inn is pleasantly old. The floors are tile and reminis-

cent of a turn-of-the-century remodeling. Many of the antiques have been here so long Ed and Lea no longer remember where they came from. In the dining room is the largest Victorian buffet I've ever seen.

In the hallway sits a straw doll carriage. You walk up the stairs beside photographs of the area in days gone by. The doors to the rooms are darkly stained and unusually tall. You open them to invitingly feminine rooms, some with lovely brass beds. It's a twist that the few adjacent motel rooms are more expensive than the inn rooms. Guess which I'd choose.

In the lobby are china closets with reproductions that you can take home. After a brief stop at the cash register you can begin your cup collection.

The bar and the adjacent sunny lunch room are friendly little places decorated with a variety of antiques and prints. Perfect for casual wining and dining.

In the dining room you can order Lea's beef stroganoff made with a brown sauce, and plenty of sour cream and mushrooms, or the steak Diane if you've been out canoeing all day. If you don't choose the cinnamon syrup for your parfait, then a liqueur might suit you nicely. There's also chocolate mint mousse and pecan pie. After all this you'd better go canoeing tomorrow, too.

How to get there: From Route 17 take Route 19 North, which becomes Route 19A North, to Portageville. The inn is a red brick building, the largest in the hamlet. The town is named Portageville because the canoes were carried around the falls that lie farther down the Genesee River.

B: *Couple-run inns have a special balance all their own.*

Olive Metcalf

The Inn at Quogue
Quogue, New York
11959

Innkeepers: Mary Finegan and Brian Moorehead
Telephone: 516-653-6560
Rooms: 7, 5 with private bath; 2 suites.
Rates: $75 to $95, double occupancy; $50, single; $125, suites; continental breakfast included. Two-night minimum weekends, 3 nights on holiday weekends. Children allowed.
Open: Mid-May to October. Dinner, tavern.
Facilities & Activities: Walking distance to beach. Low-key jazz on the weekends. Tennis in the area. Inn has 3 bicycles. Ideal area for jogging. Wildlife refuge.

The Inn at Quogue is a very easy and gentle place. Only the name is difficult. Master that by saying a "qwa" with a hard g at the end and that's the beginning of a very pleasant experience.

Quogue is part of the Hamptons. It's ☞ peaceful and quiet here. No traffic, no busy streets. It's well placed in a lovely residential neighborhood not too far from the beach, tennis, golf, and across the street from a combination newsstand—ice cream parlour. What more do you ask in an inn?

Delectable food, you say? Star Buck has been the resident chef for five years. His imaginative talents in the kitchen have earned him three stars in the *New York Times*. You'll wish Stars like him were everywhere.

The menu changes daily. It's an unassuming photocopied sheet of paper. Very unoriginal. Very unlike the food. My companion and I went for the specials. The ☛ swordfish, which is caught locally, and the ☛ sea bass were smothered with unique herbal blends. The tantalizing smoked eggplant was eaten with fresh morsels of pita bread. The arugula and endive salads were lightly seasoned to let the provocative flavors through. We finished with a ☛ chocolate cake that rested on a lemon sauce. Absolutely delicious. Mary Finegan rarely describes the food, she recommends the taste test. Good idea.

The inn is a transformed historic home. The guest rooms are ☛ summer cheer. Some have thick carpeting, others have painted wood floors. Wallpaper with bright flowers and whitewashed walls remind you this is a summertime inn. You walk down the hallway to the wooden deck. Settle in here with a new book. Pretend there's not a city for 1,000 miles.

How to get there: From 495 take Exit 70; go south to Sunrise Highway, then east to the West Hampton exit. Go south to Montauk Highway, turn right onto Quogue Street after the bridge, and proceed to the inn on the right.

The menu is consistently creative, offering fresh foods from the north and south shores of Long Island. The chef receives the food deliveries and smells, pokes, slices, tastes, and caresses each product. When he smiles, the vendor smiles.—Barbara Patterson, Quogue, New York

Olive Metcalf

The Ram's Head Inn
Ram's Head Island off Shelter Island, New York
11965

Innkeepers: Linda and John Eklund
Telephone: 516-749-0811
Rooms: 17, 5 with private bath.
Rates: $45 to $63, off season; $55 to $80, in summer and on holidays; double occupancy, continental breakfast included. Children welcome.
Open: May 1 through third week of October. Breakfast, dinner, bar.
Facilities & Activities: Sailing, 800 feet of beachfront, tennis, 6 moorings. Nearby is bicycling, golfing, swimming, boating, fishing, hiking.

The inn is located on the ☞ clear waters of Coecles Harbor.

You'll go home with tales of sailing on a summer's afternoon, biking the island roads and seeing osprey nests atop the telephone poles, and dining on fine foods by candlelight. You'll whisper the words, "perfect little waterfront inn." You want to keep it a secret. But a wonderful summer holiday can't be kept a silent memory, it must be shared.

☛ Two thirteen-foot O'Day sloops sit dockside. In seconds you're off to explore the shores of this island sanctuary of unspoiled beauty. Literally one-third of the island is a Nature Conservancy.

The inn is a large, weathered-shingle, center hall colonial, built as an inn in 1929. It is light and airy. The rooms have carpeted floors, white curtains, and maple furniture. In the dining room, light colored country ladderback chairs with cane seats give a folkish look. A late 17th-century French clock hangs near the fireplace.

There's a slate patio with flowers abloom in heavy clay flowerpots. Everything is conducive to "settle-back summer" fun. There's a hammock and two swings. A child's play set is mounted at the edge of the expansive lawn. Two paths to the water wind around either side of the tennis court.

Dinner at the inn is a saucy event with ☛ sophisticated fare that might include broiled weakfish on a bed of julienne vegetables with a cucumber and lobster cream, or rack of lamb with a honey and pine nut glaze and a port wine sauce. The shrimp graziella is sautéed with fresh tomato, mushrooms, cream, and sherry and served on a bed of capellini. The desserts have a touch of panache, like the dinners. You might try frozen strawberry souffle or ☛ strawberry gratin sabayon baked with a lovely meringue top. When you spoon it to your mouth it's gooey and pulls reluctantly from the dish. It's the only time you'll need perseverance to capture your satisfaction at the Ram's Head.

How to get there: Take Route 114 through Sag Harbor to the ferry. On Shelter Island take Route 114 North to the traffic circle and continue straight on Cartright Road to stop sign. Turn right on Ram Island Drive and go right over causeway to the inn.

B: *A ram's head hangs in the entry. No one knows the origin of the name, Ram's Head Island. A ram has never been seen in these parts and the island has no such configuration.*

olive Metcalf

Sagamore Lodge
Raquette Lake, New York
13436

Innkeeper: Sue Schafstall
Telephone: 315-354-5303
Rooms: 46, 2 with private bath; 7 dormitory rooms.
Rates: $150 per week, per person, double occupancy, without tuition (averages $150 week). July and August weekends, $120, per person, double occupancy; or $220 per couple; AP. Children's programs available. Minimum stay, week or weekend.
Open: Closes briefly in December. Breakfast, lunch, dinner. BYOB.
Facilities & Activities: On Sagamore Lake, swimming and canoeing, 18 miles of cross-country ski trails, ski lessons, tennis court, volleyball, bowling, hiking, programs. Adirondack Mountain Museum.

In the middle of the woods on Sagamore Lake is the former Vanderbilt summer estate, a historic ☞ "Adirondack Camp." Public guided tours of the "camp" are popular, but you can also stay in this beautiful setting on July and August weekends.

During the rest of the year it's the Sagamore Conference Center and you must take a course to stay at the Sagamore Lodge. You can attend ☞ fishing, hiking, canoeing, skiing, and other important "conference" programs. Summer, spring, or fall you might go on hikes and canoe trips to see other "Great Camps" of the Adirondacks. In the winter you can ski to several "Great Camps" with a guide. There's a week-long storytelling program, and photography workshops, computer courses, and a variety of human development workshops. Ask for a program brochure.

The lodge overlooks the mile-long lake that surrounds it on three sides. Of log construction, it was built in 1897 by William West Durant and is composed of fourteen buildings. The lodge is a beautiful sight in the winter, with its red trim and bark exterior in the white snow. You drive four miles through the woods from the main road to get here. It's serene and natural. I was greeted by a deer when I arrived.

Inside, the walls are highly polished and smooth. There are twenty-six stone fireplaces and Adirondack mountain furniture. The library is in another building. You walk to the dining room for your buffet or family-style meals. There is even a bowling alley. You have to hand-set your pins, just like the Vanderbilts.

You'll discover self-sufficiency reigns here in the mountains. You're not pampered. You clean your trays after dinner and strip your bed before you leave.

Carol Darling is the local chef. She prepares all-American dishes like roast beef and barbecued chicken. Just the thing after a long day's hike through the mountains.

How to get there: Take Route 28 West to Raquette Lake. On the outskirts of town, turn left at the wooden sign for the lodge. Follow the dirt road for 4 miles. Turn left at the red barn and wind around to the lodge.

☀

We enjoy . . . the good, wholesome, home-cooked meals. It's always a pleasure to return, which we do frequently.—Soini & Harry O'Connell, Apalachin, New York

olive Metcalf

Beekman Arms
Rhinebeck, New York
12572

Innkeeper: Charles LaForge
Telephone: 914-876-7077
Rooms: 38, all with private bath; 2 suites; in 4 buildings.
Rates: $50 to $70, double occupancy; $40 to $60, single; $90 to $95,
  suites; EP. Children under 12 free. Pets allowed in some
  rooms.
Open: All year. Breakfast, lunch, dinner, tavern.
Facilities & Activities: Rhinebeck Aerodrome, county fair, Crafts
  Fair in June, Antiques Fair in October, Roosevelt and Vander-
  bilt estates in Hyde Park, golfing, boating, horseback riding,
  and other sports.

The Beekman Arms is a busy in-town inn with one foot
in the past and another in the future. A sunny new glass-en-
closed garden room gives you a good view of Main Street, and
inside you can choose the seclusion of the all-wood dining
room or the ancient taproom.

The inn dates from 1766. ☛ From the rafters hang an
assortment of muskets, swords, and guns, which remind you
these thick walls have protected settlers from the area's first

residents, the Indians. You feel safe and sound here. It's a friendly little town.

On a sunny afternoon I anticipated watching a show of vintage World War I airplanes at the Rhinebeck Aerodome between bites of a savory turkey crepe, homemade barley soup, and a fresh salad. I sat comfortably knowing the audience would be the winners in the afternoon's mock battle.

The next morning I returned to my favorite table in the sun, and the aroma of the blueberry pancakes pulled me away from the newspaper. They are as good as they look and smell.

You can choose the traditional rooms with pine floors in the inn or retire up the street to the Delamater House or the Carriage House. The Delamater House is an adorable ☛ Gothic cottage built in 1844 with gingerbread trim. On the front porch are twin swings. The rooms are ☛ appealing and fresh. One is furnished in white wicker. The televisions are concealed in armoires. You can pretend they don't exist if you're on your honeymoon, or you can catch the news like my husband and I are wont to do. Then we make it disappear.

In the Carriage House the second-story rooms have wonderful skylights and soothing gray-stained wood.

The spirits are very spirited. You can order a "Cappuccino L'Amour" with rum, vodka, crème de cocoa, and brandy. A "Long Island iced tea" has gin, vodka, rum, tequila, and triple sec. Lucky your room is nearby after one of these.

How to get there: From the Taconic Parkway take Route 199 West to Route 9 South to the white wooden inn. Park in the back. Fly-in. Kingston Airport.

🍸

B: *Pineapples were the symbol of welcome in Colonial times. They are aptly stenciled on several doors in the inn. Around the corner is the inn's* ☛ *gift shop. It's delightfully large.*

Winter Clove Inn
Round Top, New York
12473

Innkeeper: Merton Whitcomb
Telephone: 518-622-3267
Rooms: 52, all with private bath.
Rates: $48, per person, AP. Reduced rate for children under 16 in the same room as parents. Weekly rates available. Gratuity appreciated. Motel units available. Two-night minimum most holidays.
Open: Closes mid-December to December 27th. Breakfast, lunch, dinner. Wine served. BYOB restricted to room.
Facilities & Activities: Outdoor and indoor swimming pools, tennis court, bowling, hayrides, 400 acres for hiking and picnicking, skiing, 9-hole golf course, basketball, paddleball, volleyball, and 5 family rooms. Family inn.

On the marvelous ☞ front porch of this Catskill Mountain inn are large ladderback rockers. You can spend your days mountain watching or pursuing the active life. Summer, winter, fall, and spring, there is a variety of things to do. In March is maple syrup making. Summertime barbecues and hay rides are followed by weekly movies. In January it might be a vigorous day of cross-country skiing followed by a float in the indoor pool. In the pool house is an impressive boulder that was unearthed when the pool was dug. There's a 🖝 garden here, where it takes a pineapple six months to grow.

American home cooking is served in the large dining room. By the light of oil lamps on the tables you're served hearty meals, such as roast prime rib of beef, with candied carrots, buttered asparagus, and a baked potato. If your appetite isn't satiated, there are seconds. With the strawberry shortcake on the way you probably won't ask for more.

Around the dining room hang photographs of inn guests taken in 1863. The ladies wear straw hats and long dresses, the men wear suits, and the boys each hold a baseball bat. It's fun to see today's guests in the same place, but in today's sporting clothes.

The inn has been in the Whitcomb family for five generations. The youngest generation has recently remodeled several sunny rooms on the fourth floor, which have a spectacular view. Pretty 🖝 hand-braided wool rugs are spread across the wide pine floors in the rooms.

In the entrance hangs a large picture of Uncle Elliot. He was found in the attic. He's the mysterious stranger dubbed with a family title. The real family portraits hang behind the front desk. Here is the founder, H. B. Whitcomb, who started a very good thing. Only the games have changed; the setting remains as inviting as ever.

How to get there: From Route 23 off the New York Thruway go to Cairo. At the first light turn left and follow the signs to Round Top. Or, take Exit 20 off the thruway and turn left onto Route 32. After the Catskill Game Farm turn left on Heart's Content Road, go 3 miles, turn left on Winter Clove Road, and follow the signs to the inn.

⏳

B: *This is an inn for all ages.*

olive Metcalf

The American Hotel
Sag Harbor, New York
11963

Innkeeper: Ted Conklin
Telephone: 516-725-3535
Rooms: 8, all with private bath.
Rates: $100, Friday and Saturday; $75, non-holiday and midweek; double occupancy; continental breakfast included. Two-night minimum on weekends, 3 nights on holidays. Separate room booking for children. No credit cards.
Open: Closes Christmas Day. Lunch Saturday and Sunday, dinner, tavern.
Facilities & Activities: One block from waterfront in downtown Sag Harbor. Whaling Museum, walking tour of town, antique shops, historic churches, water sports, bicycling, cruise ships travel between Sag Harbor and Haddam, Connecticut.

Ted Conklin emphasizes that first and foremost he is a restaurateur. There's no arguing that point. Anyone with a $1,200 bottle of Chateau Mouton Rothschild dated 1893 on the wine list and a deft chef named Arondel in the kitchen is serious about ☞ French continental dining.

But the rooms in this inn-like hotel also deserve your attention. It's ☞ difficult to pick a favorite, they are so refined

102

and stylish. There's the spacious art nouveau room that over-looks Sag Harbor's Main Street. A gigantic French poster hangs on the exposed brick wall. A vividly colored American Indian rug graces the wood floor. An oversized chair sits in the corner opposite the pair of oval mirrors and the bedroom suite.

The ☞ antiques form well-favored ensembles. The sleigh bed room is popular with honeymooners. A French sink in the bathroom will intrigue you. In the Cuckoo Room the deep red carpeting enhances the twin brass beds. You can sit at the large secretary and begin your memoirs. One room is two stories. You climb the stairs to go to bed.

In the lobby, which contrasts a bit from the rooms, you register atop a glass case. The top shelf is filled with boxes of cigars. To one side sits a ☞ Jump Spark Cigar lighter. There's a variety of antiques, and lace doilies sit under the lamps. A pair of sofas sit opposite an ornately carved library table stacked with newspapers.

The menu changes frequently. Offerings include fish, fowl, and meat. For beginnings you might select a plateful of Long Island oysters on the half shell, juiced with a squeeze of lemon, and edged into your mouth directly from the shell. One evening the chef offered two versions of weakfish, an angler fish with a shrimp sauce, and a filet of bluefish pre-pared with Roquefort, flounder, and lobster. During winter, a lovely time to come to Sag Harbor, my preferences turn to a tenderloin with a smooth, rich, béarnaise sauce, one that lin-gers in your palatable memories. That followed by a Tome de Savoie cheese or a St. Jouvin and an espresso is how to end the perfect day.

How to get there: From Route 27 in Long Island follow signs to Sag Harbor from Bridgehampton. The Bridgehampton Highway turns into Main Street; the inn is on the left side of the street as you come from the wharf. East Hampton Airport, fly-in.

Olive Metcalf

The Point
Saranac Lake, New York
12983

Innkeeper: Ted Carter
Telephone: 518-891-5674
Rooms: 9, all with private bath
Rates: $300 to $425, per couple, per night, AP (continental breakfast). Picnics, snacks, help-yourself bar 24 hours. Add 20 percent gratuity. Two-night minimum stay. Children 18 and older welcome.
Open: All year. Breakfast, lunch, dinner, alcoholic beverages.
Facilities & Activities: On Lake Saranac. On the estate: sailing, fishing, canoeing, boating, waterskiing, badminton, croquet, cross-country skiing equipment.

The Point is not for everyone. It's a 🖙 magnificent "Adirondacks Camp" built on the shores of 🖙 Saranac Lake for the Rockefellers.

"It's not an inn," protests Ted Carter. "It's our home." However, he and James open their house to paying guests with whom they share their lifestyle and entertain at black tie dinners in the great stone hall.

It's exquisite. The living room is thirty feet by fifty feet, large stone fireplaces are at each end, zebra skins are on the floors, animal heads adorn the walls, a magnificent ibex skull sits in the window. Two round tables are before the windows and from here you can see the lake. Good books and magazines lie about the tables.

Ted selected the animal heads and the ibex skull in London. He has lived and worked in Europe, and retired young as a businessman. He used to summer on the lake at his grandfather's "Camp." Now summer is year round in spirit for him.

This inn has probably received more major publicity than any other. Ted had no idea he'd open his home to guests. Or that one day he'd be the only American inn in the prestigious ☞ "Relais et Chateaux," a French publication that guides you to elegance and good tastes.

The ☞ four bedrooms in the Main Lodge have views in three directions, cathedral ceilings, stone fireplaces, and sitting areas. The ☞ woodwork is beautiful. It's never been restored. It's perfect the way it is.

James is the handsome chef. Guests are asked prior to coming what they don't like to eat. Dinner is like dining at a friend's home who also happens to have studied cooking in Europe. Imported wines and wonderful roasts, homemade pastries, and baked breads. Original foods that show style and good taste.

Ted likes to visit when you call. He has prepared a packet of information about his home. So far only one guest has left prematurely. She expected the Point to have a disco.

How to get there: Directions given upon confirmation of reservation.

B: *I visit every inn in my book. To research this inn further I've suggested an evening at the Point to my publisher. So far, no response.*

olive Metcalf

The Adelphi Hotel
Saratoga Springs, New York
12866

Innkeepers: Gregg Siefker and Sheila Parkert
Telephone: 518-587-4688
Rooms: 16, all with private bath; 4 suites.
Rates: $55 to $75, April through December; $120 in August; suite $95, and $160 in August; double occupancy; continental breakfast included. Two-night minimum on summer weekends. Children allowed.
Open: Lodging April through December. Restaurant and cafe open in July and August for lunch and dinner. Bar.
Facilities & Activities: Grand lobby. Saratoga Horse Races, National Museum of Racing, Saratoga Spa State Park, Performing Arts Center is summer home of New York City Ballet and Philadelphia Orchestra, Canfield Casino, a Victorian museum, city architecture, antiquing, parks, and lakes.

This sumptuous old building has been restored by a very imaginative pair. You are going to enjoy the ☞ ambiance, the flavor of the 1900s, the posh look, and ☞ Saratoga Springs.

They make a scene at the Adelphi. No country clothes here. Get out your finery for some downtown Saratoga fun

106

with your cronies after the horse races. This town will entertain you. There is a round of pleasures from museums, to
parks, to the ballet and symphony in the park. You might
even take the waters. Begin with a good massage.

☛ Flowers are everywhere. Exquisite gladiolas, pink
impatiens, prim tulips, whatever Sheila is in the mood for
that day. She orders flowers with abandon and that's how you
should approach the Adelphi. The ☛ lobby is turn-of-the-
century opulence. Great mirrors and lots of niches for intimate seating arrangements. Quartets play on warm summer
afternoons.

The staircase is grand. Walk up all four stories to the top
and then descend slowly. Large windows are hung with aesthetically draping curtains in scarlets, whites, pinks, browns,
and lavenders.

The lavender room is French provincial. Really! Have
you ever seen walls covered with such luscious lavender
moire? The oriental room is furnished in bamboo, russets,
golds, and browns. Baskets cluster above the beds. There are
Victorian rooms. Down the wide hallways you stroll past the
crazy quilts, the lace tablecloths, the portraits. Sheila decorates all this. In the charming bar she even has lace around
the shelves. Marvelous touch she has.

The breakfast parlor is "comme il faut" or lavish. Step
out on the second-story veranda and scan an eye down Main
Street, Saratoga.

You can order a Campari or Pernod and Saratoga Water.
Perhaps you prefer an ouzo on ice. The exotic is familiar in
Saratoga. Duck is prepared with a pungent sauce of black
currants and Crème de Cassis.

Meryl Streep has stayed here. I'm not surprised. It's like
a romantic movie setting.

How to get there: From I-87 take Exit 13-N or Route 9 North that
becomes Broadway Street. Continue to the downtown stretch of
buildings past Friendly's Ice Cream. The inn is on the left, painted
brown with yellow trim. Fly-in, Saratoga County Airport.

B: *How captivating to watch the world go by from the lobby of
the Adelphi.*

Olive Metcalf

Chequit Inn
Shelter Island Heights, New York
11965

Innkeeper: Phil Franzoni and family
Telephone: 516-749-0018
Rooms: 44, 40 with private bath.
Rates: $38 to $78, double occupancy; $30 to $72, single; $110,
   suite; EP. MAP available. Lower on weekdays. Two-day minimum on weekends. Children welcome.
Open: May 1 through Columbus Day. Call after that. Breakfast,
   lunch, dinner, bar.
Facilities & Activities: Walking distance to public beach. Game
   room in bar. Swimming, boating, bicycling, hiking in the Nature Preserve.

   Sit on the shaded patio out front. There's a view of the
boat-filled bay. At lunchtime the crowd swells with families
and friends, casually dressed duos and trios, and
stroller-driven children enjoying the summer breezes. Order
an 🖝 avocado and bean sprout sandwich with all the trimmings, a basket of fries, and a sun tea or a cold beer. Maybe
you're in the mood for a plateful of fried clams or fresh oysters. This is the life.
   Chequit is a historic summer inn composed of different

worlds. Upstairs, guests sit on the porch that's terraced into the hillside. Through the door behind them a white-wicker-filled guest lounge is bright and pretty. Ida Franzoni has selected a rose floral print wallpaper that goes well with the white original tin ceiling. There's charm here.

Downstairs is the game room and bar. There's a juke box, video games, pool, and a bowling machine, all receiving heavy use around the sandy floor.

The rooms in the inn are old fashioned with antique furnishings. Next door the Little Brown house is an older, smaller version of the inn. Across the street in the Cedar Lodge are spacious rooms with fine antiques and white sheer curtains.

The inn began over one hundred years ago as "The Restaurant." Summer guests stayed in houses without kitchens and came here for their meals. Having grown up in the inn, Phil knows most of the guests by name. Today he is the chef. He prepares a fine dinner that includes broiled swordfish, a fresh catch, lobster when available, duckling, leg of lamb, veal, and 12- and 16-ounce sirloins.

The streets hug the hills that curve around the inn. For a moment you wonder if you've been whisked away to the Italian hills, with the water in the background, and this rambling white inn with the green shutters.

How to get there: From the North Ferry take Route 114 up the hill to the inn on the right-hand side. From the South Ferry cross the island on Route 114 to the North Ferry, turn around, and come back to the inn. Ferry pickup service.

Excellent seafood ... in a charming candlelit Victorian dining room.—Barbara Foley, New York, New York; an annual summer guest

Olive Metcalf

The Sherwood Inn
Skaneateles, New York
13152

Innkeeper: Francis Lee
Telephone: 315-685-3405
Rooms: 13, all with private bath; 2 suites
Rates: $35 to $60, single or double occupancy; suite, $60; continental breakfast included. Children welcome and pets allowed.
Open: Inn open all year. Restaurant closes Christmas Eve and Day. Lunch, dinner, bar.
Facilities & Activities: Fourth of July and Labor Day sailing regattas, sailing, weekly sailboat races, mailboat cruises, boating, windsurfing, canoeing, tennis courts, enclosed ice skating in winter, August music festival. Winery tours.

Grape harvesting season is a spectacular time of fall colors in the New York Finger Lakes. You can take a lake and land tour that includes wine tastings. At day's end return home to the Sherwood Inn.

Isaac Sherwood built the inn in 1807 ostensibly to headquarter his stagecoach business. Since he weighed over 300 pounds his gastronomic interests were fortuitously met in owning an inn.

In today's dining room the chicken orlaff is baked with a

redolent mornay sauce and there's not a finer ☞ cauliflower soup to be found. The ☞ plump yeast rolls and date nut bread are excellent and should you have room for homemade pies, more power to you. There also is a tavern menu with hot chicken and sausage pies in winter and lighter summer sandwiches and soups.

The hallways are wide, pine paneled, and filled with oriental carpets that ☞ contrast beautifully with the polished woodwork. Impressive palms and other plants are strategically placed and the combination is striking.

Innkeeper, Francis Lee, half walks, half bounds through the rooms that he delights in showing. His disposition warms you to this grand old inn. Up on the third floor is one Victorian room, another is furnished in European pieces, but the majority are early American in keeping with the inn. It's quieter the higher you go. On the second floor you're closer to the library, petite guest lounge, and the action downstairs. The majority of rooms have a view of the lake. There's a bridal suite with a canopy bed and the entire room can be closed off from the parlour with light blue draperies. The enormous mirror that hangs from floor to ceiling in the hallway is perfect for a last-minute check before going down to dinner.

How to get there: Take Route 34 South from I-90 to Auburn and take Route 20 East 7 miles to the inn. It's on the left and you park behind it.

B: *Say "Skinny Atlas" for Skaneateles and the locals will accept it as correct and not a contradiction in terms.*

olive Metcalf

Zeiser's Mountain Lodge
Speculator, New York
12164

Innkeepers: John and Genevieve Zeiser
Telephone: 518-548-7021
Rooms: 6, all with private bath.
Rates: $45, double occupancy; $35, single; EP. Children welcome.
Open: Closes April. Lunch, dinner, bar.
Facilities & Activities: Fourteen lakes in 15-mile radius, skiing, hiking, camping, fishing, bicycling, swimming, golfing, boating, tennis, bear-hunting region, Kunjamuk cave. June sea plane fly-in on Lake Pleasant.

In the southern Adirondacks on Lake Pleasant you'll find Speculator. And in the town is an inn. And in the inn are John and Genevieve Zeiser and Ludwig the cat. You can tell a lot about an inn by sizing up the cat. A more content cat would be hard to find.

☛ Ludwig was once the write-in mayoral candidate in Speculator. The innkeepers were as amazed as the townsfolk. He must have been campaigning when they thought he was out prowling.

John has a light sense of humor. A group of friends once marked his and Genevieve's anniversary in an unusual way.

They sent them to Europe for a month. John was worried the tickets might be one way. They are very fond of this little town.

The heart of the inn is the bar and restaurant. Genevieve is the 🖝 expert cook. She prepares magnificent dinners. We tried to get snowed in. By 8:00 A.M. the snowplows had the roads cleared and we had to be on our way.

John is the expert bartender. He 🖝 makes everyone feel at home. Ask about John D. MacDonald. It's no mystery he's familiar with the food and drink at this establishment. Mystery fans have traced him here. Some have been rewarded with a meeting. What luck!

The rooms are fresh, cleanly inviting, and simply furnished with the basics. The windows are high and with a little stretch you see the treetops. The inn is located in a wonderful area with woodlands down the road, skiing, hiking, and plenty of things to do in the great outdoors. Driving here along the tree-lined roads is a pretty experience. Flying to Zeiser's would be as pleasurable. The airport is a few miles distant.

The crowd might be pilots, outdoor vacationers, and mystery fans. Ludwig likes all of them. He doesn't look like a hiking fan himself.

How to get there: From I-90 take Route 30 North to Speculator. The inn is on the south side of the road, marked: Zeiser's Restaurant.

Hearty broiled lamb chops or Sautéed Chicken Genevieve served with light and delicate sauces complemented by creamy potatoes and seasonably fresh vegetables are always desirable.—David H. Schrader, Amsterdam, New York

olive Metcalf

Millhof Inn
Stephentown, New York
12168

Innkeepers: Frank and Romana Tallet
Telephone: 518-733-5606
Rooms: 7, all with private bath; 4 suites.
Rates: $60 to $75, double occupancy; $50, single; $70 to $100,
   suite; continental breakfast included. Three-day minimum stay
   on July, August, and holiday weekends.
Open: Closed in April. Dinner served during the winter by reservation only. BYOB.
Facilities & Activities: Swimming pool, bumper pool table, central
   lounge. Skiing at Jiminy Peak and Brodie Mountain. Tanglewood, two Shaker Museums, Berkshires, Williamstown Theater Festival.

Millhof resembles a Swiss Mountain inn. The innkeepers are Frank and Romana, an American-Yugoslavian couple
who say, "It's no particular style but our own."
In 1971 the Tallets transformed this former sawmill
with wood paneling and beams, antiques, and a lovely dining
niche. Frank did all the carpentry work. In the dining area
are dark benches with small hearts where the back rests.

Nearby is a 🖙 patio deck. You can have breakfast and listen to the birds sing.

Children become wide-eyed to find a scrumptious stone-ground wheat cake in the shape of Mickey Mouse. Adults are pleased to discover maple syrup that's made down the road by the Tallet's neighbor. You may ask for blueberries to be blended into the pancakes and you'll ski your very best all day long. If you're lucky you'll arrive during blackberry season for Romana's delicious preserves. She makes them fresh and the flavor reflects the season.

Tanglewood is thirty minutes away and when you speak to Romana her melodious Yugoslavian accent is also like music. She collects miniature folk art from central Europe and the smallest dishes, and tiny carvings surround the dining room. Frank collects wooden toys for everyone to play with and there is a stack of readily accessible games.

The 🖙 fireplace doors in the living room were designed by the Tallet's sculptor friend. An apple-wood handle opens the lovely doors that are decorated with an apple tree. It's unusual and beautiful.

The inn is designed efficiently and attractively for visitors. The rooms are 🖙 spic and span and furnished with matching antiques. The honeymoon suite looks out to the pool. The furniture is oak and there's a fireplace. It's cozy and private.

Smoking isn't allowed in the rooms. You're welcome to go to the common room in your robe if you need a goodnight cigarette.

How to get there: From I-90 take Route 22 to Stephentown, turn right on Route 43, and go one mile. The inn is on the left. It is almost on the Massachusetts border.

♗

Mrs. Tallet presides over her kitchen providing a superb selection of foods for breakfast—our favorite being her pancakes served with slightly warmed syrup.—Rita and Gene Marokko, New York, New York

olive Metcalf

Three Village Inn
Stony Brook, New York
11790

Innkeepers: Nelson, Monda, and Whitney Roberts
Telephone: 516-751-0555
Rooms: 33, all with private bath.
Rates: $60 to $75, double occupancy; $55 to $65, single; EP. Two-night minimum on weekends from April through October. Children welcome.
Open: Closes Christmas Day. Breakfast, lunch, dinner, taproom.
Facilities & Activities: Museums at Stony Brook. Swimming, boating, and tennis nearby. Theater. Friday concerts on Village Green from mid-July through August.

If you arrive around twilight the old-fashioned street lanterns mark the way. The inn's windows sparkle with lights and the warmth of the inn draws you in.

Sequestered in the trees back from quiet little Main Street, opposite the Yacht Club, and a short walk from the city beach is this historic colonial inn. It's grown into an L-shaped inn with cottages nestled in the hillsides and modern-style rooms filled with quality colonial reproductions. Request a room in the inn and you'll rest in historic but contemporary comfort where the rooms are a little smaller than others. Those most requested are the attractive rooms with the wooden beams, which are reached by the sea captain's staircase. A sea captain originally built the inn for his home.

In the inn's common room is Lorita, the green parrot. She used to talk, but she has heard so much nonsense over the years that she's taken to silence. Nearby is a brick fireplace that burns on cold winter nights and Chippendale-style furniture where guests relax. A television is hidden behind wooden shutters.

In the bar you find a bulletin board with area activities posted. A historic flag hangs from the ceiling that reads: "Don't Tread On Me." This is a ☞ cozy place with bowls chock-full of nuts around the bar, and plenty of memorabilia to peruse. One print says, "Cake Walk: Saturday Night. Come one come all."

In the dining room the staff is dressed in colonial costume. The colonial influence is evident in the lengthy menu. Nothing could be sweeter and tastier than the ☞ chilled plum soup in summer. The clam pie is a long-standing tradition here and steamed clams are a favorite. Fresh cottage cheese arrives before dinner along with hot bread.

This is a picturesque town. Up the hill is the Federal-style shopping crescent. On the post office is the carved American eagle whose wings turn to mark the time. Farther along you'll come to the village pond filled with ducks and geese. Soon you arrive at the Museums at Stony Brook. Here's one of the ☞ best collections of carriages to be found. It's fascinating. History comes alive in this town.

How to get there: From the Long Island Expressway take Exit 62 and proceed north on Nichols Road to 25 A. Turn left at the stoplight, go to the second stoplight, and turn right onto Main Street. The inn lies straight ahead in the trees.

olive Metcalf

The Eggery Country Inn
Tannersville, New York
12485

Innkeepers: Julie and Abe Abramczyk
Telephone: 518-589-5363
Rooms: 7, 5 with private bath.
Rates: $75, double occupancy (inclusive), MAP. Two-night minimum on weekends. Children welcome.
Open: Closes one week in September. Call. Breakfast, dinner on weekends.
Facilities & Activities: Skiing Hunter Mountain. Hiking, trout fishing, golfing, swimming, horseback riding, antiquing. Woodstock is nearby. July and August are Oktoberfest, Polka, and Celtic Festivals, and a Country Western Festival.

The Eggery never was and is not a hen house. It was a working farm where fresh eggs were served to guests. They still are. Now they arrive from local farms. You can sit in the dining room with an 🖙 inspiring view of Hunter Mountain and prepare for a full day of skiing down these slopes. In summer you're more likely to be wearing your walking shoes and smothering a stack of Julie's pancakes in syrup and taking your time over a second cup of morning coffee.

Abe is the restorer and builder. He even built the bar in

the cheerful dining room. But don't ask him about what happens behind the kitchen doors. Julie is the chef. Steaks, broiled center cuts of pork chops, creamy chicken dishes, delicately stuffed shrimp, or stuffed flounder with mornay sauce are likely to find their way to your table. Desserts might be old-fashioned apple strudel or chocolate almond cake that's caressed with chocolate frosting.

The rooms are paneled or wallpapered and filled with antiques and frilly curtains. They are as clean as you'd expect, but there's nothing antiseptic about your treatment here. Julie and Abe are very ☞ guest oriented. They take time out to visit. They speak fondly of previous guests and the feeling is mutual.

Ask Abe and Julie about the area; they know all the favored places to go hiking, take a drive, where to find the best fishing, and when to arrive for which ethnic festivals. For the take-it-easy summertime crowd there are lounge chairs under the trees positioned for a mountain view. That's where you'll find me, after an early morning wildflower hike.

How to get there: From the New York State Thruway take Exit 20 onto Route 32 A toward Palenville. Take Route 23 A to Tannersville. At the traffic light, turn left and follow the road past the gas station and up the hill to the inn. It's on the right-hand side and painted eggshell white.

Absolutely the best cream of broccoli soup that I've ever eaten. Perfect constancy, with just the right blend of seasonings to bring out the smooth delicate broccoli flavor.—Bill Berger, Connecticut

Olive Metcalf

Taughannock Farms Inn
Taughannock Falls State Park, New York
14886

Innkeepers: Nancy and C. Keith le Grand
Telephone: 607-387-7711
Rooms: 5, 3 with private bath; guest house.
Rates: $40 to $55, double occupancy; single $8 less; continental
   breakfast included. $90 for guest house for up to 4, EP. Re-
   quest package rate. Children welcome. No credit cards.
Open: Closes late December to January 1. Dining room closed December 1 to March 1, but meals served to house guests. Dinner, Bar.
Facilities & Activities: Taughannock Falls State Park. Cayuga
   Lake. Swimming, boating, hiking, bicycling, roller skating,
   golfing, bowling, tennis, antiquing, cross-country skiing. Lake
   cruises. Ski shop nearby. Plane's Cayuga Vineyard in Ovid.

   Taughannock Farms Inn sits astride ☛ a high promontory directly overlooking Cayuga Lake. She's a stunning
beauty, crowned with classic widow's walk. Taughannock
Falls State Park is across the road. There's plenty to do with
all the ☛ lake activities, and hiking, bicycling, and winery
tours are a few others.
   This happy inn has a long-time staff with close ties to

the innkeepers. The pastry chef has been here for forty years, her husband and the chef for twenty-five years. Tasty ice creams are a summer specialty. After a sportive day you can cool off with bittersweet ice cream pie in an almond crumb crust, or coffee ice cream pie with a thick caramel topping. For a more traditional approach there's southern pecan pie with whipped cream.

Innkeeper, Karen le Grande, summered here as a child. She's probably the only little girl her age who played with an authentic Victorian music box. It sits in the inn. "Listen to the Mocking Bird" was her favorite song. Now guests listen to the old melodies and spin the clock backwards musically.

The rooms are beautiful and recently refurbished with new carpeting and paint. Antiques are everywhere. You'll find elegant highboys and breakfronts, original bentwoods, and inlaid tables in these bright surroundings. Several of the antiques were brought from Europe when the mansion was built in 1873 and were here when Karen's parents began the tradition of innkeeping forty years ago.

A fine inn is adopted by travelers and the community. If you hear the locals comment that the highboy has been moved, it's because they regard the inn as their own. That's the sign of a good inn. Everyone takes it personally.

How to get there: The inn is located on Route 89, 8 miles north of Ithaca. The state park signs are your cue you've reached the inn. Look up the hill for the large yellow inn and climb up to the entrance. Fly-in, Ithaca Airport.

B: *If there's one thing this inn is missing, it's pretension.*

olive Metcalf

Jeronimo's
Walker Valley, New York
12588

Innkeepers: Armand and Delores Jeronimo
Telephone: 914-RE3-1219
Rooms: 35, all with private bath.
Rates: $110 to $130 per couple, AP. One-day stay slightly higher.
Children welcome. No credit cards.
Open: From July 4 through Labor Day, and on weekends the rest of
the year. Breakfast, lunch, dinner, bar.
Facilities & Activities: Outdoor and indoor swimming pools, sauna,
indoor hot tub, tennis court. Three golf courses nearby, fish-
ing, and walking country roads.

Armand, the master builder, and Delores, the artful
chef, are two congenial hosts who inspire a comfortable so-
ciability with their savvy presence. They began constructing
modern wooden cottages in small clusters around the central
glass-fronted inn in the mid-forties. It's surrounded by eighty
acres of land and overlooks the Hudson River Valley.

This is a New Yorker's "getaway" with 99 percent of the
guests non-Kosher Jewish. It's continental in feeling, and
modern American in looks.

As you approach Jeronimo's the landscape of the New

York woods is exchanged for terraced lawns and snapdragons planted along wooden fences. There's a large ☞ outdoor pool, and a Cinzano umbrella and rustic wooden furniture on a brick patio shaded by magnificent old trees. A few steps away is the indoor pool and the hot tub. Stone pathways lead between the buildings bordered by flowers and plants and wooden decks. Some cottages are shingled, others are pale shades of brown and gray.

Two of the buildings are titled "Happenings." Some rooms have antique furnishings, and others are a 1950s style. All rooms have a good reading light and a view of the trees and countryside.

The bar has the atmosphere of a casual family room with modern furniture from the fifties. In the dining room Delores has incorporated several antiques. A former post office cabinet makes a lovely hutch.

Armand does all the shopping. He goes from market to market until he finds the freshest items: ripe and luscious pears, peaches, cantaloupes, mangos, and all the season's best. He once paid $17 for a watermelon because Delores had requested it for a salad. Delores is a natural born cook. Many of her recipes derive from their travels. They are ☞ Mediterranean and international. One night it might be shrimp harillo cooked South American fashion, another a lasagna with a special tomato sauce, or veal en papillote with stuffed olives sliced across the top. For lunch it might be a fresh tuna salad with melon, kiwi, papaya, mango, and pineapple. Ah, then for an afternoon swim.

How to get there: From Route 17 take Exit 119 and turn right onto Route 302. Proceed 10 miles to Pine Bush. Turn left at the traffic light onto Route 52 and go 5 miles to Walker Valley. Turn left at the Jeronimo's sign and proceed up the hill and over the bridge to the inn.

Numbers on map refer to towns numbered
on index on opposite page

New Jersey

Olive Metcalf

Alexander's Inn
Cape May, New Jersey
08204

Innkeepers: Larry and Diane Muentz
Telephone: 609-884-2555
Rooms: 4, 2 with private bath.
Rates: $50 to $68, double occupancy; $5 less for single; continental breakfast included and served in your room. Two-night minimum on weekends, 3 nights on holidays. Children over 14 allowed.
Open: Closes mid-December through January. Restaurant closes Tuesdays. Afternoon tea, dinner by reservation. BYOB.
Facilities & Activities: Beach 2 blocks. Victorian House Tours. Victorian Week in October. Dickens' Christmas Celebration. Emlen Physick Estate. Carriage and trolley rides, bicycling, boating, summer band concerts. Historic Cold Spring Village.

Be inquisitive. Larry and Diane are informed Victorian preservationists. They have unusual Victorian pieces everywhere in their blue and brown Victorian mansion. Examine the baby chair in the parlour. It's retractable. The marble-topped pedestal hides a washbasin, and the smoking chair in the smoking room has carved dogs smoking a pipe that support the armrests. You can't make a turn without making a discovery.

Larry and Diane harmonize authenticity around elegant dining. This superb inn beams from attention. Come to 🖝 dinner at Alexanders and discover the fine touches. The crystal salt and pepper shakers have silver caps, the wine carafes are silver, and the finger bowls arrive floating with rose petals. But even more than the accoutrements it's the food that sends you into 🖝 un-Victorian excesses.

Diane is an imaginative professional chef who offers diverse choices. Maybe it's country French rabbit braised with onions, pine nuts, and bacon, and flavored with burgundy. Or oysters gently poached in cream with sherry and subtle spices and presented in a shell of puff pastry. There also is filet mignon à la bourguignon with pâté and a dark burgundy sauce. For an appetizer try the unusual sausage nut strudel.

For those dessert fetishes some of us harbor, there is kiwi anglais, with a melba sauce served in a spider web pattern; Diane's specialty, brandy Alexander pie, a frozen white chocolate dessert; homemade ice cream; and more.

You retire satiated to one of four 🖝 sumptuous rooms. One has French wallpaper and an exquisite bedroom set. There's a gray satin spread across the bed and frilly lace curtains, a dream room. Another is in rich, deep greens. It has a huge wardrobe, imported peacock lace curtains, and wallpaper replicating that from a Victorian mansion.

The Queen herself would approve.

How to get there: From the ferry take Route 9, then Route 109 to Cape May. Continue on Lafayette Street, turn left on Franklin Street, and turn right on Washington Street. The inn is on the right at 653 Washington. From Garden State Parkway, merge into Lafayette Street.

olive Metcalf

Carroll Villa
Cape May, New Jersey
08204

Innkeepers: Harry Kulkowitz and Vicki Seitchik
Telephone: 609-884-9619
Rooms: 29, 5 with private bath; cottages, apartments.
Rooms: $24 to $36, double occupancy, off season; $30 to $48, double occupancy, in season; EP. Two-day minimum for weekends. Three-day minimum for holiday and Victorian weekends. Children welcome.
Open: April to early January. Breakfast, lunch, dinner daily in season. BYOB.
Facilities & Activities: Beach one block. Victorian House Tours. Victorian Weekend in October. Dickens' Christmas Celebration. Emlen Physick Estate. Carriage and trolley rides. Summer band concerts, biking, boating, U.S. Coast Guard Tour. Historic Cold Spring Village.

    Carroll Villa is ☞ country Victorian and only one block from the ocean. It has a ☞ "Europeanesque" veranda on a wonderfully narrow street lined with great old gingerbread mansions. It's a stroller's delight. One block away is Washington Square, a pedestrian mall where everything "beachy" is found.

There is a bounty of good reasons to visit Cape May and beach lovers, food lovers, and just plain lovers eventually find their way to the Mad Batter, the inn's restaurant. The open-air tables are busy rounds of conversations, romantic candles, and worldly foods.

During January and February Harry and Vicki travel the world. Once they took the staff of six to Thailand. The cuisine at the Mad Batter reflects these excursions. The French toast is made with fresh French bread. You'll find pad woon sen or Thai fried cellophane noodles with chicken, peanuts, and bean sprouts in a spicy oriental sauce. Drum-fish was the special one evening. This thickly textured fish was broiled lightly with a savory buttery wine sauce. To sample everything would take the entire summer. The menu changes often.

Service is famously slow here. Who wants to rush when you're about to bite into exotic fare like coquille St. Jacques with caviar?

You enter the inn by the stained glass registry. In the lounge are white wicker furnishings and eclectic antiques. The guest rooms are filled with antiques, and the floors are painted soft colors to match the rose and flowered wallpapers. Some of the hallways to the rooms are inordinately narrow, then you turn a corner and they become very wide. "Victorian houses are strange like that," says Vicki. "They are filled with surprises."

How to get there: From the Ferry take Route 9, then Route 109 to Cape May. Cross the bridge, and bear right onto Layfayette Street to deadend. Turn far left on Jackson and proceed to the inn on the left. For Lewes Ferry call: 302-645-6313. Cape May County Airport, fly-in.

ᕦ

B: *Try the homemade Mexican coffee ice cream. Delicious!*

Olive Metcalf

The Chalfonte
Cape May, New Jersey
08204

Innkeepers: Anne Le Duc and Judy Bartella
Telephone: 609-884-8409
Rooms: 103, 11 with private bath.
Rates: $69 to $98, double occupancy; $39 to $53, single; inclusive, MAP. Children's rates available. Two-night minimum on weekends.
Open: June 14 through September 9, then weekends through mid-October. Breakfast, dinner, tavern.
Facilities & Activities: Beach 2 blocks, Wine-tasting weekends, evening theater, musicals, concerts by candlelight, Murder Mystery Weekend. Victorian House Tour. October Victorian weekend. Bicycling, tennis, golfing, boating, swimming. U.S. Coast Guard Station.

In Cape May the seasons impinge themselves on you. Summer has arrived when the crowds swell, the heat changes all manner of dress and pace, and the Chalfonte opens its doors as it has for more than one hundred years.

On the veranda and in the hallways a cool ocean breeze blew the afternoon of my arrival. The air conditioning is "natural." It's 🖛 two blocks from the shore but the wide residential street promotes the breezes as far as the Chalfonte's summer guests.

Helen Dickerson is as much a part of the Chalfonte as its familiar rocking chairs on the porch. For over 35 years she's prepared ☛ Southern home cooking for the inn. She fixes American traditionals: roast beef, country ham, southern fried chicken, crab cakes, broiled bluefish, spoonbread, bread pudding, apple pie, and strawberry shortcake.

Men are requested to wear jackets to dinner. Children under age seven dine in their private dining room served by a staff all their own. That's a splendid practice.

The rooms have wooden floors, iron or wooden beds, and many have marble-topped antique dressers. Most are white-walled, and all are simple, summery, and clean.

The energetic innkeepers sponsor a variety of ☛ summer entertainments. Request the brochures before you go. The concerts by candlelight might be your cup of tea, or maybe you prefer wine-tasting parties. Ask about plays, music, or comic revue. They even "Resort to Murder" at the Chalfonte. A special mystery created by Murder To Go, Inc., revolves around an auction with some mighty suspicious bidders in the crowd. You have the weekend to discover the culprit. The sleuth goes home with a small prize.

How to get there: From the Garden State Parkway which merges into Lafayette Street in Cape May, go to the first stoplight and turn left on Madison. Proceed past 4 streets and turn right on Sewell which dead ends at Howard. The inn is on the corner of Howard and Sewell. Cape May County Airport, fly-in.

⌛

Chalfonte dinners are a pleasant surprise the first time. . . . More surprising and pleasing is that week after week, season after season, Chalfonte dinners live up to one's memory of the first time.— Michael Hillmann, Austin, Texas

olive Metcalf

Publick House
Chester, New Jersey
07930

Innkeeper: Linda Gregg
Telephone: 201-879-6878
Rooms: 10, all with private bath; 2 suites.
Rates: $43 to $64, double occupancy, continental breakfast included. Children welcome.
Open: All year. Lunch, dinner, Sunday brunch, bar.
Facilities & Activities: Sundays from Memorial Day to mid-October large antique flea market held nearby. Jockey Hollow, Ford Mansion, Black River Playhouse, parks, and contemporary sports.

Linda Gregg knows her inn from the guest's point of view. She once stayed here not knowing one day she'd become the innkeeper. She remembers it fondly as a most restful night's sleep.

Linda's bubbly personality comes through in several ways. Brides are surprised to find their antique-filled room decorated with thoughtful little things. Linda doesn't fuss over her guests, she discreetly pampers them. On the hall table near the rooms is a ☛ cornucopia of fresh fruits, coffee, and every afternoon a surprise of cookies or cakes appears.

Linda even requests your height to fit the bed to your length.

The main floor of the Publick House is a series of comfortable dining rooms. We chose a position near the fire one rainy afternoon and indulged in a Belgian Waffle oozing with chocolate syrup and crowned with heaping mounds of ice cream. The walls were busy with antiques and there's an ☞ industrial-size oak icebox that's exquisite.

Sunday brunch is served from a groaning board and after this feast of hot blueberry pancakes, omelettes, meats, and luncheon dishes, capped off with a series of delicious Danish, you can go to the flea market or walk the shop-filled town. You might run into Linda who is adding more pieces to the rooms.

In the Tack Room dining area you might brush shoulders with members of the U.S. Equestrian Team who practice nearby. If you're listening to evening music and think you see Paul Newman and Joanne Woodward in the corner, you might be right.

The brick inn opened in 1810. The first proprietor owned a line of stagecoaches that ran between New York City and Easton, Pennsylvania. Next, it was a classical school until 1862 when it again became a classical inn.

There is a maze of picture-perfect country roads surrounding Chester. Linda will start you in the right direction.

How to get there: From I-80 take Route 206 South to Chester. Go west on Route 24, Main Street, and the inn is on the left in the center of town.

B: *Innkeeper Linda still goes to country inns on her vacation.*

Olive Metcalf

The Lambertville House
Lambertville, New Jersey
08530

Innkeeper: Susan Darrah
Telephone: 609-397-0202
Rooms: 32, 5 with private bath.
Rates: $30 to $60, double or single occupancy, continental breakfast included. Children welcome.
Open: All year. Restaurant closes Christmas Day. Lunch, dinner, bar.
Facilities & Activities: Jazz entertainment Fridays and Saturdays. Children's dinner with Santa. Washington Crossing State Park, Bucks County Playhouse, wineries, antiquing, bicycling, tennis, canoeing, tubing, hiking along Delaware Canal, mule barge rides, and Sunday steam train rides July through October.

Lambertville is a walk across the bridge from New Hope, Pennsylvania. Lambertville House first opened in 1812 as a stagecoach inn when the ferry transported travelers across the river on the Philadelphia-to-New-York-run. It is stone, masonry, and wood, and located in an area with plenty to do.

The inn's restaurant is a beehive of activity. You can sit

in the dining room or go to the more casual atmosphere of the wooden bar. Here is a lighted glass display case of the Lambertville House memorabilia.

Americana is the theme here. Even the wine list is all-American. You might try a carpetbagger steak, a tender filet of beef that is stuffed with fried oysters, or an apple-stuffed chicken breast. ☛ Vegetarian dinners are available. Gingerbread just like my grandma used to make and apple walnut custard round out the delicious meal.

The innkeeper, Susan Darrah, works with her family. Her sister, mother, uncle, aunt, brother, daughter, and her best friend since childhood all work here. It's an extended family operation. I like that. If you're short of help you can always find more when the family is willing.

Every Friday and Saturday night there's entertainment in the bar. ☛ Holidays are popular occasions here. Lamb is traditional at Easter, and at Christmas there's dinner with Santa with gifts for the children.

You climb the creaky stairs to the rooms. They're plain and simple. The inn is very old and has never been anything other than an inn and restaurant. Food is at the heart of the matter here.

How to get there: From I-95 take Route 32 North to New Hope, Pennsylvania. Take Route 202 East across the Delaware to Lambertville. The inn is in town on the left-hand side of the street.

The management treated me like one of the family. The food was marvelous, always well cooked, and the rooms cozy.—Stephen John Pike, Buckinghamshire, England

olive Metcalf

Colligan's Stockton Inn
Stockton, New Jersey
08559

Innkeepers: Todd and Penny Drucquer
Telephone: 609-397-1250
Rooms: 2, both with private bath; 3 suites.
Rates: $45 to $65, double occupancy; $75 to $95, suite; continental breakfast included. Two-night minimum stay on weekends. Children welcome. Small pets welcome with $50 deposit.
Open: Closes Christmas Day. Lunch, dinner, bar.
Facilities & Activities: Outdoor dining, dancing and music occasionally. Antique shops, Washington Crossing Delaware State Park, Bucks County Theater, hiking, bicycling, fishing, golfing, canoeing and tubing on the Delaware.

Colligan's Stockton Inn has no view, and then again it has a most wonderful view. It imposes itself on the tiny Main Street of Stockton, New Jersey, and from your balcony of the Colligan Suite you can watch the world go by.

You will enjoy your stay here. This very old stone inn has young and experienced innkeepers at the helm. Todd says they wanted to return to the idea of bed and board in the full sense of a country inn. He's a fellow with a sense of place and history. In the dining rooms are marvelous ☞ murals. They were painted by artists during the Depression in return for room and board. You can enjoy your lunch and look at the 19th century displayed on the walls. I noticed that the locals are as comfortable with the old tin ceiling and the new kelly green carpeting in the bar as are travelers.

Todd and Penny have transformed the rooms into what I'd call ☞ "designer country" style and they are fresh and cheery. In the carriage house there are black and white tiles in the entrance, a floral print on black wallpaper and white woodwork. It's wonderful. One of the rooms has the loveliest canopy bed, and the mauves predominate.

In the outdoor garden is the ☞ wishing well that's mentioned in the lyrics, "There's a Small Hotel," by Lorenz Hart. You can sit here over a leisurely dinner on a summer night and listen to the piano-playing with the gentle gurgling of the trout ponds in the distance. I tried the sole stuffed with macadamia nuts; I liked its crunchy texture and the velvety smooth wine sauce on top. A rich chocolate cake followed.

That evening reminded me of the last two lines of Hart's lyrics. They are, "Good night, sleep well; We'll thank the small hotel together."

How to get there: Take I-95 to Route 29 North in New Jersey. Continue to Stockton. The inn is on the right-hand side of the street. Fly-in, Doylestown Airport.

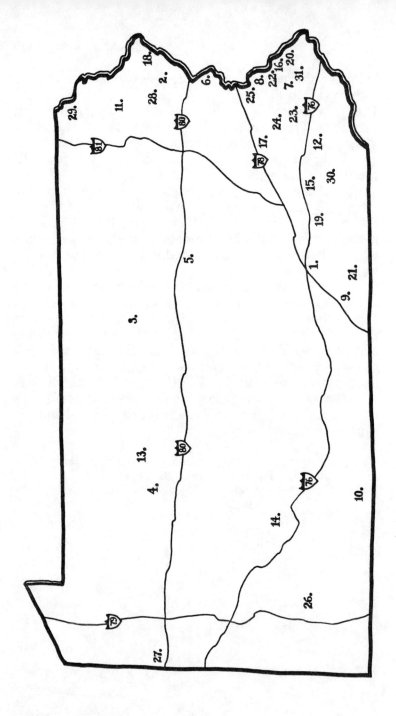

Numbers on map refer to towns numbered
on index on opposite page

Pennsylvania

olive Metcalf

Allenberry Resort Inn and Playhouse
Boiling Springs, Pennsylvania
17007

Innkeepers: John J. and Jere Heinze
Telephone: 717-258-3211
Rooms: 51, all with private bath; 3 cottages.
Rates: $48, double occupancy; $40, single; $85 to $140, cottage; EP. Children welcome.
Open: Mid-March through October. Breakfast, lunch, dinner, two taprooms.
Facilities & Activities: Professional Equity Theater, swimming pool, 2 Har-Tru tennis courts and 2 Laykold Lighted tennis courts, and trout stream. 57 acres.

Under the pine and maple trees large yellow and green city scenes are laid out to dry. They are the sets for the next show at the ☞ Allenberry Playhouse. John Heinze signed John Travolta's equity card here. You might see future stars practicing their lines as they walk under the large shade trees.

Jere Heinze admits it's exciting to run an inn with a theater. The theater has grown to accommodate 420, some of

140

whom arrive from the city by bus. The performers, many of whom return yearly, stay for two-week engagements.

The terraced inn accommodates all guests quietly and smoothly. If the theater doesn't interest you, you can sit beside the olympic size swimming pool and look out at "Yellow Breeches," a famous "Fish for Fun" trout stream that attracts anglers from around the country. You also can play some tennis on one of the inn's four courts. The grounds are inspirational, lush, and beautiful. It's an inn of multiple pleasures aesthetically hidden from one another.

The Stone Lodge has its own guest living room with fireplace and colonial reproductions in the rooms. There's a Penn State suite for football fans. The Meadow Lodge is motel style, with a lounge overlooking the stream. Directly on the stream is the charming little "Still House," rumored to have been the home of independent brewers.

Guests may walk into the self-serve wine cellar to select their dinner wine to accompany such entrees as broiled rainbow trout or barbecued country-style ribs basted in a tangy sauce.

There's an array of foods for the buffet luncheon, chicken and biscuits, meat loaf, cold meat salads, broccoli, big bowls of fruit salads, and vegetable salads. A buffet spread of no small magnitude. It puts you in a cheerful frame of mind for the comedy matinee. You won't find yourself in any other mood at Allenberry.

How to get there: From I-81 exit onto Route 34 south to Route 174 and turn west to Boiling Springs. Go though the village and on the right hand of the road you'll see the small sign for the Allenberry Playhouse. Carlisle Airport, fly-in.

Salad bars are a favorite of mine and I loved the one at the Allenberry. We were struck with the beauty and plan to return.—Margaret and Vance Boelts, Grand Island, Nebraska

olive Metcalf

The Overlook Inn
Canadensis, Pennsylvania
18325

Innkeepers: Bob and Lolly Tupper
Telephone: 717-595-7519
Rooms: 20, all with private bath.
Rates: $54 to $57, per person, double occupancy; $66, single; MAP.
    Three-night minimum stay on a holiday weekend.
Open: All year. Breakfast, dinner, tavern.
Facilities & Activities: 15 acres of woods for walks and cross-coun-
    try skiing. Swimming pool. Camelback, Jack Frost, Big Boul-
    der, and Buck Hill ski areas, 30 minutes. Indoor ice skating,
    antiquing.

Quiet, quiet, quiet it is. The 🐦 towering pine trees fra-
grantly encircle the inn, and for sounds you have the birds in
the trees by day and the crackling of the fire on a cool evening. The inn no longer overlooks the town of Canadensis as
it once did, but you can hike through the woods that have
risen to misname the Overlook.

The inn has grown from a small 19th-century farmhouse to accommodate its guests. The rooms are cozy with
homemade afghans across the beds, pretty throw-pillows
made by local churchwomen, and antique wooden dressers

where a full carafe of wine waits your pleasure. Desks and rockers are found in several rooms, but you'll really want to go down and relax in the living room that stretches across the entire front of the inn. The front porch is equally inviting on a gentle summer day. At twilight you might see deer grazing on the back lawn.

Before dinner we took a tour of the paintings by Rick Tupper, son of Lolly and Bob. They are contemporary and fit perfectly in this dear old inn. The sea oats and coral reef were among my favorites. Most rooms have a Tupper painting.

Paul Bunyan must have stayed here in the past; he left his shoe in the library. It's large enough to sit on and yet no one knows its history because it's always been here.

The meals are worth dressing up for, and men are asked to wear jackets for dinner. The ☞ prime New York-cut of sirloin steak is covered with a sour cream sauce flavored lightly with cognac and large fresh mushrooms. A Texas rancher couldn't find a better cut. The sauce left a permanently flavorful memory. The Chicken Ambrosiana is delicately accented with anisette, not too much. It's a gastronomic treat.

Homemade ice creams are popular here but don't overlook the ☞ trifles. They're made with fruit of the season and fresh moist cake and blended with a real whipped cream.

My husband still talks about our stay at the Overlook. You feel rejuvenated and a bit pampered at this large old country inn.

How to get there: Take Exit 52 from I-80 onto Route 477 North to Canadensis. Go through the traffic light in town and continue north a short distance over the bridge. Turn right on Dutch Hill Road and continue 1½ miles to the entrance on the right. Fly-in, Mount Pocono Airport.

☀

B: *The staff at the Overlook are extra special people.*

olive Metcalf

The Pine Knob
Canadensis, Pennsylvania
18325

Innkeepers: June and Jim Belfie
Telephone: 717-595-2532
Rooms: 27, 19 with private bath.
Rates: $44 to $55, per person, MAP. 10 percent service charge.
   Children over 5 allowed. Two-night minimum on weekends, 3
   nights on holidays. Stay 6 days, 7th night free.
Open: May through November open every day. December through
   April open on weekends. Breakfast, dinner, tavern.
Facilities & Activities: Ski Timber Hill and Buck Hill; 30 minutes
   from Camelback and Jack Frost Ski Areas. Golfing privileges at
   Buck Hill and other courses. Swimming, tennis, boating,
   horseback riding, bowling, racquetball, Pocono Playhouse, hik-
   ing, snowmobiling, and indoor ice skating.

   A Steinway sits in the large L-shaped living room and a
pair of white couches face off before the stone fireplace. You
may join others here and fall into discussions of music, art,
literature, movies, or the best way to pet a moody cat.
   June Belfie was an artist and pianist, Jim was in insur-
ance. They wanted to try something different, and they got

their wish. Theirs is a smoothly run inn that has the ☞ 3 C's: comfy, casual, cozy. Add an F, for friendliness.

It's a large rambling inn painted charcoal gray with white trim, that provides plenty of outdoor pursuits. Cross the road to Brodhead Creek and you find the swimming pool and the tennis court. You can hike up Pine Knob or venture out on local excursions and return to candlelight dining with classical music in the background. Around the dining room hang June's paintings. I especially like the little girl and the duck. It's reminiscent of a Mary Cassatt.

How Jim and June keep so trim is a mystery. When I tried the chef's desserts, the word scrumptious came to my lips. The chocolate ☞ Charlotte Malinkoff is soft and mousse-like, but during the summer the chef freezes it to cool the palate. The ☞ orange caramel flan is coated with a subtle sauce that made me a flan fan. Then there's a chocolate marble cheesecake that's a guaranteed palate pleaser.

Jim is the breakfast expert. He might feel like making blueberry pancakes, or buckwheat, or buttermilk during the week. For Sundays he has developed a special Swedish pancake that's wonderfully light and rich.

The clean rooms are filled with a blend of some antiques and good wooden furniture. They are not old and not new, but somewhere in between. There's a natural comfort in these avuncular surroundings.

How to get there: Take Route 390 south to Canadensis from I-84. Turn left at the light in town on Route 447 and the inn is less than a mile. Fly-in, Birchwood Airport.

Dinners are outstanding! Great appetizers, wonderful salad dressings, an intermezzo, choice of three entrees and best of all, a different freshly baked bread every night.—Dorothea Lutz, Philadelphia, Pennsylvania.

olive Metcalf

Pump House Inn
Canadensis, Pennsylvania
18325

Innkeeper: H. Todd Drucquer
Telephone: 717-595-7501
Rooms: 2 rooms, 3 suites, 1 cottage, all with private bath.
Rates: May through November, $45 to $90, double occupancy; $100 to $140, cottage; continental breakfast included. December through April, $40 to $85, double occupancy; $95 to $130, cottage; continental breakfast included.
Open: All year. Dinner, tavern.
Facilities & Activities: Skiing, indoor ice skating, horseback riding, golfing, nightspots, summer theater, antiquing.

On Route 390, one and a half miles from the village intersection in Canadensis, is the Pump House Inn. A bright red, long-handled pump sits to the left of the entrance. You enter the restaurant that is a maze of rooms and little niches. Even the petite white-walled stone basement with the black and white checkered floor appeals to a ☞ romantic diner.

The inn is known for its restaurant. The chef emphasizes ☞ French cuisine. During winter season you might find a cassoulet de poulet, saucisson, and veau, which is one of my favorite country French dishes. Rack of lamb is a year-round favorite and finely roasted with Dijon mustard. Desserts are a French assortment that varies from day to day. You might try the traditional chocolate mousse or fresh fruit bathed in a liqueur. Seasonal fruits will appear. During winter there's nothing finer than a hot apple compote in the sunny, windowed dining room.

The inn does not have a common room, but you can wander between the trees along the road or go off to enjoy one of the many nearby activities. You also could select one of the suites if you want extra space. The rooms are decorated in two styles. A few are American country with pine floors, and others are more contemporary. They're not too large or too small, but just right.

And when you arrive you'll find wine in your room and a candy morsel on the pillow for sweet dreams.

How to get there: Take Exit 52 off I-80 and Route 447 North to Canadensis. At the light in town, turn right on Route 390 and go 1½ miles north. The inn is on the left-hand side of the road.

olive Metcalf

The Cedar Run Inn
Cedar Run, Pennsylvania
17727

Innkeepers: Peggy and Randall Lounsbury
Telephone: 717-353-6241
Rooms: 13, 4 with private bath.
Rates: $14, per person, EP: $32, per person, MAP. Children welcome. Two-day minimum on Memorial Day and Labor Day weekends. No credit cards.
Open: Closes January. In February and March open on weekends. April through December closes Monday and Tuesday. Breakfast, dinner, alcoholic beverages.
Facilities & Activities: Pine Creek for shallow swimming. Innertubing, canoe rental. Rafting, horseback riding, snowmobiling, cross-country skiing, and hiking nearby. "Grand Canyon" of Pennsylvania.

However you arrive at Cedar Run, population 13, the ☞ scenery is exhilarating. If it's from the east much of the way is one lane and some of the route is dirt road. It puts the spirit of adventure in the trek. The route from the southwest is hardtop all the way.

Cedar Run is not posh and the rooms are still like olden times with linoleum on the floors and some shared baths. But everything is clean, quiet, and orderly, and when you get a taste of what's happening in the kitchen in this ☞ chef-owned inn you'll appreciate the palatable heart of the matter.

In the handsome dining room the wooden tables and buffets gleam and patterned placemats set the scene. A graduate of the Culinary Institute, Randy is an ☞ accomplished chef. One impressive dish he prepares is scallops poached with green grapes and quartered mushrooms, finished with a lobster sauce. He also prepares a loin of pork pounded thinly, filled with ground apples and hazelnuts, sautéed and covered with an apple brandy sauce. Fresh strawberries are served with a brandied sour cream sauce.

If you call, Peg will send you the dinner menu; it's a good way to get acquainted before you go.

It's a small inn with a common room filled with eclectic furniture and interspersed with fun and surprising things to examine. A straw fishing basket hangs on the porch next to the entrance. In the porch rafters is a magnificent wooden canoe. It's touchingly pretty and rustic.

Randy and Peg do it all here, which explains why they must close two days a week. They are a pair of "natural born" innkeepers. I like it when there's organization and planning behind amiability.

At the General Store across the road you can buy a bar of homemade soap or check out a book from the small lending library. Just sign your name and return it before you leave.

How to get there: From Route 287 exit onto Route 414 West. After Blackwell it's a dirt road for 5 or 6 miles, then hardtop. Turn sharply left 3/10 mile after sign: Village of Cedar Run; cross the bridge, turn left, and you'll see the inn.

The inn presents an unexpected blend of fine dining and honest hospitality. Randy's linguine appetizer, veal sauté, and a California Zinfandel are my favorites.—George R. Wertz, Akron, Ohio

oliveMetcalf

Gateway Lodge
Cooksburg, Pennsylvania
16217

Innkeepers: Joseph and Linda Burney
Telephone: 814-744-8017
Rooms: 7, 2 with private bath; 8 cabins.
Rates: $25 to $40, double occupancy; $40, cabin sleeping 4; EP.
Children welcome. Must be of age to sleep in own room if in
lodge. Dogs allowed in cabins, $5 per day. No credit cards.
Open: Closes at Thanksgiving and Christmas. Breakfast, lunch
Tuesday through Saturday during summer only, dinner Tues-
day through Saturday. Tavern.
Facilities & Activities: Stables, swimming pool, hiking trails, cross-
country skiing from inn, skis available. Fishing, hunting, golfing, bicycling, theater, Clarion River for canoeing and tubing,
near 2,599-acre Cook Forest State Park.

Gateway Lodge is a wooden jewel in the forest. Step a
foot inside the door and the 🖝 charisma of the front room al-
lures you the rest of the way. Massive hemlock timbers compose the walls, the ceiling is pine, hemlock, and chestnut.
The flooring is oak, and the trim is chestnut. It is lovely.
Summer, winter, spring, and fall the stone fireplace always has a blazing fire. Even in summer it can get cool at

150

night. Around twilight the lanterns are lit, and the wood gleams from the flame's reflections. The mood is one of pure contentment.

A circle of couches and chairs surround the fireplace, a guitar sits casually to one side, and there's an ornately refinished piano. Jars of lemon candies sit within easy reach.

I like coming here for many reasons: the ☞ beauty of the lodge, the outdoors, and the casual relaxed style of the innkeepers. You feel as if they did away with all the pressures of the world. Behind it all they are working very hard, but they make it look effortless. You also feel as if you're entering the forest primeval.

Joseph and Linda decorated the inn together. The petite and cozy country inn rooms have beige ruffled curtains, print wallpapers, little chests, and bookshelves. Linda keeps ☞ thick quilts on the beds all summer long and exchanges them for "haps" or much heavier quilts for ski season. They are the real thing, handmade from old woolen clothes. They'd keep you warm through a blizzard should you be so lucky as to get "trapped" here.

In the dining room you eat from tables gifted, inherited, and found, which shine from their daily polishings. From the walls hang tools, hats, toys, jars, a great assortment of things.

Two entrees are served nightly from a weekly selection of seven. Request the brochure, which includes the menu. The entrees are ☞ family recipes of Linda's and include a fat, stuffed chicken breast, moist and crisp; a stuffed pork chop; barbecued spareribs; sirloin steak with stuffing; and baked Boston scrod. Among the desserts is a chocolate lover's delight. I'd order with abandon; you'll not have regrets afterward.

How to get there: From I-80 take Route 36 North. The inn is on the right just before the park. Clarion County Airport, fly-in.

Olive Metcalf

The Pine Barn Inn
Danville, Pennsylvania
17821

Innkeeper: Martin Walzer
Telephone: 717-275-2071
Rooms: 45, all with private bath; 6 rooms in the guest house with 2 shared baths.
Rates: $34 to $38, double occupancy; $30 to $34, single; EP. Guest house: $20, double occupancy; $18 single; EP. Children welcome.
Open: Closes Christmas Day, New Year's Day, Memorial Day, Fourth of July, and Labor Day. Breakfast, lunch, dinner, tavern.
Facilities & Activities: Antique auctions and shops, farm markets, golfing, horseback riding, covered bridge tour in Snyder County, and Buggy Museum in Mifflinburg.

At the entrance to Geisinger Medical Center turn left into the Pine Barn Inn.

At first glance the Pine Barn hasn't the configuration of an inn. The rooms stretch out with motel-type doorfront parking. But behind the brown barn exterior lies a variety of rooms, and the past is retold in the whitewashed stone that forms part of the original barn, which is now the restaurant.

Marty Walzer is the "in touch" innkeeper who is the expert's expert on the area. There's a caring behind his casual manner that is demonstrated in the way it all works together here.

The inn's restaurant is open from 7 A.M. until 10 P.M. Besides three meals daily and anytime in-between, there is afternoon tea, which was recently instituted by Barbara Walzer.

The restaurant is very popular. The seafood comes from Foley Company in Boston and the chef prepares a long selection of seafood dinners. The meats are .equally interesting. It's impossible not to find a perfectly delicious meal that will fill you to your limits. The beef Wellington is a petite filet mignon topped with a slice of goose liver pâté and baked in puff pastry. Any chef who occasionally offers coquille St. Jacques or scallops with mushrooms in a rich creamy wine sauce wins my applause. The pies are all ☞ homemade and the blueberry and banana cream are not surpassed by anyone.

Barbara has transformed the former lobby into a wonderful ☞ gift shop filled with dolls, baskets, and fun things. She also decorated the rooms in the ☞ lovely guest house, which is a three-minute walk from the inn. It has one bath for women, and another for men. Downstairs is a living room with television and desk. In the main inn are several rooms, each with a television, and the motel-type rooms have cherry furniture and a writing desk.

Thursday through Sunday the auctions are announced in the local paper. Ask Marty for the local brochure listing antique shops.

How to get there: Take Route 54 South from I-80 to Route 11, and go east to Railroad Street. Turn left toward the Geisinger Medical Center. The inn is on the left just before the center.

B: *This is Amish country and there's a buggy museum in nearby Mifflinburg. You can still get a custom-made buggy here.*

olive Metcalf

The Mountain House
Delaware Water Gap, Pennsylvania
18327

Innkeepers: Frank and Yolanda Brown and family
Telephone: 717-424-2254
Rooms: 32, 8 with private bath.
Rates: $35 to $45, double occupancy; $25 to $35, single; continental
   breakfast included. Children welcome.
Open: Year round. Closes 2 weeks in January but call. Restaurant
   closed Mondays. Lunch, dinner, alcoholic beverages.
Facilities & Activities: Swimming pool, Appalachian Trail. Access to
   country club golf course. Hiking, canoeing, white-water rafting, cross-country skiing. Downhill skiing at Shawnee Mountain, 10 minute drive, and Camelback, 20 minute drive. 70,000
   acre Delaware Gap Park.

   This old-fashioned inn is well located on a quiet "Mountain Road." Step out the front door and you're in the 70,000-
acre Delaware Water Gap Park. Go in May and jack-in-the-
pulpits, lady's slippers, and unfurling fiddleheads announce
springtime. In fall the trees along the forest pathways are a
fury of seasonal colors.
   There's a homey ☞ doiley-frilled living room for guests,

154

comfortable sink-into-it furniture, and a piano. Who knows, you might end up in a spontaneous sing-along.

The attractive dining room is trimmed in blue and surrounded by a waist-high shelf filled with a variety of antiques and vintage photographs of women. It was decorated by Yolanda.

In this setting the shrimp Newburg is a tasty delight as is the creamy homemade banana pie. The menu offers old-fashioned favorites at reasonable prices. One of the baker's surprises is rum cake that Frank admits will "knock your socks" off. Friday night it's seafood buffet that is almost an American custom.

The rooms have an appealing quality of another time. They are spartanly old-fashioned and clean. Several bathrooms have claw-footed bathtubs, and where else could you find the original swinging wooden doors of old in bathrooms? Every room has a petite sink.

Behind the inn is the pool and Yolanda's antique shop that she opens by request. The antique shop was where the staff stayed in the old days when traveling was an expedition and guests spent weeks.

Frank and Yolanda share the old secrets of the inn with a sincere interest in the past. They have the original guest books that date back to the inn's opening in 1870. Some guests have stayed here who have found a great-aunt's or grandmother's name in the book. That's a rare pleasure.

How to get there: From I-80 take Exit 53 to Delaware Water Gap. Turn left on Main Street (Route 611) to Mountain Road. Turn right and climb the hill to the inn on the right-hand side. Fly-in, East Stroudsburg Airport.

🌹

The food at the Mountain House is the best I have eaten in many years. The cream of chicken rice soup, veal cutlet Lorenzo, and lemon meringue pie are without equal.—H.T. Goldbach, P.E., Little Ferry, New Jersey

Olive Metcalf

Doylestown Inn
Doylestown, Pennsylvania
18901

Innkeepers: Dennis Sackelson and Nick Adams
Telephone: 215-345-6610
Rooms: 22, all with private bath.
Rates: $53 to $65, double occupancy; $45, single; continental
breakfast included. Children welcome; no charge for under age
10 if share room with parents. Two-night minimum on holiday
weekends. Pets allowed.
Open: All year. Restaurant closes Christmas Day. Breakfast, lunch,
dinner, two bars.
Facilities & Activities: Jazz entertainers Wednesday, Friday, and
Saturday evenings. Mercer Museum, Fonthill, the Mercer ma-
sonry home, Moravian Pottery and Tile works, antique shops,
Pearl S. Buck's home, Washington Crossing Historic Park, and
Bucks County Playhouse.

I saw oyster pie for ten cents, lobster for twenty-five
cents, and Welsh rarebit for only thirty-five cents. Of course,
that menu was framed and dated 1937. You'll receive a more
contemporary version and can order fresh vegetables that arrive with a mellow vegetable dip, or the special might be pork
Normandy speckled with apple slivers and bathed in a light

brandy sauce. I like light fare at odd hours of the day and night, and at the Doylestown Inn you can ☞ order from the luncheon menu any time, whether you are seated in the dining room or one of the two pubs.

On the walls, throughout the small lobby and dining room hang stained glass pieces and art works by local artists. If you see something you like, you might call up the artist and meet him or her over a bowl of hot chili or a thick cheese omelette and negotiate a deal. The ☞ handmade furniture in the lobby is for sale. You might walk in for dinner and walk out with an oak table.

The rooms are plain and simple. They all have telephones so there's no excuse to lose touch with the boss if you're a business traveler. The inn is convenient to the courthouse and interesting museums and historic exhibits. In nearby New Hope is the Bucks County Playhouse.

The inn had been refurbished and then closed when innkeepers Dennis Sackelson and Nick Adams bought it. They brought it back to life.

How to get there: From I-276 north of Philadelphia, take Route 611 North to Doylestown. Where Court Street and State Street intersect at Route 611 take Court, and circle the block back to State Street, which is one way. The inn is at 118 West State Street.

olive Metcolf

Ever May on the Delaware
Erwinna, Pennsylvania
18920

Innkeepers: Ronald L. Strouse and Frederick L. Cresson
Telephone: 215-294-9100
Rooms: 12, all with private bath; one suite.
Rooms: $49 to $80, double occupancy; $35 to $45, single; $65 to
     $125, suite; continental breakfast and afternoon tea included.
     Children under 12 discouraged. Two-night minimum stay on
     weekends; 3 nights on holiday weekends.
Open: Closes Christmas Day. Five-course dinner served at 7:30
     p.m. on Fridays, Saturdays, Sundays, and some holidays.
Facilities & Activities: Croquet, canoeing Delaware River, antiqu-
     ing, fishing, golfing, tennis, Mercer Museum in Doylestown,
     Bucks County Theater in New Hope.

   "Ever May" it is, this bright ☞ sunny Victorian gem
that's comfortably spacious and meticulously restored. This
is an inn where you couldn't have a cloudy day, even if it was
raining outside, because in the parlour the snapdragons and
the lilies would be in bloom, a steaming cup of English tea
would be at your side, and you would have the expectation of
an evening to come with ☞ dinner a graceful five-course
banquet with epicurian dimensions.

Innkeeper Ron Strouse wears the chef's hat, and to keep his cooking skills sharp he takes a week every year to go back to gourmet cooking school. He should be the professor. You'll agree when you visit Ever May.

Holidays are gala at Ever May. The hors d'oeuvres might include savory fresh oysters or caviar followed by mousse de salmon delicately coated with a special lobster sauce, chicken stuffed with salmon, or quenelles poached with shrimp on top. You can tell when someone likes to cook by the way he likes to keep exploring. Ron might try a new sauce, or a hot Grand Marnier souffle with raspberry sauce. He calls his style of cooking "vivacious French." Very apt. You can't categorize a gourmet adventurer.

The beds are Victorian in keeping with the style of the house and each room is named for a Bucks County figure. In the carriage house is an amazing bathtub. The rim around the top is wooden.

In the library-parlour Ron has merged ☞ Mercer tiles into the fireplace bricks. They are figures in clear deep hues and will entice you to visit the Mansion and Mercer Museum in Doylestown where this genius lived. Ron knows all about him and a room is named Henry Mercer.

Behind the house are ☞ 25 acres where you can roam between the apple trees and watch the peacocks or pet the sheep. There's a canoe for launching in the Delaware across the road and there's croquet on the lawn. It's a soothing inn where you will want to spend the night, and the day.

How to get there: From I-95 take Route 32 North to Erwinna. The inn is on the left-hand side of the road with a half-moon driveway. Fly-in, Doylestown Airport.

ᵍ

B: *The innkeepers purchased Ever May from the Stover family who had owned it since the 1700s. The contract listed twenty-seven family members.*

159

Olive Metcalf

The Golden Pheasant Inn
Erwinna, Pennsylvania
18920

Innkeeper: Ralph Schneider
Telephone: 215-294-9595
Rooms: 14, all share baths.
Rates: $50, double occupancy, continental breakfast included. Two-night minimum on weekends.
Open: Closes mid-December to early February. Restaurant closes Mondays. Dinner, bar.
Facilities & Activities: Across the road is the Delaware River and Canal. Near New Hope, Pennsylvania. Washington Crossing State Park, antique shops, Mercer Museum in Doylestown.

In the summertime you can sit in the garden room and, as you might expect, order a ☛ pheasant gilded with sauce. Enhance the fowl with a light Pennsylvania wine. This is a superb meal. There's a console radio in one dining room and, depending on the mood of the diners, you can request a station, but mostly it's silent and interesting to look at.

Ralph Schneider was in advertising in New York City when he came to vacation in Bucks County and stayed to open an inn. "I guess it was a fluke really," he says. "But apparently it's one that's worked because ☞ I'm still here, eighteen years later."

There are six rooms in the inn and eight down the road in the Isaac Stover Mill mansion that dates from 1834. The dark Victorian furniture and deeply stained wooden floors give the impression this is real Victorian and not an updated version. In the parlour of the Mill Manse is an overstuffed red couch for guests to sink into while perusing the magazines arrayed on the marble tabletops. There's a pair of ornate and lovely marble fireplaces.

Ralph likes clocks. There are several throughout the inn and dining rooms. In the garden room is a French grandfather clock ensconced in the corner. It's a beauty.

How to get there: From I-95 take Route 32 North. The restaurant is on the left after Tinicum and just before Erwinna. The inn is one mile farther down Route 32.

⏳

The desserts are sinful. A favorite is the almond cheesecake.—Jeanette and Harry Gregor, Martinsville, New Jersey

Olive Metcalf

The Historic Fairfield Inn
Fairfield, Pennsylvania
17320

Innkeeper: David W. Thomas
Telephone: 717-642-5410
Rooms: 6, all with shared bath.
Rates: $40 to $45, double occupancy, EP.
Open: Closes holidays, first week of February, and first week of September. Restaurant closes Sundays October through April. Breakfast, lunch, dinner, tavern.
Facilities & Activities: Gettysburg Battlefield nearby. Ski Liberty 10 minutes, golf, antiquing, auctions, Miniature Horse farm, farmers markets, and annual Apple Festival.

You come for country cooking and a leisurely paced weekend in a historic inn. Bring your antique questions. During the month of March, David hosts Monday night lectures with antique experts. He is rich in knowledge about the ways and things of old, and his curiosity is infectious.

David's interests complement the inn. He has selected beautiful furniture in a blend of periods. He has hung red, yellow, and black lanterns from the tavern ceiling. You're in the right place if the electricity goes out. David also has studied landscaping and horticulture. From the dining room you can see his attractive, petite garden, surrounded by a high hedge.

Squire William Miller laid out the town of Fairfield in 1801, having begun his plantation home in 1757. In 1823 his home became an inn. It's in the middle of little Fairfield and a pre-revolutionary American flag fittingly hangs out front.

You'll find delicious seasonal cobblers served at the Fairfield. The ☞ peach version is served with ice cream. Local women prepare the food and everything arrives with hot flaky biscuits. There are tantalizing combinations of a ☞ thick filet, served with your choice of crab cakes, chicken and biscuits, or a porkchop.

There are two large rooms in the inn and two guest lounges. In one room the floor dips slightly, and tucked under the bed is a chamber pot that's for looks only. In the next is a baby carriage and a double-seated wicker chair. You can step out to the second-story porch and watch the world of Fairfield go by. Three doors away is the Guest House. The parlour is ☞ elegantly furnished and above the sofa hangs a friendly portrait of a gentleman. David selected it for the man's kindly expression. The rooms are petite, country-stylish, and inviting. You'll have a pleasant night here.

You can spend the day touring Gettysburg Battlefield, pick a basket of fresh fruit, visit the winery for fruit wines, and never be too far from the inn.

How to get there: From I-81, go east on Route 16, which merges with Route 116. Entering Fairfield the inn is on the left.

olive Metcalf

The Inn at Nemacolin
Farmington, Pennsylvania
15437

Innkeeper: Ron Lex
Telephone: 412-329-8555
Rooms: 22, all with private bath; 5 suites.
Rates: $88 to $108, double occupancy; $78 to $98, single; $108 to $118, suite; EP. Champagne Fantasy $150, per person, per night. Children allowed.
Open: All year. Breakfast, lunch, dinner, bar.
Facilities & Activities: 3,000 acres of woodlands, ponds, 18-hole golf course, tennis courts, swimming pool, indoor hot tub, horseback riding, hiking, hunting, fishing, skeet and trapshooting, cross-country skiing, camping. Downhill skiing, 45 minutes; Frank Lloyd Wright's Fallingwater, 20 minutes; white-water rafting, 10 minutes.

Park your plane on the 4,000-foot-long private airstrip adjacent to the inn or leave your car in the tree-lined parking lot, and a satisfying quiet descends. One visitor said this inn reminded her of a setting for a James Bond movie. I have to agree.

Skeet and trapshooting anyone? Or fishing in the myriad ponds? You'll need a map to find your way around the

3,000 acres that surround the inn. There are sleigh rides in winter and during the rest of the year carriage and wagon rides. For physical pleasures try golfing, swimming, hiking, or cross-country skiing.

This polished inn offers "haute camping." They call it "Champagne Fantasy." You bring your toothbrush and evening dress. The innkeeper supplies the tent, puts it up beside the lake, and around dusk dinner is served. You dine at lakeside on a linen tablecloth, are served an eight-course dinner by a waiter that begins with terrine of rabbit and includes the specialty of the house, trout. That's pretty extravagant.

If you stay in the inn the large rooms are similarly furnished and decorated with wildlife prints. The views of the trees are soothing. Everything is new and professionally managed.

You get your bearings in the lobby. In one direction is the masculine bar in deep green and shiny woods and hunting prints.

In the other direction is the Golden Trout Restaurant. The ceiling is exquisitely draped. The salad was served with a piquant hot bacon dressing, and for the intermezzo, a rainbow of sherbet balls, watermelon, lemon, and orange. The fresh trout came circled with an edible pool of irresistible dill hollandaise sauce. For the grande finale there was a feather-light chocolate mousse.

How to get there: By air: 13 nautical miles southwest of Indian Head VORTAC. By land: From Uniontown proceed 12 miles east on Route 40 past Fort Necessity Battlefield to the village of Farmington. Turn left at the Nemacolin Woodlands sign, and follow the road to the left up the hill.

B: *If you fly, call ahead for clearance.*

olive Metcalf

Settler's Inn
Hawley, Pennsylvania
18428

Innkeepers: Grant and Jeanne Genzlinger
Telephone: 717-226-2993
Rooms: 16, 9 with private bath; 2 suites.
Rates: $30 to $40, double occupancy; $45 to $60, suite; continental
breakfast included. Children welcome.
Open: Closes Christmas Eve day. Lunch, dinner, Sunday brunch,
tavern.
Facilities & Activities: Fishing streams, Lake Wallenpaupack, ski
Tanglewood and Mast Hope Mountain, downhill and cross-
country, fishing lakes, hiking, swimming, boating, antique and
flea markets, bicycling, and tennis.

Stay at Settler's Inn and you discover an interconnec-
tion of family and friends that runs through the delicious
foods, the handmade crafts, even in the flowers out front that
greet the summer arrivals. A general friendliness prevails
here.

A chef-owned inn is a sign of especially tasty dishes.
Grant prepares all the ☞ homemade soups, such as the
chicken and rice that's thick with fresh vegetables and delicious broth. The breads emerge from a heavenly smelling

bakery where Grant's mother and two assistants bake the pumpkin bread, the moist yeast rolls, and the pies and cakes. The broccoli quiche is made with tofu. What an excellent introduction to tofu. Grant prepares a wide selection of entrees. There's steak, pot roast, veal, pork, and chicken along with scallops, shrimp, and flounder. There's not much he doesn't offer.

Above the stone fireplace in the dining room hangs a petite quilt of the inn made by a friend and waitress. Full-size handmade quilts that are made by local women hang around the inn.

Children have plenty of space behind the inn to play and across the street is the park. Fishermen trek through the woods behind the inn to Lackawaxen River. Upstairs is a large common area for guests, and downstairs before the fireplace is a comfortable social area with tables and large soft chairs for enjoying a drink before dinner.

On your way to the rooms you pass three petite shops run by friends and a card player's museum. It's the only one in the country and open for limited summer hours.

The rooms are country simple and furnished, says Jeanne, with "early attic" antiques. They're clean and pleasant.

One day a curate friend came to lunch and gave the inn-keepers an inside tip. A church was replacing its chairs with pews. Would the inn like to have oak chairs with pockets for hymnals on the back? They are perfect, looking as if they were made for the inn.

How to get there: From I-84 exit onto Route 6 in Hawley. Pass through the town and the inn is on the left opposite the park.

🌺

My favorite [entree] is veal Oscar, a sautéed veal in a light brown sauce topped with crabmeat, asparagus spears, and hollandaise sauce.—Carolyn Lokay

olive Metcalf

Waynebrook Inn
Honey Brook, Pennsylvania
19344

Innkeeper: Lewis Frame
Telephone: 215-273-2444
Rooms: 17, all with private bath.
Rates: $58 to $98, double occupancy, continental breakfast included. Children welcome. No children's menu.
Open: Closes Christmas and Fourth of July. Lunch and dinner Tuesday through Saturday. Tavern.
Facilities & Activities: Amish country. Longwood Gardens, Hopewell Village, French Creek State Park, antiquing, and country auctions. Factory outlet stores in Reading, 30 minutes.

This Chester County inn is located in the heart of Amish country. I stepped out of my car and saw a horse-drawn wagon fly by. The entire family was dressed in black and three small blond-haired boys appeared to be thoroughly enjoying their ride in the afternoon sunshine.

Stepping inside the inn, I discovered a historic structure dating from 1738 that has been entirely gutted (the original staircase remains) and transformed from a 44-room hotel into a professionally run 17-room hotel-like inn. It's a small-town sanctuary.

168

The dining rooms are going to make an immediate impression on your romantic nature. They are sumptuously carpeted, and in one dining room a series of nooks provide for a tryst by candlelight.

At dinner, choose from this experienced chef's array: filet of Chesapeake sole, stuffed to the gills with morsels of crabmeat, and served with a ramekin of melted butter; a double cut of lamb chops scented with sage and served with pan juices; or an unusual blend of sautéed veal and shrimp in a poignant garlic herb sauce.

At bedtime the sheets in your room will have been carefully turned back. A mint lies on the pillow. These are such nice touches. The rooms are spacious and furnished with traditional reproductions. Several of the rooms have stainless steel kitchenettes. These are convenient if you happen to be moving to the area and are househunting from the inn. Each room is immaculately new and clean.

The tavern also sparkles with newness. It's a comfortable pull-up-to-the-bar kind where you might come for an after-dinner cocktail while you're pouring over the "Points of Interest Map" and deciding, "Is it Longwood Gardens or those irresistible factory outlets tomorrow?"

How to get there: From Route 30 east of Lancaster take Route 10 North to Honey Brook. The inn is in town on the right at the intersection of Route 10 and Route 322.

B: *If you come for the special* *"Escape" weekend, whether it's from the kids, the city, or the suburbs, a welcome tray of fruit and cheese is in your room. When you're ready, a bottle of chilled champagne appears.*

Olive Metcalf

The Kane Manor Country Inn
Kane, Pennsylvania
16735

Innkeepers: Laurie Dalton and Lynne Holmes
Telephone: 814-837-6522 (Recording until noon.)
Rooms: 9, 5 with private bath.
Rates: $42, double occupancy, Sunday through Thursday; $59, double occupancy, weekends; EP. Children welcome. Request ski package rates.
Open: All year. Breakfast available weekends during winter and most of summer. Dinner, tavern.
Facilities & Activities: Cross-country skiing from the inn and ski shop. 250 acres of fields and forests through wildlife sanctuary. Kinzua Bridge State Park and Dam. Hiking, biking, boating, swimming, fishing, and hunting.

This inn is a most unusual place. It's an ☞ homage to a diversely talented family, the Kanes. You are at will to explore and that's part of its charm. Ask to be led up into the attic room where Elisha Kane spent the last years of his life pasting maps from around the world to the walls. There's a brick fireplace in the attic room and the most wonderful view out to the Kinzua valley, the same view as from the library-dining room.

Ironically, General Kane, who had the mansion built for the family, never actually lived here. His wife, Elizabeth, called it "Anatole," or "Place that kisses the wind." Her children's and grandchildren's winsome portraits span the bureau in the "Family Dining Room."

One family member, Dr. Evan O'Neill Kane, twice made history when he performed surgery on himself. General Thomas L. Kane was the first from the state to volunteer for the Civil War. The sun-porch dining room is named for his division, the Bucktail Room.

Upstairs, the door of each room has a title painted by Elisha Kane. In the sunny Yellow Room a windowseat stretches along the wall. In the Blue Room a small windowseat and a sunken bathtub are found. The bright country wallpapers, fresh matching spreads, and frills of the curtains give the ☛ spacious rooms a warm individual personality of their own.

The basement Rathskeller has small paintings by Elisha, several a shade off-color. You can order a blend called "Passion Drink," but when you hear what's in it you might request a cold bottle of imported beer or a nice hot toddy after a day on snow.

Meals are prepared by two local cooks who work on separate evenings. They've composed a menu that lists several kabobs: beef, scallop, and beef and scallop. Consider having a Yankee pasta salad on the side, a composition of fresh vegetables blended with noodles and marinated in a vinaigrette dressing. Desserts include a homemade peanut butter pie.

When you enter the inn, it's through a small porch that leads through the gift shop. It's well placed. You can't pass without stopping and you can't stop without enjoying.

How to get there: Take Route 219 North from I-80 to Route 6 West. Proceed to Kane. At the flashing light in town, turn right or north on Clay Street and proceed to the inn on the right.

olive Metcalf

Ligonier Country Inn
Laughlintown, Pennsylvania
15655

Innkeeper: Katie Blasco
Telephone: 412-238-3651
Rooms: 11, all with private bath.
Rates: $55 to $70, double occupancy; $45 to $70, single; EPB. Children over age 8 allowed.
Open: Closes Christmas Eve and Christmas Day. Breakfast, lunch, dinner, tavern.
Facilities & Activities: Town of Ligonier and Fort Ligonier. Laurel Mountain Ski Resort. Seven Springs and Hidden Valley Ski Areas, 30 minutes. Frank Lloyd Wright's Fallingwater design, Laurel Highland fall leaves, Linn Run State Park. Hiking, cross-country skiing, golfing, huge outdoor pool, antiquing.

Katie Blasco, in her early twenties, is the youngest innkeeper in the book. In high school she convinced her father to buy a small restaurant for her to manage. It was her business debut. This continued "father-daughter" partnership has spawned the lovely renovation of the Ligonier Country Inn.

You enter into a narrow lobby with a friendly cluster of chairs around the fireplace. Next door is the dining room

172

trimmed with blue woodwork and dark wooden floors. A more casual dining nook is barnside-white with stone walls and comfortably padded benches.

"The inn," says Katie, "was professionally decorated [and most appealingly] by two decorators." The main floor and third floor rooms were by one, the second floor by another. You'll sleep in chic comfort regardless of your ☞ room for the night. The second floor has Country Lane furnishings. I like those sleek lines of the pencil four-poster bed and the matching pine wooden chests. The third floor has more ruffles and frills. Clean and pretty as a picture is what comes to mind.

There's plenty to do in the area. First make a visit to nearby Ligonier. There's a community bulletin board posted on the north side of the town square. Now isn't that thoughtful. You might find a country auction posted.

On Saturday night make your dinner reservations early so you won't miss ☞ guitarist, Bobbie Frye. He plays all types of music. And you should see those folks dance at the Ligonier.

For dinner the young chef presents a broad menu of poultry, fish, and steaks. It's not often you find a succulent roast duck glazed with raspberry sauce. Mmm, mmm. That's not something mother taught you to make. On a warm summer day I tried the chilled orange soup. It was a zesty summer diversion and the right complement for a large fresh green garden salad.

How to get there: From I-76 take Route 711 North to Ligonier. Turn right on Route 30 and proceed to Laughlintown. The inn is on the right-hand side in this wisp of a village. It's painted gray.

ᴥ

B: St. Patrick's Day at the Ligonier is a major event. The chef prepares an all-Irish menu and Katie decorates the inn in memory of her ancestors.

Olive Metcalf

The General Sutter Inn
Lititz, Pennsylvania
17543

Innkeepers: Joan and Richard Vetter
Telephone: 717-626-2115
Rooms: 11, all with private bath; 2 suites.
Rates: $50 to $62, double occupancy; $40, single; $85 to $115,
   suite; EP. Children and pets welcome.
Open: All year. Dining room closes Christmas Eve, Christmas Day,
   and New Year's Eve. Breakfast, lunch, dinner, bar.
Facilities & Activities: Saturday night entertainment. Antiquing.
   July antique show and August arts and crafts show.

Going to the General Sutter is like going to your grandmother's house. The inn is 🖝 chock-full of old and dear
pieces from the past that will stimulate your memories.

One of the lobby walls is covered with dozens of 🖝 cottage prints. One reads "Rest Haven." From here you walk up
to your cottage-like room.

Joan Vetter has chosen early 🖝 Victorian beds and
dressers, and old-timey quilts are in every room. Nearly every
room has a beautiful brush and comb set. You'll want to lie
down and take a nap and dream away the afternoon in rooms
like these. In one room there's white wicker, an oak bed, and

174

lacy, frilly curtains. The pink room on the third floor might strike your fancy for anniversaries.

The General Sutter is named for John Augustus Sutter of gold rush fame; however, he never got any of the gold. Discouraged and broke he came to Lititz to rest and recuperate beside the curative Lititz Springs that's across from the inn. The inn was built in 1764 by the Moravian Church and dancing, cursing, gossip, and bawdy songs were prohibited here. Now on a Saturday night you can hear a strolling guitarist, or the lilting strings of a dulcimer accompanied by a singer.

I think the Moravians would have approved of the church organ in the lobby and of the fact the innkeeper is a minister who knows how to play it. Richard Vetter was also assistant headmaster in a Pennsylvania school. That explains why all the rooms are named for his favorite authors. You can sleep in the Emily and Charlotte Bronte family suite, or read Dickens in the Dickens' Room. "They were named by pure accident," says Richard. "I just gave them names I like."

You step into the cranberry dining room for a juicy five-ounce hamburger cooked to order with sautéed mushrooms and steak fries and a skewer of fresh fruit thrown in for good measure. After a special herbal tea there's an antiquing stroll about town.

How to get there: From I-76 take Route 501 South to Lititz. The inn is in the center of town on the left, across from the spring. The town is east of Harrisburg, Pennsylvania.

⧗

B: *In one direction lies the chocolate factory, in the other the country's oldest pretzel factory. What a location for an inn.*

Olive Metcalf

Black Bass Hotel
Lumberville, Pennsylvania
18933

Innkeeper: Herbert E. Ward
Telephone: 215-297-5815
Rooms: 7, with 2 baths; 3 suites.
Rates: $50, midweek, $60, weekends, double occupancy; $110 to
    $125, suites; continental breakfast included. Two-night mini-
    mum stay on weekends, 3 nights on holiday weekends. Pets al-
    lowed.
Open: Closes Christmas Day. Lunch, dinner, bar.
Facilities & Activities: Three acres of woodland begin across the
    road opposite the inn. Piano entertainment on the weekends.
    Inn is located on the Delaware Canal and River, a short walk
    from the bridge to Bull Island nature preserve, Washington's
    Crossing Park. Mercer Museum, Bucks County Playhouse,
    sports, antiques.

The Black Bass is famous for leaving the famous alone
when they come here. Liza Minelli sang in the pub one
merry evening. Calvin Klein, Angela Lansbury, Ann Margaret, and Walter Mondale have stayed here. So have Joan
Fontaine and the Cassidy kids. If I listed everyone I'd never
get to the inn.

"One and all receive the same attentions," says Innkeeper Ward. They are left alone to walk in the woods behind the inn, or cross the bridge over to Bull's Island, or maybe sit and enjoy the river on the wooden balcony that extends from the waterfront rooms.

When you stay here you go into the past. Heavy antique 18th- and 19th-century beds with headboards and footboards and massive chests and armoires fill the small rooms. This is a classic built in 1745 that's stopped in time. It's for those who want an old, old inn on the waterfront with a European flavor. It's not for those who want all the up-to-date amenities.

The Black Bass is as English as deep dish apple pie. Innkeeper Ward explains apple pie is English and Americans claim it because it's good. Mr. Ward chose the English emphasis for the inn thirty-five years ago. He says that it was after World War II and we needed to pull together.

In keeping with the English tradition of a fine pub, there's the exquisite pewter bar that came from Maxim's in Paris. The pub is entirely wood. Along one wall is a fascinating collection of English royalty pictured on tin containers. They begin in the upper left-hand corner with Queen Victoria and end with Princess Diana.

The waterfront dining rooms and wooden tables with fresh flowers were just the setting I needed for lunch one afternoon. Taking in the spirit of the place I order a beef and mushroom pie. The crust was a tasty affair and the hot beef was juicy and lean. The deep dish apple pie is probably better than you'll ever find in England, even if the Brits did send it over. But then, they sent the chef, too. He's from England.

How to get there: From I-95 take Route 32 North along the Delaware to the village of Lumberville. It's on the right on Route 32; park on the left side of the road.

B: George Washington never slept here. It was a Loyalist bastion. Staying at the Black Bass is like sleeping in history.

Olive Metcalf

1740 *House*
Lumberville, Pennsylvania
18933

Innkeeper: Harry Nessler
Telephone: 215-297-5661
Rooms: 24, all with private bath.
Rates: $58 midweek, $62 weekends and holidays, double occupancy, EPB. Two-night minimum on weekends, 3 or 4 nights on holiday weekends. No credit cards.
Open: All year. Dinner, BYOB.
Facilities and Activities: Swimming pool, card room, Delaware River and Canal, Mercer Museum, Bucks County Playhouse, Washington Crossing State Park, festivals in area, antique shopping, sports, and country towns and roads to explore.

A ☞ waterfront inn is my weakness and the 1740 House is directly on the Delaware Canal and River. One side of my room was a wall of windows that opened out to a brick walkway and a split-rail fence lined with rhododendrons. Beyond the fence the river flows. It's very soothing here. ☞ Springtime it's ravishing. Pots of Impatiens hang from the covered walkways, the forsythia and azaleas are in bloom, and the tulip trees droop with their lush flowers.

You descend to the riverside inn from the village of

Lumberville. An ivy covered 100-foot-high embankment and tall trees separate the inn from the road. The swimming pool is near the entrance. In summer and winter it's a pleasant first encounter with the inn to see ☞ the swimming pool clean, full, and prettily lighted.

A conversation with Harry Nessler sparkles and shines the way his inn does. Given a chance, he probably has something to say on every topic in the encyclopedia and a few besides. Don't expect Victorian beds and lacy curtains. Harry says the style is "Early Nessler," which translates as rustic, naturally weathered board and batten, ivy covered stone, and early colonial in concept. There are ☞ brick paths and covered walkways. The rooms are up-to-date, tasteful, and have large beds that are turned down every night for the guests.

The chef serves a thick steak and a fresh salad, which are a wonderful counterpoint after a hike on the canal. Says Harry, "A filet mignon will take care of half the world." Other chef specialties include duck à l'orange, crab imperial, and fresh fish and scallops. These will probably take care of the other half.

Breakfast is a serve-yourself buffet that includes fresh Danish pastry, cold cereal, eggs, juice, and toast of every description.

How to get there: From I-95 take Route 32 North to Lumberville. The inn is on the east side of the road. You take a sharp right turn and descend to the inn's gravel parking. Doylestown Airport, fly-in.

You certainly have a remarkable talent, not only for making your guests feel at home, but for making them feel comfortable and relaxed in such elegant surroundings.—A New York Editor

Blair Creek Inn
Mertztown, Pennsylvania
19539

Innkeeper: Blair
Telephone: 215-682-6700
Rooms: 2 suites, both with private bath.
Rates: $100, double occupancy, continental breakfast included.
Two-night stay, $85, nightly.
Open: All year. Restaurant closes Mondays. Dinner, Sunday
brunch, bar.
Facilities & Activities: Six acres including woods, a lake, and Blair
Creek. Allentown Art Museum, historic homes, Pennsylvania
Stage Company, Moravian Museum and church in Bethlehem,
antiquing, factory outlets in Reading and Allentown, downhill
and cross-country skiing, golf, and tennis.

Innkeeper Blair does not serve meals. He choreographs
food and serves finished masterpieces for fine dining in this
five-star restaurant and inn.

Blair is a fine food lover who talks about food the way he
prepares it. He's an expert who often lectures on cuisine. He
goes to other restaurants in search of new tastes. One dining
room is covered with ☞ menus from the great restaurants of
America, and a few are from Europe. When you're handed

the inn's menu, you might want to begin a collection of your own. The woman's menu is without prices, the man's menu has the figures in the European tradition.

In addition to a long list of menu choices that includes veal Hapsburg, which is stuffed with jumbo lump crabmeat, Portuguese calamari and clam pasta, and broiled lobster tail with caviar, there is a host of daily specials. Baskets of wine are brought to your table for the selection. Five- and eight-course dinners are customary at Blair Creek and include a parade of desserts and candies. The ☞ frangelique cheese-cake is divine and the ☞ chocolate mousse is so light it defies gravity.

The small dining rooms are perfect for a savoring evening. In one room hang paintings of flowers that happen to be painted by women, a detail Blair noticed only after he'd collected them.

Christmas at the Blair Inn is lavish. Blair has a passion for flowers, and there are fresh bouquets everywhere all the year around. But at Christmas they are accented by angels from Rome and Budapest and over 7,500 lights that surround the inn.

Blair Inn was originally a Quaker meetinghouse, and later a farmhouse. Today, the adjacent country barn is re-modeled into two large rooms with four-poster beds. They are pleasant and cheery, and each has a fireplace. You won't find a speck of dust anywhere.

A stroll in the ☞ rose garden and around the exquisitely groomed grounds is just the thing to put you in the mood for an inspiring dinner.

How to get there: From Allentown take Hamilton Street (Route 222) west to Trexlertown. Cross over Route 100 and continue for 3.7 miles. Go left into Mertztown, and proceed just over 2 miles. Make lefts at the next two stop signs and continue for 1.2 miles. The inn is a white building with a large porch and yellow awning. Fly-in, Allentown or Kutztown Airport.

B: *The chocolate-covered strawberries are ambrosia.*

olive Metcalf

Cliff Park Inn and Golf Course
Milford, Pennsylvania
18337

Innkeepers: The Buchanans
Telephone: 717-296-6491
Rooms: 10, all with private bath; 3 cottages.
Rates: Friday plus Saturday night, $145, per person, double occupancy; Sunday through Thursday, $70, per person, double occupancy; AP. Gratuities $7.00 daily, per person. Two-night minimum on weekends.
Open: Late May through October. Breakfast, lunch, dinner served, taproom.
Facilities & Activities: Golfing, hiking, antiquing, October Fest.

The Cliff Park Inn is a ☛ gourmet golfer's paradise. It's a wonderfully relaxing and soothing inn neighbored by the luxuriant golf course. Even if you've never acquired the game, a visit to the inn might convince you otherwise.

Golfers visit and chat on the front porch, and the shade trees give respite to guests stretched out on the lawn chairs. The pink Impatiens blooms in the flower box beside the porch. On the door is a brass plate that says: Please no spikes.

You notice the please comes first. That's the nature of this accommodating inn.

The two ☞ guest lounges are to the right as you enter. Even in May and October the fireplaces burn to take the nip out of the air. The Victorian furnishings are simply lovely. They fit in with the soft rose colored couches and chairs. These are the fat stuffed kind that give you the "I never want to leave" feeling.

In the first of the three ☞ dining rooms are lovely round oak tables covered with lace tablecloths. The largest dining room has the Buchanan plaid on the walls. It's accented with matching carpeting and rich pine walls.

In the inn proper are ten ☞ spacious rooms with wooden floors and sparkling clean windows, each framed with white sheer curtains. Fresh comforters and sheets await your nightly rest. Nearby are cottage rooms furnished in fifties contemporary style. The Augusta House is tastefully redecorated and has two bedrooms.

Chef's elegant menu reads like a ☞ gourmet's dream. He's young, certified, experienced, and willing to try anything that he thinks will tantalize. He might serve filet of lemon sole, stuffed with wild rice dressing and topped with sauce beurre blanc. Another dish he prepares is quail stuffed with raisins and apples and flamed in brandy, then napped with a truffle sauce perigeux. I go prepared for a special surprise each time.

How to get there: From I-84 take Route 6 South to Milford. Turn right in town at Luhrs Hardware Store, proceed 1½ miles to the inn signs.

olive Metcalf

The Cameron Estate Inn
Mount Joy, Pennsylvania
17552

Innkeepers: Betty and Abe Groff
Telephone: 717-653-1773
Rooms: 18, 16 with private bath.
Rates: March through November, $45 to $90; December through February, $40 to $70; double occupancy, continental breakfast included.
Open: All year. Restaurant closes Christmas Day. Lunch, dinner, Sunday brunch, alcoholic beverages.
Facilities & Activities: Fifteen acres of woodland and walking trails, trout stream. Swimming pool access at Groff's home. Hot air ballooning, Nissley Vineyards' Winery, Donegal Mills Plantation, Susquehanna Glass Factory, Wilton factory outlet, antique auctions, farmers markets, golf, tennis, and bicycling.

This is a perfectly lovely ☞ country inn that combines the best of everything. Scenic farmlands, history, peace and quiet, and farm-fresh, delectable, French cuisine.

Abe and Betty have restored the summer mansion of Pennsylvania's political czar, Simon Cameron. It's ☞ simply elegant. Each room has received its own distinctive attentions and the setting gives every window a view of the pretty Lancaster countryside.

The Green Room has a queen-size four-poster bed, kelly green Queen Anne chairs, and a green marble fireplace. The cameo room has a cameo-shaped window that looks out to the tallest pine trees. Most rooms have handmade quilts. One room is rumored to be haunted. Evidently ghosts can have good taste, too.

You have fifteen acres of woodland to roam. Under the arching stone bridge runs a trout stream. You can catch your dinner and the chef will prepare it for you. Another favorite walk is the neighboring Donegal Church that dates from 1721.

Over the Sunday brunch Betty and Abe refreshed my history. Cameron was the first secretary of war, a senator, and ambassador to Russia. "National politics were decided in these dining rooms," said Betty. Now I was making important decisions like whether to order the eggs goldenrod or artichoke bottoms stuffed with crabmeat. I ordered both.

The dinner menu includes a fresh rainbow trout dredged in crushed pecans and sautéed in lemon butter. The fresh country chicken is wrapped around ham, sautéed in garlic butter, then coated with a tantalizing wine and cheese sauce and served with white asparagus.

You're in good hands here. Betty Groff has written two cookbooks. She created a four-star Pennsylvania Dutch farm restaurant in her family dining room.

How to get there: From Route 30 take Route 441 West after the Susquehanna River to Route 141 North. Turn left at the geodesic dome on Colebrook Road. Turn left on Donegal Church Road and right at the Donegal Church and right again into the inn's estate. Fly-in, Maytown Airport.

☀

B: *The adventurous take a hot air balloon ride from a nearby field over the ripening vineyards and expanses of wheat and corn of Lancaster County.*

Centre Bridge Inn
New Hope, Pennsylvania
18938

Innkeeper: Stephen Du Gan
Telephone: 215-862-2048
Rooms: 7, all with private bath; 2 suites.
Rates: Available upon request by writing inn at Box 74, Star Route, in New Hope. Two-night minimum on weekends, 3 nights on holiday weekends.
Open: All year. Continental breakfast, dinner, bar.
Facilities & Activities: Located on Delaware Canal and River. Mercer Museum, Bucks County Playhouse, antique shops, and flea markets. Fishing, bicycling, golf, and tennis. Washington's Crossing Park south of New Hope.

If you approach Centre Bridge from the Pennsylvania side, the white and burgundy colonial inn looks sedate and conservative. But approach from New Jersey via the bridge over the Delaware, and you'll see a glamorous ☞ waterfront view of terrace dining with thousands of sparkling lights scintillating from the trees.

"Centre Bridge is brand new," says Stephen Du Gan. "Everyone expects a very old inn, but the old one burned down and this was built during the 1950s." This classy colonial reproduction is directly on the Delaware River and Canal.

The expansive living room is trimmed in Williamsburg blue, the chairs are big comfortable Queen Annes, and the fireplace is ready to chase the chill on a rainy night. The rooms are ☞ updated colonial, pleasant and clean. Some have floral print wallpaper and carefully chosen antiques. In the hallway are lampshades drawn with the Centre Bridge image.

The downstairs suite has a canopy bed and a large blue and beige checked wallpaper. The bathroom is rough-hewn cedar paneling. The adjoining sitting room is a wonderful place to nestle before the fireplace. In the springtime you can relax on your private terrace.

In summer ☞ dining is a waterfront combination of scene, music, and atmosphere, blended around a series of most palatable tastes. Innkeeper Dugan believes, "Dining is more than food." At Centre Bridge it's mood evocative.

Several champagnes are on the menu. You might have one flavored with a raspberry liquor followed by escargots. Then a roast rack of lamb glazed with mint béarnaise. The after-dinner drinks are as enticing as the before-dinner champagnes. A Frangelico is served with steamed milk, fresh whipped cream, and nutmeg. That really caps the evening after a quality day of doing your favorite activities. You end with a toast for the pianist who's playing your favorite song.

How to get there: From I-95 take Route 32 North along the Delaware to Route 263. The inn is on the right before the bridge. Fly-in, Doylestown Airport.

ᶁ

B: New Hope, Pennsylvania, is nearby. There is a plethora of things to do in this area, but relaxing is a priority at a fine inn.

Olive Metcalf

Hotel du Village
New Hope, Pennsylvania
18938

Innkeepers: Omar and Barbara Arbani
Telephone: 215-862-9911
Rooms: 19, all with private bath; one suite.
Rates: $50 to $65, double occupancy; $80, suite for four; continental breakfast included. Two-night minimum on weekends, 3 nights on holidays. Children welcome. American Express card accepted.
Open: Closes January 15 to February 15. Restaurant closes Mondays and Tuesdays. Dinner, bar. Dinner reservations required.
Facilities & Activities: Swimming pool, two tennis courts. Washington's Crossing Park, Mercer Museum, Bucks County Playhouse, New Hope, antiquing, near Delaware Canal and River, barge rides, bicycling, and golf. Annual flower festival in spring and antique automobile show.

    Hotel du Village looks very much the country estate it was built to be circa 1900. In the mansion is that elegant Tudor restaurant where the woodwork is dark and richly polished with age. Around the fireplace are ☛ embedded copper oak leaves. The inn was originally called White Oaks and there are still white oaks on the estate, one immediately outside the dining room window. The petite bar is formed from the rare wood of the 🖝 chestnut tree and offers several tiny round tables. You can step down from the bar into a cozy alcove for dining.

The rooms of Hotel du Village are in the former dormitory, from the days when the estate became first a girls' school, then a boys' school. Barbara has wallpapered the rooms with subtle flower prints. The furnishings are conservative and clean.

It's a family inn, run by the energetic Arbanis. Omar is a 🖝 European chef who runs one of the largest kitchens with the smallest staff I've ever seen. "I'm organized," he says, and that's probably an understatement.

Omar does all the cooking and baking. His perfect chocolate eclairs and cream puffs came from the oven while I was there and the aroma pervaded the kitchen. A large tray of crisp chicken awaited the attention of white wine and a blend of tomato and herbs before it would be devoured by guests later in the evening. Omar admits his sweetbreads are very much in demand and laughs that he doesn't know why. Everyone says they are especially tender.

Behind the lodgings is a cornfield. From the swimming pool you can watch the corn sway with the wind in the July sun, followed by a brisk round of tennis, and then, of course, dinner. Fall is exquisite here when the massive oaks turn to shades of amber and gold and the ripening corn rustles in the breeze.

How to get there: From I-95 east of Philadelphia, take Route 32 North to New Hope. Continue on Route 32 North to River Road. Turn left and left again at the "Hotel" sign into the estate.

☷

We discovered this hotel only by accident. We went to dinner and were hooked. The food is just excellent and the price is really too inexpensive for such quality.—William R. Schaick

olive Metcalf

The Inn at Phillips Mill
New Hope, Pennsylvania
18938

Innkeepers: Joyce and Brooks Kaufman
Telephone: 215-862-2984. Call between 10:00 A.M. and 2:00 P.M.
Monday through Friday, or a recording will answer.
Rooms: 4, all with private bath; one suite.
Rates: $55 per room; $65, suite; EP. Three-night minimum on holi-
day weekends. No small children.
Open: Closes Christmas Day and January 7 through February 10,
but call. Continental breakfast available for guests. Dinner.
BYOB.
Facilities & Activities: Patio dining. Antiquing, Bucks County
Theater, rafting and canoeing on the Delaware, tennis and
golf, Mercer Mansion and Museum, hiking and bicycling, his-
toric homes and buildings, and Washington Crossing Delaware
State Park.

Above the doorway to the Inn at Phillips Mill hangs a
pig. Around his neck hangs a wreath and from that wreath
hangs a red bow. Innkeepers Joyce and Brooks have created
a French country inn in a stone building that's been a barn, a
girls' school, and a tearoom. It was next door to a piggery and
that's why the smiling pig greets guests.

190

It's a whimsical kind of place where the most delightful surprises happen. It might be purple violets or tiger lilies set in a basket, or startling colors made compatible, or the handsome fireplace that moves out from the stone wall to reveal an arched doorway for a passageway to the patio. The inn has been charmingly decorated with plaids, and prints, and checks. Many of the rooms are small with hand-stenciled wooden chests, and pretty fresh spreads, and the pink room has the tiniest pink chair.

Even at this romantic little hideaway you'll find the occasional business traveler during the week. They must share my love of French food. The steak au poivre is served flambéed in brandy with a cream and mushroom sauce, and the pork chops are stuffed with fresh prunes and delicately braised. The desserts were described ad infinitum by a friend who has sampled everything in the house. Two pastry chefs prepare this exotic fare. One recipe is Joyce's. C'est fantastique: Fresh Strawberry Japonnaise with a light, whipped meringue base. The blond chocolate mousse comes dripping with chocolate sauce. Another is the lemon meringue ice cream pie. It's three to four inches high with layers of lemon, homemade ice cream, and a topping of white meringue. Can you tell that my friend and I both love desserts, especially when they show originality?

The inn is located in the hamlet of Phillips Mill at the turn in the road. William Lathrop arrived here in 1900 and gathered his friends around. That's how the New Hope area became known as the artists' haven that it is to this day.

How to get there: From I-95 take Route 32 North through New Hope to the inn. Three flags hang from the inn on the right and you park on the left side of the road. Fly-in, Doylestown Airport.

※

B: *On Wednesday evening a woman comes to entertain with French songs. Melodies and a fine French meal make a splendid combination in a country inn.*

Olive Metcalf

Logan Inn
New Hope, Pennsylvania
18938

Innkeepers: Carl Lutz and Arthur Sanders
Telephone: 215-862-5134
Rooms: 10, 5 with private bath.
Rates: $50 to $60, double occupancy, EP. Two-night minimum on weekends, 3 nights on holiday weekends. Well-behaved children welcome.
Open: Closes January to mid-February, but call. Restaurant open daily from Memorial Day to Labor Day; closes Mondays the rest of year. Lunch, dinner, bar.
Facilities & Activities: Washington Crossing State Park, Bucks County Theater, Willmot Lapidary Museum, Mercer Mansion and Museum, Delaware River and Canal, antiquing, hiking, bicycling, canoeing, fishing, golfing.

☛ "People watching" from the front of the Logan Inn is the fair-weather sport in downtown New Hope on the Delaware River. You find your niche around an umbrella table, order a fresh tangy lemonade, a box of fried chicken Logan-style, and settle back for some serious people-watching.

The little town swells from 1,400 to 8,000 and 10,000 every summer says the former three-time mayor and innkeeper, Carl Lutz. He should know. He seems to know just about everyone and everything else that's happening. If it's foul weather, so much the better. You go in before the fire that's warming the entire bar and let Carl slip you into conversation with new friends.

Carl oversees this bastion of history from his niche behind the bar. If you want to know where George Washington slept, and when the Battle of Trenton was planned here, you can ask, but you'll have more fun pulling up one of the high chairs that surround the bar and joining the crowd. Carl says he can't figure it out. Strangers come into his bar and in a matter of minutes they start visiting like old friends. But it's no mystery with a master conversationalist like Carl Lutz at the helm. You become acquainted without knowing he's made it happen.

On the top of the bar sits a silver water pitcher. It belonged to Carl's grandmother, as did much of the furniture in the inn. To get the full picture, go look at the oil painting in the dining room of Carl's grandparents as they looked when they were first married. And upstairs in one of the rooms is grandmother's ornate brass bed. The rooms are filled with antiques.

One dining room is hot pink, the other a plant-filled glass conservatory with a white piano and a summertime mood the year around. Carl has composed the excellent menu over the years. His collection of cookbooks rivals many bookstores. He says someday he's going to sit down and read nothing but cookbooks. What a delicious idea.

How to get there: From I-95 take Route 32 North to New Hope. The Inn is on Main Street, on the left before the cannon. It's white with black shutters.

B: *New Hope has 181 buildings that were built before 1876. The Logan Inn is the oldest of all.*

olive Metcalf

Hickory Bridge Farm
Orrtanna, Pennsylvania
17353

Innkeepers: Nancy Jeane Hammett and Mary Lynn Martin
Telephone: 717-642-5261
Rooms: 7, including cottages, 6 with private bath.
Rates: $55, double occupancy; $35, single; EPB. Two-night mini-
mum on weekends from May through October. Children wel-
come.
Open: Closes Christmas. Breakfast, dinner served Saturday eve-
ning. BYOB.
Facilities & Activities: 50-acre farm. Country museum, collection of
antique farm implements, pond, trout fishing, hunting, and
walking. Gettysburg Battlefield, 10 minutes. Antiquing. Ski
Liberty, 15 minutes.

You drive through orchard country to reach Hickory
Bridge. In the fall the tree branches are laden with ripening
red apples. In the spring the hillsides are snowy white with
apple blossoms.

Turn off the paved road, and follow the signs to the
green-pastured farmstead. The buildings are painted barn
red. The grounds are charming and well groomed. ☛ A trout
brook ripples behind the inn, and up a short rise you find the

spring-fed pond where guests swim on warm summer afternoons.

The petite office of the inn is in the farm kitchen that dates from 1750. Here a large pot once simmered the whole day. It's no longer used for cooking, but it is a beauty to ponder.

On Saturday nights you go to the barn, now transformed into a ☛ country restaurant of the first order. Dinner is Pennsylvania Dutch-style with two entrees and bounteous servings of vegetables. Wagon wheels, a sleigh, a large brick fireplace, and Nancy's granite pots and pans decorate the high shelf. The restaurant is entered through Mary Lynn's gift shop.

Monday through Friday guests usually dine at the nearby Fairfield Inn.

The inn rooms are homey and inviting. In one is a Pennsylvania Dutch chest that represents the innkeeper's roots. There are all kinds of interesting antiques. They fill the china closet, sit above the fireplace, and decorate the guests' living room.

For more privacy you may go up the road a short distance to the inviting cottages. They have porches, woodburning stoves, and look out on the trout stream.

Behind the barn is a small ☛ country museum and several old tractors and farm implements.

Adams County is famous for its fruits. Orchards cover the hillsides. One afternoon we visited a fruit winery where fruit wines are a delicious specialty. Ask for the Hickory Bridge map to find your way on the maze of country roads.

How to get there: From I-81 take Route 16 East, which merges with Route 116 before Fairfield. Continue into the town and turn left at the gas station toward Orrtanna. Go 2 miles and at the sign turn left, then a short right, and a short left again. Go over the tracks and down into the farmstead. Signs lead the way.

olive Metcalf

Innisfree
Point Pleasant, Pennsylvania
18950

Innkeeper: Marie A. Balla, Estate of John R. Huestis
Telephone: 215-297-8329
Rooms: 10, 3 with private bath.
Rates: $55 to $75, double occupancy; single $10 less; EPB. $5 service charge per room. Two-night minimum on weekends, exceptions made. No small children on weekends.
Open: All year. Dinner served to small groups by reservation. Wine served. BYOB.
Facilities & Activities: Creek. Near New Hope, Mercer Museum, and Washington Crossing Delaware State Park. Antiquing, spring antique auto show, flower show, fall foliage.

The door to Innisfree is a double-Dutch worn with the beauty of age. Its stone walls are over 200 years old. It is a former gristmill that dates from 1749.

Innisfree is Celtic for Ireland. There's a poem by Yeats of the same title that describes the inn. It's a wild and poetic kind of place with rustic tones, but 👉 comfortable in every way. The inn borders on a creek, which roars and tumbles like a river during the spring melts and periods of heavy rain. At other times of the year, the sound of the creek has the most lulling effect. During late summer you can rock-hop barefoot across to the parkland opposite the creek.

Every room overlooks the ☛ creek and trees. Some have large picture windows, others the original deep casement windows.

In the living room where wine and cheese are served every afternoon, two walls support the ☛ library. Cow bells, sheep bells, and goat bells hang from the windows, and sprigs of wildflowers and fresh pine scent the room. On the piano is a collection of musical instruments awaiting their players. An impressive collection of cookbooks lines the shelves. Not surprising when you taste the masterfully prepared ☛ crepes and omelettes that Marie prepares in moments.

At dinnertime everyone is seated around a long oak table in front of the fireplace, and from the kitchen emerges roast rack of lamb dripping and moist in its own natural juices, or delicately poached salmon. At breakfast there are special light crepes puffed with a savory filling and coated with a fruit sauce. On Thanksgiving there's a traditional Thanksgiving dinner, at New Year's there's a special buffet, and other holidays are given special significance with Marie's carefully chosen menus.

Innisfree has been beautifully restored. I departed refreshed and restored myself.

How to get there: Take Route 32 North from I-95 to New Hope on the Delaware. Continue north on Route 32 8½ miles to Point Pleasant. Immediately after crossing over the bridge turn left onto Cafferty Road. A sign points the way to take a left turn down the hill.

B: *This is a poetic inn tamed and made gentle by hospitable hosts.*

Olive Metcalf

Coventry Forge Inn
Pottstown, Pennsylvania
19464

Innkeeper: Wallis Callahan
Telephone: 215-469-6222
Rooms: 5, all with private bath.
Rates: $45 to $58, double occupancy on weekends; slightly lower in
    midweek; continental breakfast included. Children allowed.
Open: All year. Restaurant closes Sundays and Mondays; during
    daylight savings time, closes Sundays only. Dinner, taproom.
Facilities & Activities: Swimming pool. Antiquing, factory outlets
    in Reading, country walks, Hopewell Village Historic Site,
    Brandywine River Museum, Brandywine Battlefield, and
    Longwood Gardens.

It began in 1717 as a little log cabin that now forms the
tiniest pub. It grew and became a family home, an inn, and
then reverted back to a home. This is where the innkeeper,
Wallis Callahan, comes in. He grew up here. He took a bud-
ding cooking talent and combined his love of food with a
country inn.

Today his cooking talent is in full bloom. Wallis experi-
mented, learned, traveled in France, and tested and tasted
wines to accompany his cuisine.☞ This is still the place to

order a Bordeaux and expect a nicely prepared lamb or grilled magret de canard. Other dishes are veal accompanied by a finely seasoned mustard sauce, and crab Wallis, which has surely been misnamed by the gentle and quiet innkeeper I met. For an after-dinner delicacy you might find fresh peaches poached in white wine and served with slivered almonds.

One concession to the times has been made with the windowed porch. You look out on the lawn and trees and the cluster of houses that make up Coventryville. In the taproom is a small desk for the innkeeper. It looks like something from a tavern museum, but it's most suitable right here. There's a magnificent wooden bar that serves the dinner guests.

The rooms are one hundred yards away and are pleasantly furnished, some with Empire style antiques. The bathrooms have bidets and black and white tiles on the floors. The woodwork is blue gray. Hunting scenes are appropriately hung in several rooms. There is horseback riding nearby and riding to the hounds is a popular local sport.

Antique lovers are in their element in this area. A walk in the country, a swim in the pool, and a ☞ fine meal in a historic stone inn, these are the simple pleasures of the Coventry Forge Inn.

How to get there: Take Route 202 North from I-95 to Route 100 North in West Chester. Continue to Route 23 and turn left at the light. Proceed 1½ miles to crossroads, turn right, and follow directional arrows up the hill to the inn. The inn is actually in the village of Coventryville, in Pottstown.

Olive Metcalf

Sign of the Sorrel Horse
Quakertown, Pennsylvania
18951

Innkeepers: Karl Ratz and Kass Ratz-Kilian
Telephone: 215-536-4651
Rooms: 6, 4 with private bath.
Rates: $50 to $55, double occupancy, continental breakfast included. Two-night minimum stay on weekends in summer and fall.
Open: Closed January, and Mondays and Tuesdays. Picnic lunch on request for guests, dinner, Sunday brunch, bar.
Facilities & Activities: Swimming pool, patio dining, and 5 acres of woodlands to roam. Canoeing and hiking at nearby Lake Nockamixon, cross-country skiing, antiquing, the Moravian Museum, and four other museums in nearby Bethlehem.

The Sign of the Sorrel Horse is the second night's stage-coach ride from Philadelphia. Kass says before the majority of people learned to read, tavern and inn signs used symbols and pictures. The Sign of the Sorrel Horse pictures a chestnut-colored mare, and appropriately soft shades of browns and beiges are the colors throughout the intimate inn.

Karl and Kass are a handsome couple who love the restaurant business. They have been at the Sorrel for several years and last year became the owners. They've discovered the inn is the best of both worlds. They enjoy meeting their guests who appreciate a fine French restaurant with a friendly atmosphere.

The Sorrel is one of those inns where there's not a book or magazine in sight. I can appreciate that. It's very small, and provides an intermezzo to calm the senses against the flood of daily stimulation. The rooms are sparsely furnished with antiques and fresh fruit. Every evening Kass puts out sherry.There's a ☞ lovely pool out back for swimming. It's painted black. How sensible, it retains the heat long after the sun has set. Behind the inn are several acres of woodlands you may roam. If you take up the notion of going for an afternoon of rowing on nearby Lake Nockamixon, then Kass might ask the chef to prepare a light duck salad with fruit and cheeses tucked in for good measure. Very appropriate for a boating party.

If you're going for a walk in the woods go past the ☞ herb garden. In the springtime it's a flurry of blooming scents. During winter it's covered with hay. Fresh thyme, mint, rosemary, and other herbs supply the kitchen during the winter.

Chef Mark Matyas is American, but he speaks French. It's necessary when you study at the ☞ Cordon Bleu. A fresh shipment of ☞ truffles had just arrived and he proudly pulled them out for me to sniff. He calls them "black gold." They are bulbous, ugly things, but they transform veal dishes into a delightful sensation, with the help of the chef, of course.

How to get there: From Quakertown take Route 313 East to Route 536 North. In 2 miles turn left on Old Bethlehem Road. The inn is on the left in ¼-mile. Fly-in, Penridge Airport in Perkasie.

B: *Duff is the Labrador retriever who lives in his own house between the pool and the inn. Lucky dog.*

olive Metcalf

The Riegelsville Hotel
Riegelsville, Pennsylvania
18077

Innkeepers: Fran and Harry Cregar
Telephone: 215-749-2469
Rooms: 10, 4 with private bath, 2 with half-bath.
Rates: $40 to $65 double occupancy, EP. No small children.
Open: All year. Closes Mondays and Tuesdays. Breakfast for guests, dinner, bar.
Facilities & Activities: Golf privileges at nearby country club. Rafting and canoeing on the Delaware River, museums and Moravian churches of Bethlehem, State Reservoir with swimming, boating, fishing. Riding stable. Hiking. New Hope area.

This inn is a family affair. Harry, Jr., the dad, Fran, the mom, and Harry III, the son, have restored this old-timey hotel dating from 1838 into a friendly small-town inn. The first time I met Harry, we shook hands to the sound of the telephone and he said, "Sometimes life is a series of interruptions connected together by the clock." Fran has decorated the ☞ second-story sun porch with white wicker and fresh pinks, and Harry III is the chef.

The Riegelsville Hotel overlooks the Delaware River at a ninety-degree bend in the road. From the enclosed sun porch you can look upon the ☞ bridge. It was designed by John Roebling of Brooklyn Bridge fame, and it's wonderful. People come here just to see the bridge. But while you're looking at the bridge you may sample peanut butter cheesecake and the deep dish kiwi cream pie.

Chef Harry prepares continental European cuisine with a dash of French. The filet Béarnaise is a broiled tenderloin with two blended sauces. I like the sound of Palourde à la co-quilles, a casserole with clams and scallops bathed in a cheese and cream sauce, with mushrooms and duchess pota-toes.

If you really want to treat yourself reserve a place ahead of time in the dining room around the raised hearth fireplace. It is a former ☞ cooking fireplace that has been raised to just the right height to enjoy during dinner.

The rooms have antiques and brightly colored solid quilts and five have river views. In the morning when you rise, an opportunity awaits. Your breakfast is set out for you to prepare in the chef's kitchen. That's unique. Only in a small inn could something like this happen.

Last year Harry planted over 1,000 bulbs. Every year he adds more. The Riegelsville Hotel gets brighter and brighter.

How to get there: From I-95 take Route 32 North to Riegelsville. The inn is just before the bridge on the right.

Ⴏ

Desserts have expanded each year to include a sinful variety of pas-tries, but my favorite dessert is tutti-frutti flambé. It is never on the menu, but available whenever there is fresh fruit—just ask.—
George Herzog, Riegelsville, Pennsylvania

olive Metcolf

Century Inn
Scenery Hill, Pennslyvania
15360

Innkeepers: Megin and Gordon Harrington
Telephone: 412-945-6600
Rooms: 3, all with private bath; one child's room; 2 suites.
Rates: $40 to $50, double occupancy; $10 to $20, child's room; $55
   to $85, suite; EP. Children welcome.
Open: Closes before Christmas to mid-March, but call. Breakfast for
   guests, lunch, dinner, bar.
Facilities & Activities: Hiking and walking on 22 acres behind the
   inn. Antiquing, boating, rafting, cross-country and downhill
   skiing, countryside of rolling hills.

A sampler on the wall says: "To a friend's house the way
is never long."
Megin and Gordon are second-generation innkeepers
who obviously love their beautiful inn. You will, too. It's furnished from head to toe with enticing antiques. The ☞
Chippendale highboy is one of a kind.
Each room has its special attributes. One dining room
has a lovely view to the rolling hills, in another the walls are
hung with large samplers, and a third is the old kitchen
where the original cook's fireplace was discovered in the

1950s. The pots and pans were still hanging on the rack inside the fireplace when it was accidentally uncovered.

In the front parlour hangs a flag used in the Whiskey Rebellion. Have a seat on the long wooden bench for a perspective of the Albert Gallatin glass atop the large china chest. Off the parlour is the 🐖 coziest bar. It's beautifully stenciled and has a gas fireplace that works like the others throughout the inn.

Upstairs the hallway woodwork is painted deep pink. You won't believe it's beautiful until you see it, then you'll agree. The guest rooms are enchanting with handmade quilts on the beds. Each room has special antiques. One has a boat-shaped cradle that's exquisite.

Children are not forgotten here. Tom the Tinker's room has two beds for the young ones. Early American portraits of children hang here. How thoughtful of the innkeepers. One room is on permanent reserve. It's filled with a wonderful collection of 🐖 antique toys. The whole inn is a delight to explore.

When I finally settled down to lunch I ordered a ham and asparagus roll. It was delicious. For dessert the 🐖 light coconut cream pie was a refreshing spring fare. It was a cool day so I sat beside the kitchen fire and found dozens of things to visually examine as we ate.

The inn is a National Landmark of Historic Places and was built in 1794 by the Hill family who founded Scenery Hill on a hill.

How to get there: From I-79 take Route 40 East to Scenery Hill. The inn is in the village on the north side of the road. Fly-in, Washington County Airport.

B: *You can know an inn by its portraits. This one has friendly faces.*

Olive Metcalf

Shenango Inn
Sharon, Pennsylvania
16146

Innkeepers: Jim and Donna Winner
Telephone: 412-981-5000
Rooms: 67, all with private bath; 3 suites.
Rates: $49 to $69, double occupancy; $99, suite; continental break-
fast included. Request "get-a-way" package information.
Open: All year. Lunch, dinner, tavern.
Facilities & Activities: Horse-drawn carriage. Swimming pool, ex-
ercise room, bicycles, dinner theater. City park with free golf,
tennis, fishing, boating, a par course, and Sunday band con-
certs.

The inn is located in a quiet neighborhood where large
well-kept homes line the wide streets. Two blocks away is a
verdant ☞ 650-acre city park, "the only one in the United
States," says Jim, "that offers free golf." Borrow one of the
inn's bicycles and pedal down to the park. You'll have a perfectly enjoyable afternoon and won't even need your wallet.
Sharon isn't a town where battles were fought and won
or a resort where the rich and famous settled. It's a quiet, all-
American town where you'll find the Avenue of Flags where
444 flags were raised, one a day, until the hostages in Iran

were released. It's a place where relaxing comes naturally. You can find an evening ball game in the park, read a book, or book a seat in the theater in the inn.

Jim and Donna have furnished the former hotel-style brick colonial that dates from 1950 with wonderful 🖙 antiques discovered at local estate auctions. Several are one-of-a-kind, and others are appealing for their simple beauty. The lobby is a maze of antiques, and most rooms have Victorian or Colonial pieces. Pick your period when you call, or ask for the suite with the pretty canopy bed where John Kennedy stayed. One room has an exquisite marble-topped Victorian set.

The Twelfth Colony Tavern is reached through the hallway art gallery where the works of Nate Dunn hang. The paintings tell the story of Dunn's life through his changing styles. Jim has collected the majority of Dunn's paintings. Art and antiques throughout the inn reflect Jim's interests. The tavern is filled with delightful things, gracefully worn oriental carpets, a mix of country and linen tablecloths, and the fragrant scents from the kitchen.

The special one lunch was 🖙 vegetable lasagna. It arrived steaming with melted cheese and spinach and was a tasty blend. Upstairs a buffet was offered. Dinner offers several meats, veal, steaks, lamb chops, and seafoods. Among the appetizers is garden vegetables served with a gallipot of piping hot cheese.

After dinner you might go for a ride in the horse-driven carriage through the park.

How to get there: From I-80 take Route 60 North. Turn right on Route 18 North and proceed 5 miles to Route 62 West where you make a left. The inn sign is in about two miles. Turn left on Kimberly Road. The inn is on the left.

Olive Metcalf

The Sterling Inn
South Sterling, Pennsylvania
18460

Innkeepers: Ron and Mary Kay Logan
Telephone: 717-676-3311
Rooms: 60 in the inn and cottages, all with private bath; 6 suites.
Rates: $47 to $60, per person; $65 to $70, per person, suite; AP.
  Special rates for children under age 12. Children welcome.
  Two-night minimum on weekends, 3 nights on holidays.
Open: All year. Breakfast, lunch, dinner, alcoholic beverages.
Facilities & Activities: 103 acres of hiking and cross-country trails.
  9-hole putting course. Golf course, tennis court, Lake Wallen-
  paupack, ice skating, tobogganing. Family inn.

  The Sterling Inn is surrounded with rhododendrons and
mountain laurel. In spring the tulips, daffodils, hyacinths,
lilacs, and flowering apple trees blaze your path around the
grounds. A special wildflower hike is taken to welcome the
warblers back to the Poconos.
  In winter call ahead to reserve your cross-country skis.
You can take a lesson from Mary Kay. In the evenings she
might show a ski film so you can practice in your sleep. Ron
will direct you to the ☞ ski trails that weave through the
inn's 103 acres. Ice skating and sledding are nearby.

At other times of the year, don't be surprised if Butter-scotch and Peanut Butter, tastefully named by the Logan children, waylay you with wagging tails as you stroll to the tennis court or out to the duck ponds.

The Sterling Inn makes special events out of holidays. At Easter, the Easter Bunny is an invited guest, and on July Fourth there are barbecues and dancing.

The guest lounges are large with a television and comfortable contemporary furnishings. They have stone fireplaces. Several rooms have antiques, others are furnished with a stylish blend such as the bamboo in the brookside suite. Others are 1950s style, a trend the Logans are reversing with quality antiques. You might request a room in the back of the inn near the Wallenpaupack Creek or one of the cottages nestled in the trees. The 🐾 suites are very spacious and have televisions.

Dinner at the inn is informal, but men are requested to wear jackets. You dine on handsome Royal Doulton china. The meals are prepared by local women who specialize in all-American cooking. Roast beef, chicken, and seafood are likely to be found on the menu. During spring and summer, blueberry, rhubarb, and blackberry pies are served. An open-top apple pie receives rave reviews every time. These are honest-to-goodness local fruits. You might consider a diet when you return home, but don't even think the word while you're here.

This is an 🐾 inn for all ages with plenty of room to spread out. Whether you're coming for a honeymoon or a golden anniversary or somewhere in between, there are the mountains to roam, the seasons to enjoy, and the mix and match of all the ages.

How to get there: From I-84 take Route 507 South through Greentown. In Newfoundland take Route 191 South. It's 4 miles to the inn.

B: *Ron teaches hotel courses at a nearby college. His students must love having an experienced innkeeper for their professor.*

olive Metcalf

The Inn at Starlight Lake
Starlight, Pennsylvania
18461

Innkeepers: Jack and Judy McMahon & Family
Telephone: 717-798-2519
Rooms: 29, 21 with private bath.
Rates: $78 to $106, double occupancy; $46 to $65, single; MAP.
  Weekly rates available. Children welcome. Two-night mini-
  mum stay on prime weekends in high season.
Open: Closes first two weeks of April. Breakfast, lunch, dinner, bar.
Facilities & Activities: Spring-fed lake, 18 miles of cross-country ski
  trails, ski shop, canoeing, small sailboats, rowboats, clay tennis
  court, swimming, and hiking. Nearby are 140 more lakes, golf
  courses, Upper Delaware trophy trout fishery, riding stables,
  downhill skiing at Mt. Tone and Elk Mountain. Family inn.

This is a ☛ quaint and beguiling lakeside inn in the
northeastern lake district of Pennsylvania. It's on a quiet little road that fronts Starlight Lake where boats float gently
along the docks. You enter to a busy and friendly lobby. In
cold weather two woodburning stoves crackle and burn.
Through the glass doors is a busy game room with pool,
Ping-Pong, and plenty of children's toys to keep the young
ones occupied.

210

During the winter there's a professional ski instructor on the staff and a 🖙 ski shop forms part of the inn. In the taproom hangs a cross-country ski map and your day on snow begins directly behind the inn. In the summertime you might take a sail on the lake, swim, or go into the woods for a hike.

The rooms are country-simple and pleasant. Prints are on the walls, and magazines are in the large racks. Keep in mind the inn dates from 1909. The sounds of the inn blend in with the frogs and the silence outdoors. It's the way you might imagine the perfect little country inn.

Jack and Judy and their four children came from New York City over ten years ago to the inn. Jack left the recording business and Judy brought her theatrical talents that she had honed at the Yale drama school. Their love of music permeates the inn. A collection of albums is easily accessible as is the grand piano stacked high with song sheets. On top sits "The Best Hits of the 1920s and 1930s."

It's nothing short of wonderful to have a fine meal with Starlight Lake for a view. The jaeger schnitzel is a tender pork cutlet sautéed in brown sauce, brandy, and mushrooms. The 🖙 beef medallions are coated with a delicious smooth sauce. The chef prepares a vegetarian dish. I do like it when you can order freshly brewed coffee with dessert. The 🖙 lemon cheesecake is not the usual; it's lined with a special lemony layer as an added attraction and very light. Afterwards you can take a lakeshore stroll in the fresh evening air with the stars lighting the way.

How to get there: From Route 17 in New York, take Exit 87 and go into Hancock, New York. Take Route 191 across the Delaware to Route 370 and turn right. Follow the signs to the inn.

Olive Metcalf

Historic Strasburg Inn
Strasburg, Pennsylvania
17579

Innkeeper: Bob Cook
Telephone: 717-687-7691
Rooms: 95, all with private bath; 8 suites.
Rates: $59 to $89, double occupancy; $93 to $109, suite; EP. Children under age 18 free and welcome. Pets allowed with $25 deposit. Three-night minimum for major holiday weekends.
Open: All year. Restaurant closes Christmas Day, but inn open and serves breakfast. Breakfast, lunch, dinner. BYOB.
Facilities & Activities: Organized activities, call for brochure of dates and events. Small swimming pool, bicycles free on site, video game room, gift shops, and bakery. Train museum, Longwood Gardens, Amish Village, Mansion Tour.

☛ Horse-drawn buggies are a familiar sight on the country roads around this new Lancaster County inn. You'll pass one-room Amish schoolhouses where the boys dress in straw hats and black pants and the girls wear long dresses and bonnets. You can't come to this area without experiencing a jolt of nostalgia.

The Historic Strasburg Inn is composed of three main buildings, twelve years old and similar in style to the historic

Washington House that stood on the square in Strasburg. They are immaculately maintained in this professionally run hotel-like inn.

The inn crowns a small hilltop on the edge of town and overlooks the Pennsylvania Dutch countryside. It is set well back from the road without trees to break the view. The only outdoor sound you're likely to hear is a tractor working in a nearby field.

There's a colonial theme in the rooms, and the Dutch Overlook rooms have a ☞ lovely vista. The bridal suite, also known as the anniversary suite, is charming in mauve with colonial reproductions.

The inn provides every modern convenience, a small pool, soft drink machines in the hallways, a video room for the children, and organized activities. It publishes an informative newsletter that's helpful for planning your vacation.

You might see the elegant mansions and plantations of the area, arrive for a theater experience called "Murder at the Inn," or come in the fall for the hot-air balloon championship hosted along with the horseshoe competition.

Tuesday through Sunday entertainment in the dining room features 18th-century stories, songs, mime, and theatrical skits. You can order the crab and corn bisque soup, and sophisticated fare like beef Wellington, or roast duckling Montmorency with a brandied bing cherry sauce. There also are simple favorites like the calves liver sautéed with onions and rashers of bacon.

Follow your nose to the bakery. All the inn's breads come from here. Those cinnamon twists are a sweet treat for "carry-homes" from the inn.

How to get there: From Route 30 east of Lancaster take Route 896 toward Strasburg. The inn is on the left before you enter town.

Olive Metcalf

Wycombe Inn
Wycombe, Pennsylvania
18980

Innkeepers: Michael Short and Jacki Ochs
Telephone: 215-598-7000
Rooms: 6 suites, all with private bath, breakfast kitchen, and most with fireplace.
Rates: $70 to $95, double occupancy, includes a do-it-yourself hearty breakfast in your suite. Two-night minimum on weekends, 3 nights on holiday weekends.
Open: Inn open all year. Restaurant closes Christmas Day, New Year's Day, Memorial Day, Labor Day, July Fourth, and Thanksgiving. Lunch, dinner, bar.
Facilities & Activities: Inn-top theater with piano and exercise equipment. Hot tub, creek, jazz piano several nights a week. Antique shops, Washington Crossing Delaware State Park, Bucks County Theater, Mercer Mansion and Museum, hiking, bicycling, canoeing, fishing, golfing, tennis, and relaxing.

Innkeeper Michael Short has sailed the oceans of the world as the restaurateur aboard the Cunard Line ships. He's also started over thirty restaurants, mostly in New York City and the New Hope area. Put these talents into an inland village and folks will come for miles, and they do, to enjoy his

214

☞ steak and kidney pies. They are scrumptious. So is the salmon dish he prepared as a special for lunch.

Michael is one of those people who can tear out a whole kitchen in an afternoon and think nothing of it. He's made most of the furniture in the inn. He made the bar tables from wood and leather. He's an abstract-functional sculptor. In other words, he makes useful things from unusual combinations of materials and makes them look interesting.

Jacki Ochs comes from an academic background, but she certainly doesn't look like a professor when she sings French chanteuse songs in the style of Piaff at the piano in the evenings. All those years of French grammar paid off.

The ☞ suites are very large, light and sunny rooms. All but one have modern fireplaces. They have contemporary beige carpeting, large floor pillows, and several have black desks and headboards that were made by Michael. There are small kitchenettes for fixing your own private breakfast from the generously stocked refrigerator.

This is a contemporary inn built in a historic hotel. You can climb to the inn-top ☞ theater painted black and white, which makes it wonderful for photographers—in fact they can rent it—but as a guest you can use it for stretching your muscles with the weight machines or to simply enjoy the view.

How to get there: From I-95 take Route 413 North to Pineville. Take Township Line Road left (west) to Wycombe, and before the railroad tracks turn left. Fly-in, Doylestown Airport.

If you're partial to duckling, as I am, you won't find a more beautiful dish than the way Michael prepares it, crisp on the outside, and moist inside with a fruit stuffing.—Sandra Nell Ruch, Southampton, Pennsylvania

Numbers on map refer to towns numbered
on index on opposite page

Delaware—Maryland

olive Metcalf

The Corner Cupboard Inn
Rehoboth Beach, Delaware
19971

Innkeeper: Elizabeth G. Hooper
Telephone: 302-227-8553
Rooms: 18, 16 with private bath, 2 with half-bath.
Rates: Memorial Day weekend to mid-September: $95 to $140 double occupancy; $75 to $120, single; MAP. Rest of year, $65, double occupancy; $55, single; EPB. Children allowed. Pets, $5 a day.
Open: All year. Closes Thanksgiving, Christmas, New Year's, Easter, and Mother's Day. Breakfast and dinner in season, breakfast rest of year. BYOB.
Facilities & Activities: Beach is 1½ blocks. Tennis, bicycling, and golf nearby. Historic town of Lewes, 15 minutes.

The summer lighting is special. The sun filters through the tall, old shade trees onto the inn's ☞ cozy patios and creates a mood of total leisure. You mix yourself a drink on the cocktail patio and chat with new friends.

Around dinnertime on a summer Saturday night Scotty begins playing jazz in the screened dining room. Your waiter opens a fine wine, the one you brought in a little brown bag. The ceiling fans turn. Dinner begins: Crab imperial with just a touch of green pepper, or beautifully fried ☞ soft-shell crab, homemade bread, and more. After dinner go for a moonlit stroll on the ☞ beach.

This is a year-round inn in a lovely residential neighborhood. Elizabeth has added next door "Me Wood," formerly Homewood. Its large attic room has a private wooden patio nestled in the trees. "Eastwind" has two small cottage rooms, each with a private brick patio. Each room is different. One is small, with white walls and green and blue curtains, and green iron beds.

The rooms change according to the season. During summer the inn is floored with grass mats that are exchanged for carpeting in winter. In the inn some rooms have antiques, and wooden or iron beds.

Elizabeth's decorating is a tasteful homey blend of family heirloom and eclectic furnishings. The antique corner cupboard is in the living room. The long porch room, called the hat room for all the straw hats on the wall, is paneled and breezy in summer.

In the winter, guests return from a brisk walk on the beach and meet around the fireplace, sipping brandies, and discussing everything but what they do for a living. Here, the cares of the world are washed away.

How to get there: From Route 1 exit onto Rehoboth Avenue and follow it to the deadend, make a U-turn, go one block, and turn right on First Street. Cross over bridge, turn right, then left on First Street. Go 3 blocks to one-way Park Avenue and the inn is on the left.

Z

Oh, those soft-shell crabs were delicious. And try the pecan pie with the homemade crust for dessert.—Dr. Francis Watson and Diane Watson

olive Metcolf

The Maryland Inn
The Historic Inns of Annapolis
Annapolis, Maryland
21401

Innkeeper: Peg Bednarsky
Telephone: 301-263-2641. Washington 261-2206. Baltimore 269-0990.
Rooms: 129 rooms, 55 suites, all with private bath.
Rates: $80 to $95, double occupancy; $60 to $75, single; $110 to $150, suite; EP. Request holiday package specials. Children welcome. Pets allowed, $25 deposit.
Open: All year. Breakfast, lunch, dinner, three taverns.
Facilities & Activities: Music. Historic walking tours, harbor tours. William Paca Mansion, State House, U.S. Naval Academy. Boating, outdoor theater.

Beware: You may never want to leave. The Maryland Inn is a temptress of pleasures with your happiness at heart.

In the center of Annapolis is the triangular-shaped inn, a peculiarity that affords striking views of the Chesapeake Bay and this port town from several windows. Built in the 1770s as a ☛ "house of entertainment," it has not been deterred from that purpose for over 200 years.

Request the tavern's "Entertainment Schedule" before you go. Many nights of the week you'll find professional entertainers here. This is home base for Charlie Byrd, a guitarist whose classical training and roots in jazz give versatility to his performances.

Chesapeake Bay delicacies are served in the Treaty of Paris Restaurant. Before lunch or dinner delicious hot cornsticks and popovers arrive. Try the creamy crab bisque along with one of the chef's daily 🖙 whimsies. One afternoon it was a chunky lobster–filled sauce covering a light rice. The dinner menu offers a dish called Treaty of Paris, which includes plump scallops, shrimp, lobster, oysters, and clams, simmered together in wine, herbs, and cream. To be different you might order duckling with lingonberries, orange zest, and port wine.

During Christmas and New Year's there's an outpouring of festivities that brings music to your ears and wassail to your lips. Garlands, holly, and ribbons festoon the inn. The tree is trimmed with traditional handmade ornaments, and troubadours entertain in the King of France Tavern.

Every room in the inn is decorated for 🖙 deep comfort with antiques and superb colonial reproductions. You don't pick favorites here, because each room has its unique charms.

Annapolis is a delightfully 🖙 walkable town. The elegant State House across from the inn's Calvert House is where the Treaty of Paris was signed. The city dock and the Naval Academy are only a short walk away.

How to get there: From Route 50 take Rowe Boulevard and continue straight to the deadend. Turn right on College Avenue, turn right into circle, continue to Duke of Gloucester Street, and turn right. In 2½ blocks park in the garage on the left. Walk on Conduit Street to Main Street and turn left to the inn. Limousine service to inn from Baltimore-Washington Airport.

olive Metcalf

The Inn at Buckeystown
Buckeystown, Maryland
21717

Innkeepers: M.G. Martinez and Daniel R. Pelz
Telephone: 301-874-5755
Rooms: 7, all share baths.
Rates: Monday through Thursday, $85 to $95; Friday through Sunday, $105 to $115; per couple, MAP. Children 16 and over allowed. Two-night minimum on holidays and some weekends.
Open: All year. Breakfast, dinner. BYOB.
Facilities & Activities: Pre-Civil War graveyard on the property. Antique co-op and potter's shop in town. Walking tours of Frederick and Haymarket, antiquing, rafting, and canoeing. Gettysburg Battlefield, one hour.

You are warmly greeted at the side entrance by Marty, the innkeeper, and Amos. Marty leads you around Amos who briefly welcomes guests before returning to his sheepdog duties.

Buckeystown is a Nationally Registered Historic Village on the Monocacy River. The inn is a rambling Victorian mansion in a town of Victorian and Federal mansions. In the spring pink and purple azaleas, lilacs, and forsythia accent the inn.

Marty describes the house as Victorian/eclectic. There's enough Victorian furniture to make it interesting, but enough modern furniture to make it comfortable. I do like sensible innkeepers like Marty and Daniel. Authenticity can be very uncomfortable.

The rooms reflect the house: comfortable and well decorated. The beds have been widened to accommodate new mattresses within their Victorian frameworks.

When guests arrive the first thing they do is look for the menu on top of the hall bureau. "Cooking was a hobby that exploded," says Marty who changes the menu according to mood. One night his Basque heritage influences the Spanish-style dishes. The next it might be German according to Daniel's influence. Whatever it is, good home cooking needs no other title.

Dinner is served at seven around the two long dining room tables on a mix and match of antique rose china. Generous portions of wine accompany the "Tournedos of beef à la Inn," shrimp bisque, avocado salad, followed by the simple but delicious West Virginia black walnut apple cake. Dinner has five courses on weekends and three courses during the week. Guests have no choice for dinner but the choice to come, and that's the best of all choices.

You'll enjoy the three living rooms in this very guest oriented inn. Marty collects American pottery and you can peruse his collection. Daniel collects clown paintings. In the hallway is an intriguing case full of clowns of every description and size.

How to get there: From I-270 north of Washington, D.C., take Route 85 South to Buckeystown. The inn is on the left.

One of our most memorable feasts was over New Year's '83 when we indulged in fresh Chincoteague oysters, rabbit pâté, Eastern Shore roast goose, and a midnight supper ... Yes, you can go home again!—David and Joanne Hilton, Baltimore, Maryland

olive Metcalf

The Tidewater Inn
Easton, Maryland
21601

Innkeeper: Anton Hoevenaars
Telephone: 301-822-1300
Rooms: 113, all with private bath; 7 suites.
Rates: $50 to $56, double occupancy; $42, single; $130 to $195, suite; EP. Children welcome and no charge under 12. Pets allowed.
Open: All year. Breakfast, lunch, dinner, taproom.
Facilities & Activities: Swimming pool. Boating, fishing, hunting, tennis, and golfing nearby. Bicycling. St. Michael's Chesapeake Bay Maritime Museum.

As pretty as she is rich, Talbot County's 602 miles of shoreline allure hunters, fishermen, boaters, bicyclers, and bench sitters to her shores. The county seat is Easton where the Tidewater Inn stands landlocked in the midst of more than one hundred historic buildings.

The handsome brick colonial inn was built in 1949, shortly after the original inn burned. The street opposite the inn is a row of diverse shops selling chic clothing, American crafts, and waterfront estates. Enter the inn and to the right is an elegant jewelry shop. Don't get the idea this is a snooty inn. It's not. Not with a congenial innkeeper like Mr. Hoevenaars on the scene. "I'm from the south," he says, "south Holland."

If you arrive during the annual ☞ Waterfowl Festival in November the inn will be bursting at the seams, like the town. The highlights are the auction of antique decoys and exhibits by the world's foremost bird carvers. The inn makes no small mention of its local carvers in its decorations. In the Decoy Tavern a large photograph shows a local carver at work

Talbot County is on the Canada Geese flyway. During hunting season there's a 4:30 A.M. breakfast for early risers. The dining room dress code obviously stretches at this hour to include camouflage.

The menus offer traditional meat entrees and a long array of ☞ Eastern shore specialties that include backfin crab imperial, broiled fresh fish, crab cakes, and soft-shell crabs. At breakfast grits and scrapple are available as well as malted waffle made with walnuts, corned beef hash, and smoked salmon.

The rooms are cleanly decorated with a variety of traditional fabrics and wallpaper that rises from the rust colored wainscotting. Wooden blinds hang at the windows. There are nice fresh rust colors in the hallways.

There are many ☞ wonderful things to do in this area, from sailing to historical sights. You might come for the log-canoe races, an old-time specialty on the bay. During my visit the athletic crowd was in town for the annual summer Oxford International Triathalon. My heart went out to them, but I preferred a few hard laps and then a sit in the sun beside the inn's inviting little pool.

How to get there: From Route 50 south of the Chesapeake Bay Bridge take the second Easton exit, turn right on Dover, and the inn is on the right at the intersection of Harrison.

olive Metcalf

Oxford Inn & Pope's Tavern
Oxford, Maryland
21654

Innkeepers: Patricia and Gerry Mullins
Telephone: 301-226-5220
Rooms: 3, all share one bath.
Rates $45 to $50, includes continental breakfast. Children welcome.
Open: Closed two weeks in January. Call. Lunch, dinner every day except Tuesday. Tavern.
Facilities & Activities: Boating, bicycling, antiquing. Annual Waterfowl Festival in Easton, two tennis courts across street, Chesapeake Bay Maritime Museum in St. Michaels, Blackwater Refuge. Annapolis to Oxford Regattas. Relaxing.

A rousing sail across the Chesapeake Bay brings many a guest to the Oxford Inn. That's what first brought Pat and Gerry Mullins to this 17th-century port town.

In 1982 Pat first noticed the FOR SALE sign on the old Oxford general store. "The rest was destiny," she says. And a lot of work. Walls were built, woodwork painted, floors sanded, and the magnificently ornate tin ceiling was painted gold.

Today, Pope's Tavern in the inn looks beautiful with its

pink tablecloths and country print napkins. The woodwork is trimmed in a rich pink and the curtains are navy. There's a comfortable portable bench along the wall. In winter it's arranged cozily around the woodburning stove. The windows in Pope's tavern are artistically sandblasted with the forms of two ships, America's Cup winners.

If you arrive starving at lunchtime, Pat might be in the kitchen preparing a fresh crabmeat salad and crispy Idaho potato skins topped with melted cheese, bacon bits, and crab. If you arrive tired and late it's she who'll lead you upstairs to your room. She's one of the busiest innkeepers I've met, yet she takes the time to meet her guests.

The rooms have mauve carpeting, tangerine print wallpaper, and two have Laura Ashley curtains, ceiling fans and ☞ queen-sized beds. The two larger rooms each have an antique dresser.

Though there's excellent shrimp in all its various forms, scampi, stuffed, and fried, and three types of steaks, dinner is synonymous with the Chesapeake Bay blue crab. The crab imperial, called ☞ Oxford Imperial, is delicious, light and superbly spiced. The crab cakes vie with the imperial for "special" attentions.

We were debating dessert when we heard someone mention English trifle. We debated no longer. It was superb.

How to get there: From Route 50 take Route 322 South, then Route 333 North to Oxford. As you enter the town you'll see the inn to the left of the first stop sign.

B: Oxford is a pretty little charmer and fun to explore on a bicycle.

olive Metcalf

Robert Morris Inn
Oxford, Maryland
21654

Innkeepers: Ken and Wendy Gibson
Telephone: 301-226-5111
Rooms: 35 in inn, lodge, cottages, and apartments, 27 with private
   bath.
Rates: $32 to $116, double occupancy, EP. Children over 10 al-
   lowed.
Open: Closes Christmas Day. Breakfast, lunch, dinner, taproom.
Facilities & Activities: Beachfront on Tred Avon River reserved for
   guests. Boating, bicycling, tennis courts in town, golf in 10
   miles. St. Michael's Chesapeake Bay Maritime Museum, Wye
   Mills Summer Theater, Easton Waterfowl Festival. Adult inn.

Poor Robert Morris. It's ironic he died accidentally from
the very guns that were fired in his honor. But his tragic
story doesn't deter from an interlude in this fine inn that was
his home in the 1700s.

The inn faces North Morris Street. One block away is
the Robert Morris Lodge, a grand old Victorian home with
beach frontage on the Tred Avon River.

Want to put yourself in a good frame of mind? Come to
this inn, select a lodge room with a waterview, find yourself a

chaise lounge, and soak in the sun or bask in the shade.
There are couples who come every spring and fall, bring a
book, and spend all their time right here. Leave the kids with
mother. This weekend is for the 🖝 two of you. You can
watch the sailboats heading out for the Chesapeake or the
crabbers bringing in their daily catch. Or you can just close
your eyes and listen to the water lapping the shoreline.

If you want a little activity, a delightful summertime trip
involves the simple procedure of renting bicycles, crossing
the ferry, and riding to St. Michaels to see the Maritime Museum. In wintertime wrap in a warm coat and take the ferry
ride to see the working boats coming and going on their blis-
tery cold journeys.

The rooms are all 🖝 traditional American country, but
some are old country and some are new country. The brochure explains the diversity of rooms. A number of rooms
have lovely waterviews. I do like the enclosed screened
porches and the claw-footed bathtubs in some of the newer
rooms. You can ask for a nonsmoking room.

Dinner at the Robert Morris is a love affair with food. 🖝
Crab cakes are the house specialty. They are filled with big
morsels of crabmeat. You can order meat or fowl if you like,
but the Eastern Shore is seafood heaven. If you feel like
going overboard, order the seafarer's platter with baked
stuffed shrimp, crab imperial, seafood imperial, broiled sea
scallops, and broiled filet of fish. Try and swim after that. To
help you celebrate your favorite "non-event," there's a selection of five champagnes that precede the wine list.

How to get there: From Route 50 take Route 33 West to Route 329
to Royal Oak and turn left at the ferry sign. The inn is directly opposite as you land on the other side of the river. Easton Airport, fly-
in.

Olive Metcalf

The Inn at Perry Cabin
St. Michaels, Maryland
21663

Innkeeper: Ron Thomas
Telephone: 301-745-5178
Rooms: 6, all with private bath.
Rates: $80 to $120, per room, continental breakfast included. Children may share room with parents at no extra charge.
Open: Closes Christmas Eve after lunch and Christmas Day. Lunch, dinner, taproom.
Facilities & Activities: Located on Miles River. Entertainment Friday, Saturday, and Sunday evenings by local groups. Chesapeake Bay Maritime Museum and downtown harbor walking distance. Boating, bicycling, golfing, tennis, and hunting. Indoor ice skating. Historic sights. Waterfowl Festival in Easton. International Triathalon in Oxford.

Some say Spectacular Bid restored the Inn at Perry Cabin. But it's not true. The owners, the Meyerhoff family, were in the midst of restorations when their horse, Spectacular Bid, won the Kentucky Derby. That explains the photographs of the horse and other celebrities in the bar.

But don't come here for the fast life. Come for the food . . . the music . . . the comfortable rooms . . . the river. This is a 🖝 classy updated inn with antique furnishings, reproductions, and distinctly different rooms. You pass through the dining rooms to reach the registry and to climb the stairs to your room. Three rooms have a view of the Miles River. One has a brass bed with part of the brass painted red. Looks good. I like the double pillows stacked on the beds. Feels good. There are colonial furnishings, and china closets throughout the inn filled with bright and pretty collectibles, the kind you'd not mind collecting yourself.

The 🖝 music is contemporary. It changes often. During summer it might begin midweek and last through Sunday. One night a singer with guitar entertains, the next it might be bluegrass or a small instrumental group; occasionally it's jazz. It makes for an upbeat evening at Perry Cabin.

Seafood is very strong on the menu. Crab in every form is served, perky crab imperial, young soft-shell crabs, and mellow crab Norfolk. For those who prefer meat, a plump 14-ounce steak au poivre is a spicy choice as is a more surprising lamb au poivre. Year around the 🖝 Fogg Cove mile-high pie is an acclaimed dessert. This masterful composition is six inches high. Embedded on a graham cracker crust it's a layer of chocolate ice cream, coffee liqueur, and mint chocolate chip ice cream topped with whipped cream. Because that's too slenderizing it's dribbled with chocolate sauce.

How to get there: From Route 50 East across the Bay Bridge continue to Route 33 to St. Michaels. The beige inn with blue shutters is beyond the town on the right-hand side. Easton Airport, fly-in.

B: *Don't miss seeing the lighthouse.*

Olive Metcalf

Frances Kitching
Smith Island off Ewell,
Maryland
21824

Innkeeper: Frances Kitching
Telephone: 301-425-3321
Rooms: 5, all share a bath.
Rates: $35, per person, MAP. Children under 12 half-price.
Open: April 15 through November 1. Breakfast, lunch and dinner
   by reservation. Alcoholic beverages not allowed.
Facilities & Activities: A way of life to be experienced. Island is 4-
   by-8-miles. Sitting on porch. Relaxing.

"Word of mouth does my talking," explained Mrs.
Kitching. She has no brochures, never advertises, and can
only be visited by boat. You must call ahead for reservations
for meals and lodging.
   The inn is Mrs. Kitching's home. It's very much like
going to a relative's home, but it qualifies as an inn because
after one taste of her mouthwatering cooking, people talk for-
ever.
   The Smithsonian regards Mrs. Kitching as a "living cultural treasure." She'll dismiss that as an empty mouthful,

but during the 1984 Folklife Festival she and her husband spent two weeks in the Nation's Capital. She shared her pickled watermelon and passed her Smith Island Cookbook around.

This small Chesapeake Bay Island is home to 650 people who are premier "watermen." There are no policemen, no malls, movies, clothing stores, banks, or fast food places. There is peace and quiet, and lots of boats. Before paradise status is accorded, I must mention there are flies. In summer pack Cutter's insect repellent. Mrs. Kitching has a wonderful screened porch from which to watch a continuous stream of bicycles, pedestrians, and very occasionally an automobile. Island speed limit is 15.

Meals are served family style. This means liberal helpings of crab cakes, chicken casserole, ham, and other seafoods. There may be spiced apples, pickled watermelon, pickled carrots, potato salad, homemade rolls, and crab or vegetable soup. For desserts ☛ fresh cakes and pies, and to quench the summer heat, large pitchers of iced tea. If you reserve ahead of time you can ask for a light sandwich for lunch. ☛ Crabmeat salad is an excellent choice.

The rooms are small, wood paneled, and have shag carpeting. The living room is filled with Mrs. Kitching's afghans, pillows, and family portraits.

In some respects Smith is like any other seacoast town where the main industry is crabbing and the boats are more useful than cars, with one exception. It has Mrs. Kitching.

How to get there: From Crisfield take the mailboat, $5 round trip. Tyler's Cruises depart Crisfield June through September, $12 round trip. They also leave from Point Lookout State Park, June through September, $16 round trip.

olive Metcalf

Harrison's Chesapeake House
Tilghman, Maryland
21671

Innkeeper: Captain Buddy Harrison
Telephone: 301-886-2123
Rooms: 56, 34 with private bath. Children welcome.
Rates: $35 to $55, double occupancy, EP. $50 to $60, per person, AP. Fishing packages available.
Open: Closes mid-December to early March. Breakfast, lunch, dinner, taproom.
Facilities & Activities: Charter fishing boat trips. Sailboats, paddleboats, motorboats, and bicycles available for rental. Swimming pool.

Captain Buddy's grandparents started taking guests because they had so many friends coming they decided they might as well invite the public, too. That was over sixty years ago. Today Captain Buddy has the ☛ Chesapeake Bay's largest fleet of charter fishing boats moored right outside the door. It's not uncommon for him to get several calls on a Friday night asking where the best fishing is.

The Chesapeake House is a rambling farmhouse that's grown into a busy restaurant and fishing and boating center. There's a hospitable "let-you-be" attitude with plenty of assistance when you need it. Captain Buddy offers a "buddy" system that matches up singles and pairs of travelers for a day of fishing. He also offers a Ladies' Day. One of his guests caught a record fish on her first try. Not bad for beginner's luck.

If you're wondering who's doing all the cooking while Buddy is riding the waves, it's his mother at a youthful 80. Her stewed tomatoes are famous around the United States, explained one guest. He should know, he's been coming here since the age of 15 and he's now 84. He gets a hankering for soft-shell crabs every spring and isn't content until a plateful sits before him here.

Huge breakfasts are the order of the day here. Mrs. Harrison's homemade breads are the perfect complement to every meal. For dinner small concessions are made to land-lubbers with a rib, steak, and pan-fried chicken, but ☛ seafood is the specialty. I do like the combination of fried chicken and crab cakes; those are pure Eastern Shore specialties since those two are produced here. Every meal is served family style, with five vegetables. The in-season strawberry pie is lusciously large.

The rooms are simply furnished in both the inn and the newer motel units. A long enclosed porch is filled with white summer furniture. Inside, a homey, grandmotherly living room is popular in cool weather. The dining rooms have a waterview and are decorated with handsome models of local working boats.

From November through April the Skipjacks work the bay. They are the last fleet of working sailboats in this country. If you are lucky enough to see them at work it's an experience you'll not forget.

How to get there: From Route 50 take Route 33 West to Tilghman. Go over the drawbridge to the inn.

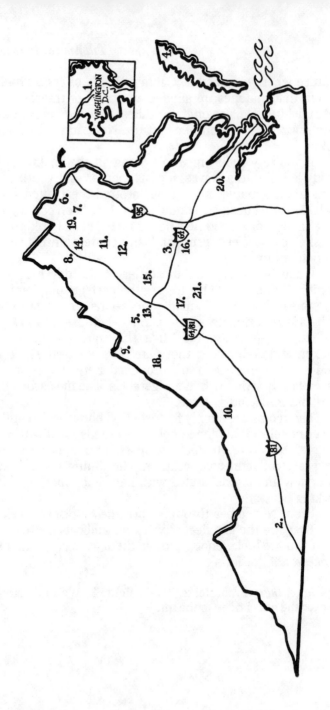

**Numbers on map refer to towns numbered
on index on opposite page**

Washington, D.C.—Virginia

Olive Metcalf

The Tabard Inn
Washington, D.C.
20036

Innkeepers: Fritzie and Edward Cohen
Telephone: 202-785-1277
Rooms: 42, 23 with private bath.
Rates: $59 to $100, double occupancy; $35 to $82, single; continental breakfast included. Children welcome.
Open: Inn open all year. Restaurant closes Christmas and July Fourth. Breakfast, lunch, dinner, bar.
Facilities & Activities: Walking distance to underground Metro. All the sights of the city. Bicycling the city bike path.

The Tabard Inn is an anomaly. It's in the heart of the fashionable Dupont Circle section on a brownstone-lined street, yet it's quaint and cozy as a favorite pair of worn slippers. It can momentarily startle you with its lemon-yellow hallway, and its unusual paint colors in the rooms, yet in the next moment you enter a ☛ cozy parlor that's a throwback to the past.

Couches and chairs are everywhere in this maze of a place. I like that. The petite lobby is filled with dark empire-style couches. Around the corner is the first parlor. Rich wood paneling covers every square inch of the walls, ceiling, and floor. The room nurtures good conversation. Pick up your drinks around the corner at the bar and meander back here.

When you're ready for dinner you enter the black and white tiled French bistro-style restaurant, a look that's not changed for years. Colorful international folk art hangs on the walls. The tables are cozy. The food is terrific.

One evening my companion and I ☞ relished our dinners of fresh fish stuffed with crabmeat and coated with a lobster sauce, and a thick steak with Béarnaise sauce. To the side was an artistic array of steamed fresh vegetables. Other offerings included a cold lobster salad with fresh figs and grilled garlic sausage with raddichio.

In the summertime you may eat on the brick patio. Sunday brunch is served here with desserts like lime caramel flan, chocolate blueberry cake, and strawberries with crème fraiche. Go for a bike ride afterwards and see Washington at a glide while you work off those delicious calories.

The rooms vary. The spacious sky-lit "penthouse" has a kitchenette, light wooden floors, country furnishings, and an extremely ornate mirror. The tiny single bedrooms are the smallest I've seen. Most of the rooms with the tile fireplaces and those that overlook N Street are more spacious (with exceptions). Nothing can be generalized about this inn, except it's like none other in the city.

How to get there: Walking: From Dupont Circle Subway take the Dupont Exit, continue one block south on Connecticut, and turn left on N Street one block to the inn. Driving: From I-95 in Virginia, take the 14th Street bridge and 14th Street until you turn left on K Street. Turn right on Connecticut. Turn right on 18th Street before the underpass and take an immediate short right on one-way N Street. Park and pay in the garage on the immediate right. The inn is in ½-block on the left.

olive Metcalf

The Martha Washington Inn
Abingdon, Virginia
24210

Innkeeper: Jim Watts
Telephone: 703-628-3161
Rooms: 66, all with private bath; 4 suites.
Rates: $40 to $49, double occupancy; $35 to $39, single; $65 to $85,
   suite; EP. Children welcome.
Open: All year. Breakfast, lunch, dinner, tavern.
Facilities & Activities: Barter Theater April through August. 154,-
   000 acre Mount Rogers National Recreation Area with hiking,
   cross-country skiing, horseback riding, and fishing. White's
   Mill for fresh ground cornmeal. Virginia Highlands Festival
   first two weeks of August.

First private home, then girls' school, and eventually
inn. The Martha Washington has served all purposes with
her stately and proper appearance.

Across from Virginia's famous ☛ Barter Theater in
busy downtown Abingdon is the inn that dates from 1832.
The common rooms are expansive, elegant, and sparsely furnished with exquisite and rare ☛ antiques. Each lounge has

240

central configurations of comfortable couches and chairs. The windows reach clear to the floor; the ceilings soar to impressive heights.

Schoolchildren are given tours through the inn, and the little girls are fascinated with the petticoat mirror in the front hallway. The young ladies who attended school here long ago would check their petticoats before they went out onto the front porch. Among those who attended was Ellen Louise Axson, who later married Woodrow Wilson. The Wilson Suite is where she stayed as a student and later with her husband.

Eleanor Roosevelt preferred the room that looks out to the back and the railroad track. She directed the formation of Mount Rogers National Recreation Area from here. Lady Bird Johnson's visits named the Johnson Suite, which has a large canopy bed. From the corner window you can see the Barter Theater. The Napoleon Suite is furnished magnificently with a bed and dresser said to have been owned by the Emperor himself.

During the summer the large dining room expands into the inner brick courtyard. You might find fresh strips of pork bathed in a nicely flavored gravy on the menu. For dinner the steak selections outnumber the seafood selections that include two styles of shrimp. For dessert you might order the cherries jubilee and watch your dessert go up in flames just as it should just before you begin. The chef appreciates a touch of theatrics.

Elizabeth Taylor has stayed here. She recognizes a good scene.

How to get there: From I-84 take Exit 8 onto Route 75 North to Route 11. Turn right, and the inn is a short distance on the right. From the Interstate you can follow the signs to the Barter Theater.

B: *Barter Theater actually bartered theater tickets for farm foods during the Depression. The saying was a "ham for Hamlet."*

olive Metcalf

Boar's Head Inn
Charlottesville, Virginia
22905

Innkeeper: Jerrod L. Godin
Telephone: 804-296-2181
Rooms: 175, all with private bath, 9 suites; Children welcome. Pets
   allowed.
Rates: $73, double occupancy; $63, single; $105 to $115, suite; EP.
   Two-night minimum for home football games.
Open: All year. Breakfast, lunch, dinner, bar.
Facilities & Activities: Sports' Club (extra fee) with swimming,
   tennis, squash, racquetball, paddle tennis, gym, clinic, and
   sauna. Hot-air ballooning. Holiday dances and dinners. Fox
   hunting, rabbit hunting, wineries, Monticello, Ash Lawn, and
   Michie Tavern nearby.

Traditions old and new are found at the Boar's Head
Inn. In the same day you can follow the centuries-old fox
hunt that begins a short drive away, join the sport of foot
hunting for rabbits with a pack of hounds, take a hot-air balloon ride, and work out at the sports club with the latest in
athletic equipment and the most-up-to-date methods.
   At Christmas there's a "Feast before forks," a seven-
course Medieval-style banquet served without forks, followed

by dancing, Christmas caroling, and wassailing. For those who prefer not to soil their fingers, the Elizabethan ball and dessert banquet might be their cup of tea. There are ☞ activities and ☞ facilities to suit every taste.

The inn is in a residential suburb in gently rolling hills in northwest Charlottesville. The inn was built in 1965. Its dining room was constructed out of an old gristmill that was dismantled plank by plank, brought to this spot, and reassembled.

I arrived on a misty day and saw a pair of graceful swans swimming on the small lake opposite the inn. The natural board and batten looked lovely and it was quiet enough to hear the loud crunch of my footsteps across the gravel.

The rooms are similarly furnished. The original fifty-four that date from 1965 are the most interesting. Some have partial alcoves around the beds and exposed pine beams. You can request an original, but they are never promised for reservation.

In the dining rooms a Virginia ham was served with a sweet raisin sauce to balance the natural saltiness of the ham. From the luncheon menu came a London broil prepared with a juicy wine sauce and the ☞ chocolate satin pie rested delicately on a layer of lemon custard. The two flavors were a tangy contrast.

How to get there: From I-64 take Exit 22B to U.S. Route 250 West. Go west 1½ miles and turn left into the inn.

B: *The Boar's Head Inn in London was famous during Shakespeare's time. The boar was chosen as its symbol because it represents hospitality.*

Olive Metcalf

Channel Bass Inn
Chincoteague, Virginia
23336

Innkeeper: James S. Hanretta
Telephone: 804-336-6148
Rooms: 8, all with private bath.
Rates: $63 to $100, double occupancy; $156 for 2-room suite; EP.
No children under 10.
Open: Closes December and January. Restaurant closes Mondays.
Breakfast on weekends, dinner, alcoholic beverages.
Facilities & Activities: Wild beach on Assateague's National Sea-
shore nearby. Chincoteague National Wildlife Refuge. Hunt-
ing, fishing, wildlife, boating, swimming. Annual wild pony
roundup and auction. Fall Osyter Festival. Adult Inn.

Some fine inns are in the most unlikely places. On little
Church Street across from a gas station, one block from the
Intercoastal waterway and a few miles from the wild beach is
this four-star restaurant and inn.

James Hanretta is the handsome, tanned, and muscular
innkeeper who resembles John Irving. He and his wife fell in
love with the 🖝 natural and wild beauty of the Chincoteague
area over ten years ago. They bought a 100-year-old farmhouse that had begun as a guest house and created the inn.

You enter a low-ceilinged lounge to shades of beige that predominate throughout. There's nothing that will jar the senses. A pair of sofas caress you with softness. You walk on thick carpeting everywhere. Even in your room.

The rooms are of two types. The "more quaint," as Jim describes them, are on the second floor, and are smaller and have more antiques than the third floor rooms, which are spacious, newer, and have carefully selected art works. Some rooms are wallpapered with soft shades of rose or fine prints. Every one is ☛ spotless and a potted plant either hangs from the ceiling or sits in a sunny window.

The inn is styled for the gourmet getaway. Only twenty-eight people are served a night. Always make reservations before you come; it's too far not to. There's no dress code for dinner, but some prefer coat and tie. A woman wouldn't be uncomfortable here during summer in a silk or cotton sundress.

You can take cooking lessons from Jim. You'll probably want to after dining here. The ☛ filet mignon is served soaking in a tantalizing mushroom and wine sauce. Do ask for a side dish of the saffron rice made with green pepper, onion, pimiento, chicken stock, and chorizo sausage. The Spanish salad tossed in pure olive oil is a wonderful blend of pasta, fresh tomatoes, green pepper, onion, and seasoned to a perfection. Try ☛ strawberries continental, strawberries marinated in lemon and orange juices, flambéed in cognac, coated with rich chocolate syrup, and crowned with fresh whipped cream. It's divinely delicious.

How to get there: Take Route 175 East to the deadend in Chincoteague, or Main Street. Turn left and go one block to Church Street. Turn right and the inn is on your immediate right at 100 Church Street. Fly-in, with advance permission to land, Wallops Island Airfield (military).

Olive Metcalf

Buckhorn Inn
Churchville, Virginia
24421

Innkeepers: Eileen and Roger Lee
Telephone: 703-885-2900
Rooms: 6, one with private bath.
Rates: $28 to $38, double occupancy; $18, single with shared bath; continental breakfast included. Children welcome.
Open: Closes Christmas Eve and Christmas Day. Restaurant closes Mondays, and in January and February also closes Tuesdays. Breakfast, lunch, dinner, beer, wine.
Facilities & Activities: Hiking, bicycling, and hunting in nearby George Washington National Forest. Shenandoah Mountains.

The Buckhorn Inn was born a modest Southern mansion, but for 180 years it has served as a tavern, waystation, and inn. Travelers on their way to the Virginia hot springs often stopped here before "taking the waters."

My favorite thing about this inn is the woodwork in the three petite dining rooms. It was laboriously stripped by the previous owners; they did a commendable job. The wooden fireplace mantels are attractive, and the Pine Room is toasty during the winter months with the fire blazing away.

Food is an important part of this inn. The dining rooms

are just the right size for you and the family or friends. The ☞ fried chicken is crispy crunchy, and with it you have a choice of two vegetables, one of which is the salad bar. Vegetarians can order a plateful of four vegetables. The spiced apples are served hot with a tangy red sauce and are uncommonly tasty. It's a sign you're in the South when the choice of vegetables is so long it takes a second repeating from the waitress. The peanut butter pie is divine and not something you'll find often.

Special dishes are offered on various evenings. On Wednesdays it's a German buffet with schnitzel, sauerbraten, hot potato soups, and German desserts. Thursday evenings you can have bar-b-que beef and short ribs, and on Fridays the seafood buffet features fried clams, crab balls, steamed and fried shrimp, and broiled whitefish. For the Sunday buffet there's a steamship round of beef, fried chicken, shrimp, and usually a line out the front door waiting for seats.

The rooms are clean and furnished with a variety of old and new furniture. In the Stonewall Jackson Suite you'll find an office desk and ☞ a jacuzzi in the bathroom. There's no common room, but the front porch with long benches is a nice place to rest your legs and visit after a day's hike.

It's debated how the Buckhorn got its name. Some believe it's from the deer crossing near the inn, which is appropriate because during November hunters are in the majority at the Buckhorn.

How to get there: From I-81 take Route 250 West. The inn is 12 miles west of Staunton past Churchville on the north side of Route 250. It's painted white with black shutters.

B: *A good meal in an inn picks up even the weariest of travelers.*

olive Metcalf

The Laurel Brigade Inn
Leesburg, Virginia
22075

Innkeeper: Ellen Flippo Wall
Telephone: 703-777-1010
Rooms: 6, all with private bath.
Rates: $32 to $53, double occupancy; $22, single; $43 to $64, for three sharing a room; EP. Children welcome. No credit cards.
Open: Closes January to mid-February. Restaurant closes Mondays and Christmas Day. Lunch, dinner, alcoholic beverages.
Facilities & Activities: Chesapeake and Ohio Canal, mansions, August Court Days, an 18th-century street celebration, fall carriage and steeplechase races, antiquing, and horseback riding.

The Laurel Brigade Inn was an "ordinary" or tavern built out of stone in 1759. In 1817 it became the Peers Hotel that once served Lafayette. Later the Mott family used it as a family residence for nearly one hundred years. Dr. Mott added the marble fireplaces in the two small street-side dining rooms and the Swiss brass fixtures on the doors. Ellen Wall's father purchased the mansion from the Mott family and installed the cypress wood throughout the main dining room.

The name, Laurel Brigade, refers to the Civil War Brigade that was consistently recognized for gallant valor. You can easily walk historic Leesburg from the inn's downtown location, using street maps provided by the inn, and return in time for lunch. Above the door to the dining room is a hand-stenciled cornucopia to whet your appetite.

Meals are preceded in the inn with a relish tray. For lunch I had creamed chicken in a pastry shell and the barley soup. The apple dumpling dessert arrived with a mound of hard ☞ brandy sauce that's the consistency of cream cheese frosting. The menu changes frequently. Traditional entrees such as filet mignon, fried chicken, and crab imperial are on the dinner menu.

The carpeted hallway to the rooms is wallpapered in pink rose up to the wainscotting. The hand-stenciled walls are a nice touch. The rooms are pine floored and furnished with period reproductions.

On the outskirts of town an ☞ unusual trail ride begins each May. It lasts twenty-four hours and goes nonstop through the Virginia countryside. Most enter the race for the opportunity to go for a nice ride with genial company.

How to get there: From I-66 take Route 15 North to Leesburg. At the intersection of Route 7 turn left. The stone inn is located opposite the small theater on the north side of the street ½-block from the Court House.

☒

B: *There is a good antique shop within walking distance of the inn.*

olive Metcalf

The Red Fox Tavern and The Stray Fox
Middleburg, Virginia
22117

Innkeeper: Turner Reuter
Telephone: 703-687-6301
Rooms: 6, all with private bath; 5 suites; one cottage.
Rates: $65 to $110, double occupancy; $90 to $175, suite; continental breakfast included in Red Fox only. Children welcome.
Open: All year. Sometimes closes for 10 days in February. Breakfast, lunch, dinner, bar.
Facilities & Activities: Night Fox Pub. Garden terrace. Upperville Colt and Horse Show in June, Hunt Country Stable Tour in May, horse races, Foxhound Show in May, house and garden tours, Point to Point Races, fox hunts, equestrian meets, antiquing, bicycling, polo every Sunday from June through September.

A Sunday drive out to the esteemed Red Fox Inn in Middleburg for dinner is a worthwhile Washington tradition. It can only be improved upon by staying the night. It's fifty miles from the city, yet worlds away.

"The Oldest Original Inn" reads the sign outside the

stone inn that dates from 1738 and under various names has warmed, nourished, and rested guests ever since. It's a refined jewel.

In 1976 Innkeeper Reuter's mother and sister thoroughly researched how an 18th-century inn should look in furnishings, fabrics, wallpapers, and bedspreads. The rooms and suites have canopied beds, some have hand-woven rugs, and most have working fireplaces. In the closets hang ☛ fresh terrycloth robes. Potpourri scents the rooms, and chocolates and fresh flowers are almost taken for granted here.

In the nearby Stray Fox the elegant Belmont Suite has a living room spacious enough to host a large hunt party after the ride. In the petite Furness Room upstairs, the floor has been beautifully stenciled. As you descend the staircase a thoughtful brass sign reads, "Duck." Where to stay in these two lovely buildings is a tossup.

☛ Middleburg is a treat. The town is small, has antique shops and a horse and bridle shop, and the area hosts many posh events. If you've never seen polo, a Middleburg horse race, or gone on a stable tour this is the chance.

The Red Fox serves inspiring dinners. The specials equal the menu listings. I've tried the ☛ Shad en Papillote flavored with sprigs of fresh herbs, carrot slices, and anise, ☛ the Escalloppe de Veau, the Pork Roquefort served on Fettucine, and the steak. Four out of four and each excellent. To help you make your dessert decision there's a two-tiered tray with selections on a small table near the entrance. The pecan pie and strawberries are perfection.

You'd have to hunt a long time to find an inn that equals the Red Fox in every respect.

How to get there: From I-495 west of Washington, D.C., take I-66 South to Route 50 West. In the heart of Middleburg is the inn on the right side of the street. Fly-in, Dulles International Airport.

Olive Metcalf

Wayside Inn
Middletown, Virginia
22645

Innkeeper: Chuck Alverson
Telephone: 703-869-1797
Rooms: 21, all with private bath.
Rates: $50 to $100, double occupancy, EP. Children welcome.
Open: All year. Breakfast, lunch, dinner, tavern.
Facilities & Activities: Wayside Theater a short walk, Skyline Drive, four wineries nearby, antique shops, auctions, Belle Grove Plantation, and Winchester hosts annual May Apple Blossom festival with parades and special activities. Canoeing, bicycling, and horseback riding.

From the moment you reach for the black latch door handle of the Wayside you're reminded it's been accommodating guests ever since 1797. First you're greeted by yourself in a very old fisheye looking glass. Then you're warmly hosted into a choice of several worlds.

In one direction lies the ☞ tavern, and it's a splendid one. I'll wager it's the only pub in the world with a back-lit single-piece carving of the seventh crusade of Louis IX. Inside the tavern is the "discovered room." When the inn was under restoration during the early sixties, a secret room was uncovered behind a wall. It was the 🖙 Old Slave Quarters Kitchen, which is now a most romantic dining room floored with bricks and lighted with candles.

Another petite dining room accommodates two couples. In the corner stands a three-sided corner cabinet that so intrigued a local furniture maker she copied the design. Today she sells the "Wayside Corner Cupboard."

Every one of the rooms is a distinct 🖙 pleasure. The navy-blue room has a canopied bed that barely misses the ceiling. The Chinese room is authentic because Chuck explains, "During the 1800s Chinese styles were popular."

Anna Rose Newman started at the Wayside at the age of seventeen, and nineteen years later she prepares the "southern regional cooking" that adorns the menu. I was delighted with the roast duckling braised with a ginger sauce. The fresh broccoli was served family style with a whole loaf of homemade bread that came fresh from the oven. The prime rib comes with one of the largest popovers ever seen. The Huntsman's Pie, composed of venison, duck, and rabbit with mushrooms and port wine sauce is for those who love a tasty crust on their meat. "We serve Huntsman's Pie," says Chuck, "because they would have eaten it here in the 1800s."

Dinner followed by 🖙 Kentucky Derby pie, pecan pie with a thin coating of chocolate, and a nightcap on the patio provide the best winning combination I can imagine. Chuck suggested it. He was right.

How to get there: From I-81 take Exit 77 onto Route 11 South to the stop sign. Turn left, and in ½-mile at 7783 Main Street is the white brick and frame inn.

B: *I can't imagine a cross word being uttered here. It's a classic inn in every way.*

Olive Metcalf

Highland Inn
Monterey, Virginia
24465

Innkeeper: Bob Campbell
Telephone: 703-468-2143
Rooms: 15, all with private bath; 4 suites.
Rates: $39 to $49, double occupancy; $50, suite, double occupancy;
$60, suite for 4 people; EP. Children and pets welcome.
Open: All year. Breakfast, lunch, dinner, tavern.
Facilities & Activities: Hiking, mountain climbing, hunting, pic-
nicking, fishing, downhill and cross-country skiing. Annual
Maple Festival in March and Fall Festival in October. George
Washington National Park.

Your drive to the Highland Inn is an immersion in the
Allegheny Highlands, which are great canvases of natural
beauty. You'll rejoice in the views of the area that has been
called the "Little Switzerland of America."

If you take the southern valley route to the inn, the
herds of sheep you'll encounter are more than pretty idyllic
pictures. They are Highland County's economy, and in the
inn you'll find the popular Black Sheep Tavern.

The inn is at the center of things in the valley town of
Monterey, population 700, just as it was back in 1904 when it

was built. On a Saturday night Bob brings in local musicians who play for the love of their music and the magic they weave through the crowd.

This is a casual, friendly inn with a down-home atmosphere. There are two guest parlours filled with books and magazines. A big-screen television has video movies available. Along the hallway off the lobby are craft shops and a newsstand.

Travelers once arrived here with trunks of clothes. Today trunks are in some of the rooms. Beige ruffled curtains frame the windows. Two rooms have natural pine floors, as does the ☛ dining room where the tables are covered with fresh white linen tablecloths.

Devour a meal of Allegheny Mountain trout fresh from the nearby fishery or Virginia country ham, and you get a flavor of the old days in Monterey. Bob also prepares a south Florida dish, a taste he acquired from his twelve years as a chef in Florida. His ☛ pecan pie is made with Highland County maple syrup.

Early Sunday morning you can order a full breakfast with all the trimmings. Then Bob serves a large midday country dinner, the kind grandma used to made. Sunday supper is light with perhaps, a reuben sandwich stacked high with corned beef, cheese, and sauerkraut, smothered with a rich sauce, and then grilled to a melted perfection.

The Fall Festival takes place on two weekends in October. The fall leaves are a glorious and showy spectacle in the Highlands and the whole world, it seems, comes to Monterey.

How to get there: From I-64 take Route 250 West. The inn is in town on the right.

olive Metcalf

Mountain Lake Hotel
Mountain Lake, Virginia
24136

Innkeeper: J. W. McMillin
Telephone: 703-626-7121
Rooms: 116 in lodges and cottages, 90 with private bath.
Rates: $74 to $112, double occupancy; $46 to $80, single; AP. Children's rates. Gratuity of $4 a day per person. Two-night minimum on weekends, 3 nights on some holidays. Pets allowed in some cottages.
Open: May 1 through October 15. Call. Breakfast, lunch, dinner. Wine and beer in dining room. BYOB restricted to room.
Facilities & Activities: 2,800 acres. Horseback riding, swimming, tennis, golf course in 1½ miles, pool tables, nightly bingo, movies, aerobics, ceramics, and nature hikes. Canoeing, paddleboats, and fishing. Fee charged for riding and golf.

    In a world unto itself on a hilltop, overlooking a 🐾 pristine, clear, and deep mountain lake, is the Mountain Lake Hotel. To circle the entire lake on foot is a peaceful endeavor that covers one-and-three-quarters miles. If you begin near the white picket fence, you'll get a perspective of the grand stone lodge, most of its small cottages, the handcraft house, and the pretty gray barn.

Many ask how they carried this much stone up to this mountaintop. They didn't. "It was here," says J. W. McMillin. "We could build six more lodges if we desired, but one very fine one is quite enough." J. W. used the rare wormy chestnut wood also found on the property to build the Chestnut Lodge. The interior paneling is offset with mustard-colored walls. From its small private balconies you can barely see the lake through the trees, just as J. W. planned it.

If you choose a room in the stone lodge, they are convenient and hotel-like. You might prefer a lake view. The handsome brass fixtures on the doors are lovely. There also are rooms in cottages throughout the hillside. Those recently remodeled are preferable. Some of the older cottages are rustic.

For dinner coats are requested for the men. Fresh white linen covers the individual tables. The inn calls it all-American cooking. You have a choice of meats and fish. It might be flounder stuffed with crabmeat, or New Zealand lamb chops served with mango chutney, or roast duckling and ginger sauce. For dessert a lemon pecan pie or chocolate bourbon pie and ice cream are the occasional selections. I'd call it fancy American cooking.

Outdoor lovers are in good company here. You can be as active as you like. You can reach the Appalachian Trail and National Forest hiking trails from a lakeside route. The canoes line the shore when not in use. If you don't choose to be active you may sit on the hilltop porch or the lakeside gazebo to watch the lake.

Spring comes late in Mountain Lake. You have the advantage of experiencing blooming alpine wildflowers in late June.

How to get there: From I-81 exit onto Route 460 West. After Newport take a right at the small Route 700 sign. Follow the road to the hilltop for a distance of 6 or 7 miles.

Olive Metcalf

The Conyers House
Sperryville, Virginia
22740

Innkeepers: Sandra and Norman Cartwright-Brown
Telephone: 703-987-8025
Rooms: 7, 2 with private bath; 2 cottages with 1½ baths.
Rates: $80 to $100 for couples, includes breakfast and afternoon
   tea. No credit cards. Guests prefer to leave their children
   home.
Open: All year. Dinner for guests only by advance reservation.
   BYOB.
Facilities & Activities: Antiquing, golf, tennis, trail rides, cham-
   pagne flight in a hot-air balloon, canoeing, and fishing. Skyline
   Drive nearby.

The Conyers House sits on a little country road in the
foothills of the Shenandoah Mountains. It was known as
Conyers Old Store back in 1850. Sandra and Norman bought
the house for their country retreat from Washington, D.C.
They installed plumbing, stripped woodwork, plastered, and
walled. Then they decided to open as an inn. Guests have
been arriving ever since. They don't advertise and they aren't
listed in the telephone book. Word travels fast when roman-

258

tics discover a country hideaway with engaging worldly hosts.

Uncle Sim Wright's Room is named for the neighbor's grandfather who dwelt here. The faded chintz curtains are perfection with the paintings by Richard Cull of Munich. The open book on the desk downstairs shows the painting that hangs upstairs. The fireplace in this room has art nouveau lines.

Helen's Room is named for Norman's mother who lives in Yorkshire. Sandra has combined three different wallpapers in reds, grays, and blues. She has a good eye for juxtaposing the unexpected.

Sandra rides with the hunt club and can arrange for guests to go horseback riding. Twice the local hunt club has left from the inn. She serves a hearty hunt breakfast on fine bone china. The jams are delicacies. The red pepper jelly is the house specialty and deserves its reputation. Nathan's bread is a deep healthy grain and the cheese strata a baked multilayered affair. On the second morning she serves a rich breakfast pudding with raisins smothered in coddled cream. A dish like that and you're in a good mood for the rest of the day.

For dinner Sandra requires advance notice. She serves Warden Robinson's fresh trout. Guests generally dine at least one night at the Inn at Little Washington, a renowned gourmet restaurant that's fifteen minutes away.

How to get there: Take Exit 29S from I-66 to Warrenton. Turn west on Route 211 to Sperryville. After Sperryville Emporium turn left at the blinking light at Route 522. Then turn right on Route 231 (¾-mile at the cemetery). In 8 miles turn left on Route 707, and the inn is ⁶/₁₀-mile. Fly-in, Dulles International Airport.

❋

B: *Two wooden decks are perfectly positioned around this inn. One to capture the sunrise, the other to watch the sunset.*

Olive Metcalf

Jordan Hollow Farm Inn
Stanley, Virginia
22851

Innkeepers: Marley and Jetze Beers
Telephone: 703-778-2209
Rooms: 20, all with private bath.
Rates: $30 to $47, double occupancy; $24 to $41, single; EP. $67 to
   $85, per person for 2 nights and 5 meals. Children welcome,
   under 4 free. Two-night minimum on weekends, call Thurs-
   days for exceptions. No credit cards. Horses boarded.
Open: All year. Breakfast, lunch, dinner, wine and beer served.
Facilities & Activities: Horseback riding and trail rides, swimming
   pool, occasional hayrides, barn dances. Luray Caverns, Blue
   Ridge Mountains, Skyline Drive, canoeing, bicycling, cross-
   country skiing, antique auctions and shops, hunting, golf, and
   tennis.

In the Shenandoah Valley surrounded by the Massanu-
ten Mountains to the west and the Blue Ridge to the east is
the eighty-acre Jordan Hollow Farm Inn. It's home to seventeen horses, black rottweiler dogs with wrinkled faces, and
two porch cats.

Marley Beers was a Washington, D.C., educational con-
sultant the day she fell in love with the farm and its dilapi-

dated house. Jetze Beers was a nautical engineer whose work took him around the world. They met in Monrovia, Africa. Today Jetze speaks his native Dutch and Freesian along with French and German to guests from foreign countries. He is captivating in any language. Marley is an experienced A-rated instructor, teaches horseback riding, and leads trail rides.

Jordan Hollow is a 200-year-old farm that began as a single log cabin. Later a second cabin was added, and around these two hand-axed gems the inn has grown.

In one of the three small dining rooms hang a pair of African masks Marley brought back from Africa during her Peace Corps stint. One is a cheerful face that is a mood setter for the Beers' home cooking. You will certainly feel cheerful after eating the orange-glazed baked ham, the juicy broiled chicken breast, or the boneless butterfly chops, followed by Marley's Profiterole, a cream puff filled with mocha ice cream, drenched in chocolate sauce, and crowned with whipped cream and pecans.

The guest rooms are new and have a variety of country wallpaper prints. Several have oak antiques. They are a hundred yards from the front porch of the main house. They all share their own long porch. There are many activities to keep you busy on Jordan Farm, but Jetze and Marley admit porch sitting is the favorite. This is a nice way to appreciate the beautiful countryside and the lovely views. I was glad to hear Marley say, "We are surrounded by national parks, which means no one can ever take our views away."

How to get there: From I-66 exit onto Route 55 to Front Royal and turn south on Route 340. Continue 6 miles past Luray on Route 340 and turn left on Route 624. Signs direct you from here.

ᗺ

B: *I love a* *country inn with horses, dogs, and cats. It reminds me of the farm where I grew up.*

olive Metcalf

The Belle Grae Inn
Staunton, Virginia
24401

Innkeepers: Michael Organ and Ken Hicks
Telephone: 703-886-5151
Rooms: 8, 6 with private bath.
Rates: $38 to $55, double occupancy, EPB. Business rate available.
Children welcome.
Open: All year. Breakfast, lunch, and dinner by reservation. Wine,
beer, cocktails served by request.
Facilities & Activities: Woodrow Wilson Birthplace, Mary Baldwin
College, self-guided architectural tour, Trinity Church,
antiquing. End of April is Garden Week and private homes
open their doors. Location: heart of Shenandoah Valley.

Settle into a wicker rocking chair on the front porch and
you can see a pair of double hills named Betsy Belle and Mary
Grae. The early Scottish settlers found the hills reminded
them of the green hills at home mentioned in a poem by Robert Burns.
Ken Hicks and Michael Organ have beautifully restored
and ☞ decorated this Italianate mansion that sits high above
the street in Staunton. Brass fixtures in every bathroom,
original claw-footed bathtubs, antiques and other quality fur-

nishings form the scenes for a wonderful time where casual and friendly innkeepers oversee the manse.

Sit deep into the red chairs in the green room and pet Bell Boy, the friendly boxer. He's been through obedience school. Put your drink on the marble top table and utter a restful sigh as the summer breezes waft through the French doors.

The meals are ☞ southern style cooking. On Derby Day the luncheon began with mint juleps on the porch, then a "camp" meal of heavenly fried chicken, potato salad, baked beans, all served on silver platters followed by fresh strawberry shortcake made with homemade pastry shells. On a warm summer afternoon lunch might be served on the back patio where you can listen to the mockingbirds sing.

The ☞ burgundy dining rooms with their exquisite marble fireplaces, candelabras, and fine china set the perfect tone for other meals. One entree is served each evening for dinner. It might be fried chicken or a thick cut of a tender stuffed pork chop. Breakfasts are at the innkeeper's whim, and during winter a scrumptious sausage gravy is often served.

From the inn you can walk to the historic Woodrow Wilson House, Mary Baldwin College, and other historic sights. "We're a city inn," says Ken. There are pleasant small-town activities to do or not to do. Decisions of pleasure are the best kind.

How to get there: From I-81 take Route 250 West to Staunton. Follow the signs to the Woodrow Wilson Birthplace, then turn left on West Frederick Street and go past the inn on the right at 515 West Frederick. Turn right on Jefferson Street, go right one block on Baldwin, and park behind the inn. Shenandoah Valley Airport or Waynesboro Airport, fly-in.

Olive Metcalf

Hotel Strasburg
Strasburg, Virginia
22657

Innkeeper: Michael Paper
Telephone: 703-465-9191
Rooms: 17, all with shared baths; 3 suites.
Rates: $35 to $40, double occupancy; $60, suite; continental breakfast included. Children welcome.
Open: All year. Breakfast, lunch, dinner. Tavern opens at 11 a.m., and serves light fare daily.
Facilities & Activities: George Washington National Forest, 4 cross-country ski trails, hiking, biking, antiquing, Skyline Caverns, 45 minutes from downhill skiing.

Built as a hospital in the 1890s it became the Hotel Strasburg in 1910, but it's really a cheery, sunny Victorian inn in a small-town neighborhood.

Take the time to linger over a before-dinner cocktail in the ☞ Depot Lounge. You'll admire the 18th-century stove, the railroad photographs, and the wooden bar with the old foot railing. After shopping the town for antiques or spending an invigorating day on the cross-country ski trails, you'll find this a very inviting place.

Upstairs the wallpaper in the honeymoon suite matches

the couch, white lace curtains frame the windows, and in the bathroom stands a claw-footed bathtub. You'll want to take a second honeymoon. The eclectic rooms range from small to large, and the 1979 renovation makes them comfortable and inviting. In the wide hallway sit two big Queen Anne-style chairs, my favorite.

Take your time to see the antiques. Innkeeper, Michael Paper, has fourteen years of experience in the antique business. In the lobby is a wooden postcard stand filled to the brim. There are portraits of ladies and paintings, golden mirrors galore, handsome buffets, and chests filled with dolls and things. It's Victorian at its ornate best, and everything is for sale. Michael has even sold the dining room tables on occasion.

Michael has another innkeeping talent. Having begun cooking at the age of eleven, he oversees all the daily specials, menus, and often does some of the cooking. You should try the pecan cheesecake or the pecan pie. It's a delicious experience and a perfect cap to the herbed pork chops or the hickory barbecue baby back spareribs. The inn has its own smoker. Fish is another special, and depending on what's available you might try swordfish, seafood kabob, or rainbow trout stuffed with crabmeat.

I saw old friends meet in the lobby. They were coming from distant points to have lunch. What a lovely idea, to meet old friends at the Hotel Strasburg.

How to get there: From I-81 take the Strasburg Exit to Route 11 South. Go 1½ miles to the first traffic light and turn right, staying on Route 11. Go one block to Holliday Street, turn left, and the inn is at 201 Holliday Street.

❦

We came here to celebrate a family birthday and were delighted with the setting. The pecan cheesecake is especially delicious.—Dr. Don and Ceretha Karolyi

olive Metcalf

Graves' Mountain Lodge
Syria, Virginia
22743

Innkeepers: Jim and Rachel Graves
Telephone: 703-923-4231
Rooms: 38, all with private bath. 7 cottages.
Rates: $29 to $57, per person, double or single occupancy; children aged 10 and under half price; AP. Two-night minimum on weekends. Children welcome.
Open: April through November. Breakfast, lunch, dinner. Serves wine. Other alcoholic beverages not allowed.
Facilities & Activities: Guest lounge, swimming pool, tennis courts, mountain streams, horseback riding, hiking, basketball court, trout fishing in pond, rock hunting, and golf privileges nearby. Hoover Camp.

"It's too bad you didn't meet Elvin Graves," said a neighbor of Graves' Mountain Lodge. "He'd work on his tractor all morning. Around noontime he'd go into the lodge in his jeans and greet guests around the bounteous noontime spread that decorated the tables." She and others speak fondly of this man. It was Elvin's great-grandfather, Paschal Graves, who opened the first "ordinary" back in the 1850s. Today Elvin's son and daughter-in-law are the fifth generation of the Graves family to continue the innkeeping traditions.

The rooms are simply furnished. Wildwood and Blackwood cottages are white cinder block construction and pine paneled inside. The more remote log cabin is dormitory style, older, and more rustic. The farmhouse is a pleasant series of small rooms, several of which have fireplaces. The motel units up the hill have a long front porch that overlooks the valley.

Depending on the location of your room, you'll probably walk to the lodge for your meals. This is a ☞ family inn where you're seated at a long table as you arrive. The ☞ view is spectacular from the dining room. You can see the mountain peaks, the stream, and the cottages down the hill. Breakfast consists of a heaping plateful of pancakes, hot sausage and eggs, English toast, juices, and coffee.

Sunday dinner includes ☞ fried chicken, mashed potatoes, gravy, corn, green beans, harvard beets, congealed salad, three-bean salad, hot homemade yeast rolls, and dessert which depends on the seasonal fruits. It's a spread my grandma would be proud of.

After savoring your meal, there are two large common rooms with fireplaces, a piano, and space to relax in the lodge. Up the hill are the apple and peach orchards that lead to a labeled nature hike. You can trout fish in "no-kill" streams, hike a myriad of superbly beautiful trails, rappel down the mountainsides, or go horseback riding. You might lie in the sun by the pool or wear your swimsuit and hike to the waterfalls in White Oak Canyon. You can cool off in the pools at the base of the falls. This is a pleasant inn for every member of the family.

How to get there: From I-64 take Route 29 North. Take Route 231 North toward Madison. In 7 miles turn left on Route 670 West toward Syria. The lodge is ½-mile past the Syria General Store.

olive Metcalf

Prospect Hill
Trevilians, Virginia
23170

Innkeepers: Bill and Mireille Sheehan
Telephone: 703-967-0844
Rooms: 5, all with private bath; 2 suites.
Rates: $60 to $75, per person, double occupancy, MAP. Two nights'
stay may be required on weekends.
Open: Closes Christmas Eve and Christmas Day. Breakfast, dinner
Wednesday through Saturday. Wine served.
Facilities & Activities: Countryside. Nearby are swimming, horse-
back riding, fishing, and golfing, Monticello, Ashlawn, and an-
tique shops.

Lovers in search of an 18th-century ☞ hideaway, your
search has ended. Turn in at the tiny Prospect Hill sign, drive
down the boxwood-bordered lane, then walk down the
hedged pathway until you reach the sunny house. There in
the sunlight you can shed your cares.

Bill, sporting a handsome handlebar mustache, greets
you cheerfully with a firm handshake and ushers you into
this pretty inn that dates back to 1732. Over the years it grew
in size to accommodate the families that lived here, and cot-

tages were built as slave quarters. Today the cottages make ☞ romantic dwellings.

Bill is the chef. Mireille is the behind-the-scenes decorator. Together they've transformed the inn into a peaceable country estate. Its French flavor derives from Mireille's French heritage and Bill's French-flavored cuisine.

Behind the inn stretches a lawn shaded with massive old leafy trees. A hammock is suspended between the trees. Large white wicker chairs cuddle the afternoon reader on the small porch. Inside there's a more formally comfortable common room with a stereo for classical music. You won't find a television.

Two rooms are in the main house and down the stone pathways are the picturesque cottages. Each ☞ room and suite has its special attributes. One is pure sunshine, another richly hewn with original logs, a third has long windows that open to the green lawn. They're all decorated with attractive antiques.

Around eight o'clock Bill rings the dinner bell. Guests eat at small separate tables. Bill's escalope de veau, roti de porc, and medallions filet de boeuf are prepared in the ☞ French manner. He presents one entree and one dessert every evening during the four-course dinner. Often requested is the chocolate amaretto mousse. Special diets are discussed when reservations are made.

This isn't really a farm inn for children, although children are welcome. As Bill says, "We even have two of our own." It's a ☞ haven. A place to lie in the sun, nap in the hammock. There's no rush, no fuss, a casual ambiance, and a friendly innkeeper who prepares a wonderful meal by candlelight. Oh, for a weekend in the country.

How to get there: Take Exit 27 from I-64 to Route 15 South to Zion Crossroads. Turn left on Route 250 East. Go one mile to Route 613, turn left, and go 3 miles to Prospect Hill on the left. Gordonsville Airport, fly-in.

olive Metcalf

Sugar Tree Lodge
Vesuvius, Virginia
24483

Innkeepers: Dean Gregory and Melisse B. Faulds
Telephone: 703-377-2197
Rooms: 10, 9 with private bath.
Rates: $59, double or single occupancy, EPB.
Open: Closes December 1 to May 1. Breakfast. Lunch and dinner
every day but Mondays. Alcoholic beverages served.
Facilities & Activities: Adjacent to 38,000-acre Big Levels Game
Refuge, woods, trails, creeks. Swimming short distance, rock
hunting, wildflower walks, hunting, fishing, and horseback rid-
ing. Skyline Drive. Request: "Exploring Sugar Tree Country."

Deep in the Shenandoah Mountains is Sugar Tree
Lodge. It's rustic at first glance, but behind that authentic
log exterior is a cultured and unpretentious inn of the high-
est order. This grand masterpiece was composed of hand-
hewn oak, chestnut, and poplar logs garnered from six buildings, all over 125 years old.

The art collection that hangs throughout the inn is just
one of the many indoor pleasures. In addition to drawings,
photographs, and prints, there are pieces of wooden sculp-

ture from around the world. A guardian angel carved in wood sits above the fireplace.

The three rooms in the main lodge each have their own stone fireplace as does the main living room. They are ☛ American rustic charm with homemade quilts and art pieces. A step or two away is the living room. Above the hearth hangs a deer head and above that a moose head. A bearskin hangs over the railing. Across the road from the inn is the ☛ 38,000 acre Big Levels Game Refuge.

If you prefer to shoot from behind a lens there are plenty of pretty areas to see. Return from your nature hike and you might settle into the hammock that's slung across the front porch.

You can reach the inn via Skyline Drive. Driving to the inn is an exhilarating experience in either direction. The roads wind and turn through shades of green and the sun shines in intermittent explosions through the trees. Along the ☛ Skyline Drive you see the Virginia Highlands between broad valleys and distant hilltops. Autumn is vivid in its golds and russets.

As if the setting wasn't fulfilling enough, there's the food. The chef changes the menu daily. Everything is written on a little chalkboard with brief descriptions of the French-style cuisine. A sampling of his gastronomic renditions are rabbit pâté, hot oriental vegetable soup, a spirited red raspberry chicken, broiled rainbow trout, Greek shrimp, and ham mousse. Chocolate lovers are going to think they've reached heaven. The Sugar Tree Lodge ☛ chocolate whiskey pie is sensational. Be sure to ask for the recipe.

Sounds idyllic here? It is.

How to get there: Take Exit 54 off I-81. Turn east on Route 606, go 1½ miles to U.S. Route 11, turn left, go 50 yards, and turn right on Route 56. It is 4 miles through Vesuvius to the lodge.

olive Metcalf

The Inn at Gristmill Square
Warm Springs, Virginia
24484

Innkeepers: Janice and Jack McWilliams
Telephone: 703-839-2231
Rooms: 12, all with private bath; 2 apartments.
Rates: $60 to $85, double occupancy; $50 to $68, single; $85 to $90,
    apartment; continental breakfast included. Children welcome.
Open: Closes first two weeks of January. Dining room closes Mon-
    days. Lunch May through October, dinner, pub.
Facilities & Activities: Swimming pool and tennis courts. Natural
    hot springs. Maple Festival in Monterey. Carriage rides, horse-
    back rides, golfing, fishing, hunting, and skiing at the Home-
    stead nearby.

      Nestled in a ☛ quiet village around a brook is the per-
fectly enticing and romantic Inn at Gristmill Square. It's a
Europeansque scene, a combination of five petite buildings
that surround the stone covered square. The flavor is intimate and the Warm Springs' area a joy to explore.
      Janice and Jack are friendly, down-to-earth innkeepers.
They had an inn in Vermont for twenty years. They left that
and came South, but they couldn't resist another inn. It's in
their blood.

The inn is composed of the ☞ Water Wheel restaurant in the original mill, which is white-walled, historic, and lovely. There's the tiniest pub, and delightful country stores. Cross the brook to reach the swimming pool and three tennis courts. Or you can play two of the three beautiful golf courses at the nearby Homestead resort.

There is a ☞ diversity of rooms for every mood. The Silo is a round, white, shingle-roofed building. You can sit before the fire in the round room or on the patio. In the Quilt Room Americana addicts will feel comfortable, and there's a room with an oriental flavor with a lovely window that looks out to the brook. The little Miller's House offers its coziness and the Board Room is spacious and sided with natural board siding. Continental breakfast is brought to your room in the morning.

For lunch you might try the ☞ rich king crab souffle. For dinner a filet mignon might tempt you or steak au poivre smothered in green peppercorns served with a brandy and pepper sauce. The fresh mountain trout, grilled and served almandine, is a trusted classic. The chef is French so don't leave without tasting his caramel custard or chocolate mousse.

Ask for the ☞ trail map to the Cascades, one of the most satisfying hikes in the area. Even driving these lovely hills is a rewarding pleasure.

How to get there: From I-64 take Route 220 North to Warm Springs. In the village turn left on Route 619 and right on Main Street at the deadend. The inn is on the right in less than a block. Closest airport is at the Homestead.

olive Metcalf

L'Auberge Provençale
White Post, Virginia
22663

Innkeepers: Alain and Celeste Borel
Telephone: 703-837-1375
Rooms: 4, all with private bath.
Rates: $85, double occupancy; $75, single; EPB. Well-behaved children over age 10 welcome.
Open: All year. Restaurant closes January through mid-February, and Tuesdays. Breakfast for guests, dinner, Sunday brunch, bar.
Facilities & Activities: White Post Restorations tour, Millwood, a restored mill, antique shops, Blandy Farm, an experimental plant and tree farm, Blue Ridge Hunt Clubs, Point to Point Races, and Winchester Apple Blossom Festival.

White Post, Virginia, population 200, has a white post marked by George Washington for surveying. On a hillock outside of town is L'Auberge Provençale, where country inn connoisseurs take their appetites for fine food in a friendly setting.

Alain Borel is a fourth-generation chef from Avignon. He and Celeste, both young but experienced restaurateurs, sold their Key West business and were flying their small

274

plane to Colorado when they stopped in Virginia. They were drawn by the state's beauty and tranquility. After a search they found their 19th-century stone farmhouse and became its restorers.

From the herb garden Alain and Celeste gather their own spices. From nearby farmers they've nurtured a market for ☞ quail, partridge, and lamb, and in Washington, D.C., they shop for fresh seafood. Alain's preparations are influenced by his provencale background. Do try the soupe de poisson provençale followed by fresh salmon with sauce provençale.

In the dining room hangs a Bernard Buffet painting of a castle in France, a gift from Alain's father. On the next wall is a poster of the same castle. It's a rare castle because it was built by a woman and has four rooms. Alain and Celeste recently went to France, saw the castle, and, of course, toured French inns.

The ☞ rooms are country fresh with Normandy-print wallpapers, white eyelet spreads during summer, wicker, and antiques. Each one is charming, different, and spotless. Out the back windows are 300 cows for company.

White Post might be small but it has another important distinction, ☞ White Post Restorations where connoisseurs take their classic cars for restoration. If your Dusseldorf is looking shabby or you've just purchased another 1937 Cord and you need the best of everything for it, you come here. A tour can be arranged. A local man, Billy Thompson, began this quality shop in 1940. It's recognized worldwide for its quality. It has a nickel Coke machine. How can one town be so lucky?

How to get there: From the junction of Routes 50 and 340, proceed south on Route 340 one mile to the inn. Fly-in, Winchester Airport.

olive Metcalf

The Williamsburg Inn
Colonial Houses
Williamsburg, Virginia
23187

Innkeeper: Bruce P. Hearn
Telephone: 804-229-1000
Rooms: 82, in 26 houses.
Rates: Complete house for 2 to 8 people, $175 to $395, per day, EP.
   Request package plans. Children welcome.
Open: All year. Breakfast, lunch, afternoon tea, dinner, bar in
   nearby tavern and inn.
Facilities & Activities: All facilities of the Williamsburg Inn: golf,
   swimming pools, parlors, Sunday recitals, Christmas yule log
   ceremonies. Colonial Williamsburg.

In the heart of Colonial Williamsburg are tiny houses.
They are named for the former owners or for their uses. One
is so small it's only one room and is called the Lightfoot
Laundry. Another is Peter Hays' Kitchen.

They are charming comfortable places near the ☛ historic district and the archeological dig. You may step out the
door of your home to see a shepherdess and her flock going
down the street or hear the sounds of guinea hens in the yard

276

next door. In Williamsburg, where authenticity is the by-word, colonial life is 🖝 nurtured and made a modern pleasure.

The houses are decorated with curtains made from colonial patterns and filled with furniture that are reproductions and naturally worn like mine. Wooden window blinds are hung at the windows and upstairs the latch doors on the closets remind me it's hard to improve on some old but good inventions.

The Orell House has been so well preserved that it's been repaired back into its original state. It was here that the prime minister of Italy stayed when he came to town. You don't have to be a prime minister or even a cabinet member to stay here, but if they're holding an economic summit as they did in 1983, it helps.

Across the street is the Lewis House. It's a lovely reproduction and has a brick patio with a small garden in the back surrounded by a low picket fence.

Families and friends usually share the houses. One family has spent the last sixteen Christmas holidays in their favorite tiny home here.

When you stay in the Colonial Houses you eat in the old taverns and the Williamsburg Inn. Everything is within walking distance. The Regency Dining Room is where we went. My husband felt underdressed without his bow tie at lunch. When his eggs Benedict arrived on a thick bed of fresh crabmeat he forgot about the tie and commended the chef. The 🖝 veal marsala was authoritatively flavored in wine and sprinkled with large mushrooms. The Black Forest cake was a visual spectacle. The view of the golf course is lush and relaxing.

How to get there: Directions given by the inn. Fly-in, Williamsburg Airport.

☙

B: *Colonial Williamsburg is intriguing. You relive the past.*

Olive Metcalf

Rodes Farm Inn
Wintergreen, Virginia
22938

Innkeeper: Marguerite Wade
Telephone: 800-325-2200, 804-325-2200 (This is the Wintergreen
  telephone. Ask for houses at Rodes Farm.)
Rooms: A 3-bedroom, 2 bath, house that converts to 1-bedroom for a
  couple. Other houses available through Marguerite (ask for
  Ext. 813).
Rates: $202 per night for entire house; $120 per night for double
  occupancy; EP. Request brochure with package rates from
  Wintergreen. Children welcome.
Open: All year. Breakfast, lunch, dinner, beer and wine. No BYOB
  in restaurant.
Facilities & Activities: Horseback riding, swimming pool, tennis
  courts, & hiking. Ski area, golf course, mountain hiking trails,
  and seasonal holiday events at Wintergreen Resort, 15 minutes
  away.

   Imagine a pretty brick farmhouse with a wooden porch
swing. It's noontime and the bees are buzzing the lilac bush
and the early summer flowers. Down the hill is the stable and
a small cluster of houses where guests stay. You catch the

inviting aroma of 🖝 barbecue sandwiches and banana pudding. This is Rodes Farm Inn.

Marguerite Wade greets you with a warm smile, as if she has known you for years. As she seats you in one of the four petite dining rooms you'll pass the sign that reads: "Down Home Cooking, Prepared with Love."

This is a wholesome 🖝 family inn, that also welcomes romantically inclined couples, and singles who need a break from the fast lane to country lanes.

You stay in the small houses a short walk from the farm restaurant. They were built in 1978 and are natural wood and furnished with antiques and fresh quilts and country curtains. As a guest at Rodes Inn, which is in the valley, you're entitled to use all the facilities of Wintergreen Resort that spans the nearby mountaintop. It's a fifteen-minute drive away.

The Rodes Farm Restaurant originated as a girls' school in the mid-1850s, but reverted back to a family home for the Rodes family. Miss Ethel Rodes was a favorite teacher of Marguerite's. Marguerite was a bus driver when the ecologically minded Wintergreen Corporation came to the area and began the Wintergreen Resort. Marguerite liked them, and one afternoon she took them lunch. They were so impressed with her delicious cooking that they asked her to turn Rodes Farm into a restaurant. That was over ten years ago.

On Sundays you sit down at your private table to heaping plates of fried chicken, country ham, creamed potatoes, fresh green beans, corn, homemade biscuits, and cherry cobbler, all served family style. It's a true American country Sunday dinner.

How to get there: From I-64 take the Crozet exit, go west on Route 250 to Route 6 East, and turn left. Proceed 8.7 miles to Route 151 South. Proceed on 151 one mile to the inn's sign.

Trillium House
Wintergreen, Virginia
22958

Innkeepers: Ed and Betty Dinwiddie
Telephone: 804-325-9126
Rooms: 12, including 2 suites, all with private bath.
Rates: $80 double occupancy; $60, single; $35, per person for triple; $120, suite; EPB.
Open: All year. Closes 2 weeks for "mud week" in April. Call. Dinner by reservation. Full Virginia ABC license.
Facilities & Activities: All the privileges of Wintergreen Mountain: skiing, nature trails, swimming, golfing, tennis, horseback riding, picnicking, 16-acre lake for boating and fishing, hot tub, and whirlpool spa. 5,550 acres of mountains and valleys. Monticello, Ash Lawn, Woodrow Wilson Birthplace, antiquing, universities.

Trillium House is a stunning, brand new, twelve-room inn built by Ed and Betty on the top of Wintergreen Mountain. In the spring pink and yellow trillium flowers surround the yellow pine inn, in winter it's frosted with snow. A brief walk down the hill puts you on the ☛ ski slopes. A walk up the hill and you're on the golf course.

The entrance is a pair of double glass doors. Overhead is

the ☞ exquisite Jefferson Palladian window. You enter a spacious sunny living room where three golden pipe organs are mounted on the white chimney. The chimney reaches twenty-two feet to the ceiling and is the flue for the wood-burning stove that you can circle on oriental carpets. On the balcony above is the well-stocked library. The sun shines in from every direction.

In an alcove behind the chimney is a big screen television and a collection of movies. There are occasions when guests like to watch a favorite late movie on a winter night. The inn has the ☞ niftiest bar. Order something and you'll see it appear. Very clever.

The rooms have contemporary bedding. One room holds a child's desk that belonged to Betty's grandfather. Very comfortable here.

In the dining room hangs a collection of ☞ Hans Christian Andersen plates that depict fairy tales. They belong in this dream of a woodland inn come true. Guests dine on Betty's "traditional American" cooking. She likes "favorite recipes," and if you are the first to make a reservation, you can even make a request.

Ed and Betty are well organized, so they can relax and enjoy your visit. They make you feel like part of the family, and some weekends the family grows to include the college-age Dinwiddies who are inn assistants between semesters.

Trillium House is a year-round destination inn. Skiing in the winter, golf, tennis, swimming and hiking. Ed recommends the triptych guidebook with twenty miles of hiking trails. This is a wildflower paradise and bird watchers are as happy as larks here.

How to get there: Directions sent with enclosed parking sticker when reservations are made.

Numbers on map refer to towns numbered
on index on opposite page

West Virginia

Olive Metcalf

The Country Inn
Berkeley Springs, West Virginia
25411

Innkeeper: William North
Telephone: 304-258-2210
Rooms: 35, 20 with private bath; 2 suites.
Rates: $40 to $75, double occupancy, EP. Two-night minimum stay
   on holiday weekends. Children welcome. Pets permitted.
Open: All year. Breakfast, lunch, dinner, bar.
Facilities & Activities: Art gallery. Hot baths and public swimming
   pool adjacent. State park. Hiking, antiquing, swimming, golf-
   ing.

The Country Inn is in town. It's adjacent to the mineral
springs and Roman baths of Berkeley Springs. Members of
warring Indians laid down their weapons and came here for
peace and tranquility. Things haven't changed. People still
come for the same reason.
   The Country Inn actually glows from all the attention it
receives from Innkeeper William North. I think he'd whistle
a happy tune all day if he didn't think it might disturb the
guests. William is a long-time inn lover. His thesis in hotel
school at Cornell University was on country inns. What a
smart man.

There's another reason the inn is so well cared for. I found Mr. Barker, the owner, with a screwdriver repairing a light in one of the rooms. He's an art lover who began his print collection years ago the way he bought the inn, by accident.

Mr. Barker's prints are wonderful. Beautiful black and white engravings hang in the bar. These are the ones that Mr. Barker discovered in an antique shop one day. He bought them as a bundle and that started him on his way to an interest he obviously enjoys. Everyone used to ask if they could buy his prints. Finally he opened an art gallery in the inn.

The rooms are decorated with brass beds which Mr. North says are really iron, steel, and brass built by a local craftsman. Whatever they are made from they look good in the rooms, and so do the different colors of wallpaper.

The Country Garden is a sunny plant-filled indoor dining room with a small sunken dance floor. Saturday night this is the place to trot out your foxtrot. It's also the place to dine. The lunch I had here with good friends amidst hundreds of healthy plants is a cherished memory. I ate creamed turkey and gravy over a flaky hot biscuit. My friends thought their liver and onions the tenderest and tastiest possible. We all lingered over the marvelous Bavarian cheesecake and cups of hot mocha.

On the way back to the gallery after lunch I paused in the lobby, where a large woodburning stove heats the entire room and saw the sign: "Tarry Long at Rest and Table, Haste ye Back if ye are able."

How to get there: From I-81 take Route 522 North to Berkeley Springs. The inn is just before the town square. Fly-in, Potomac Air Park in Hancock.

B: *You care for a* *cared-for inn.*

olive Metcalf

Mountain Village Inn & Cabin Lodge
Horseshoe Run, West Virginia
26769

Innkeepers: Bill and Sheila Reeves
Telephone: 304-735-6344
Rooms: 3 in inn, 3 in lodge, 2 baths.
Rates: $45, per person, double occupancy; $55, single; MAP. Children welcome. No credit cards.
Open: May through October, reservations necessary. Breakfast, dinner, alcoholic beverages.
Facilities & Activities: Lakefront inn with swimming and boating. Downhill and cross-country skiing. Canaan Valley, Blackwater Falls State Park, Alpine Lake, Deep Creek Lake, Swallow Falls, each a 25-mile drive. The "Smallest Church in 46 States" is across the road.

On the shores of pretty Silver Lake, 3,000 feet up in the ravishingly beautiful Allegheny Mountains, is a small inn. The beavers, ducks, and trout are only a whisper away. You'll find the ☞ peace and contentment of nature when you arrive. It's in the tiniest of villages.

This is an inviting wooden and ☞ warmly rustic inn.

It's a former small resort that dates from the 1930s. Look at the fascinating postcards from that time. The growth of the trees is phenomenal. Across the lake are tamaracks, very rare in these woods. Innkeeper, Bill, says they amaze the scientists who love to explore the unusual flowers and plants at these elevations. Closer to the inn is a huge beaver dam. At this altitude the most bothersome species of insects are a rarity, so you'll delight in the great outdoors.

With Sheila's eye for decorator touches in colors and Bill's builder's talents they've created an inn with a bright homey atmosphere. The rooms are petite and each has a ☞ lake view. The fresh quilting is charming. You can step outside and settle into a handmade rocker.

Dinner is served at lake side on the covered patio or in the intimate dining room. Bill prepares scallops, steaks, chops, and ham. Dinner begins on a satisfying note with homemade rolls and a tangy ☞ apple butter that's especially tasty. The seafood is shipped daily up to the mountains. The shrimp scampi is toothsome and juicy, made with plump fresh shrimp. Heaping servings here and no fried foods. Come breakfast and Bill's buckwheat pancakes whet your appetite anew.

You'll find myriads of business cards in the hallway. It's a custom that began serendipitously. Now guests like to add theirs. Mine is on the lower left. Was that yours above it?

How to get there: From Route 50 take Route 24 south to Horseshoe Run. The inn is on the left after the church. Fly-in, Garrett County Airport, Deep Creek Lake.

olive Metcalf

General Lewis Inn
Lewisburg, West Virginia
24901

Innkeeper: John McIlhenny
Telephone: 304-645-2600
Rooms: 24, all with private bath; 2 suites.
Rates: $35 to $55, single or double occupancy; $60, suite; EP. Children and pets welcome.
Open: All year. Restaurant closes Christmas Day. Breakfast, lunch, dinner, wine, beer, and cocktails.
Facilities & Activities: Historic walk through Lewisburg, August State Fair in Fairlea, golf at Greenbriar Hotel 7 miles, Pearl S. Buck's Birthplace 32 miles, hiking and fishing in mountain parks.

You register at a desk that's over 200 years old and see spinning wheels, stereoscopes, tools, kitchen utensils, and a myriad of antiques before you even reach the stairs to your room. In every room are substantial wooden beds, antiques, and pretty rose and print wallpapers. A rocker or petite chair sits invitingly to one side of the room. The inn probably has more antiques than an antique emporium.

The General Lewis is an ☞ old-fashioned kind of place with big white pillars and a carriage out front. A few hundred

288

yards from Lewisburg's main street, the inn exudes a secure and serene sense of the perfect country haven in town.

Lewisburg deserves its own accolades. At the desk request "A Walking Tour of Historic Lewisburg," and you'll find fifty-four historic buildings within walking distance of the inn.

The General Lewis was a home built in 1834 that later became an inn. A magazine article dating from 1931 shows the inn ☞ favorably unchanged over the years. It's warm, homey, and has a large, comfortable common room from which it's very difficult to move once you're ensconced before the fireplace.

If you come for that big event, the West Virginia State Fair in nearby Fairlea, you're going to have a busy holiday seeing the prize farm animals, blue ribbon cakes, and country entertainers. Off-season touring can be just as much fun. Arrive here on a wintery snowy day and a warm fire rewards you for the journey.

Dinner is ☞ good old-fashioned cooking. The ham is salt cured, the chicken southern fried, and the pork chops juicy and tender and served with baked apples. Or perhaps you'd prefer a T-bone or meat loaf in puff pastry that comes with brandied tomato-mushroom sauce. For dessert the cobblers are served piping hot with a dip of vanilla ice cream.

In the morning over ☞ fresh biscuits served with brimming pots of apple butter, preserves, and honey, and hot coffee, you'll notice many local businessmen enjoying the same breakfast. There are friendly, softly spoken greetings. Why is it that in a good inn everyone is so polite?

How to get there: From I-64 take Route 219 South to Lewisburg. In town turn east (left) on Route 60 and go 2 blocks to the inn. Fly-in, Greenbriar Valley Airport.

Olive Metcalf

Smoke Hole Lodge
Petersburg, West Virginia
26847

Innkeeper: Edward W. Stifel, III
Telephone: None. Write: P.O. Box 953, Petersburg, WV 26847.
Rooms: 5, one with private bath; 2 dorms. (4 shared baths total.)
Children welcome. No charge if under four. Pets allowed.
Rates: $45 per person per night; children 5 to 11, $35 per night; AP.
Charge for horseback riding. Two-night minimum.
Open: Mid-April through October. Breakfast, lunch, dinner. BYOB.
Facilities & Activities: 1,500 acre to explore. Inner-tubing, fishing,
hiking, horseback riding, swimming, and bird watching. Short
trail ride and overnights can be arranged, but bring tents.
Canoe rides from Petersburg to lodge can be organized
through outfitters in town.

No electricity, no telephones, and you'll never find the
place. That's part of its remote charm. You have to write to
get reservations. It's small, yet it's huge. You have ☞ 1,500
acres of private land to roam. It's low key, primitive, and
wildly ☞ beautiful alongside the clear flowing South Branch
of the Potomac River.

Ed meets you in town, either at the airport or Alt's
Country Grocery. You proceed by four-wheel drive an hour

and twenty minutes through spectacular mountain scenery. Unless you hire a helicopter, or travel by canoe, this is the only way in or out. It's a 🖝 ride you'll not forget.

Along the way Ed narrates stories about the cabins you'll pass. It's a sampling of Ed's good-humored Smoke Hole House Tour. You might see deer or a mother turkey and her brood as we did. The farther into the mountains we went the more I appreciated this way of life.

The lodge began in 1876 as a schoolhouse. Additions consistent with the original log structure have been made. The rooms are petite and plain. The hallway is richly pine paneled and hung with kerosene lanterns for lights. The stone fireplace and casual furnishings in the common room are "down home" and comfortable. The front porch has plenty of rocking chairs to go around.

The food is expertly prepared on a woodburning stove with propane gas burners used for back-up. It's 🖝 prodigiously delicious. Cook Pete welcomes you into his domain, shows you where the cola is, and lets you snack between meals from the larder. After his bountiful meals of chicken and dumplings, or a roast, fresh vegetables, and homemade breads you won't need in-between snacks, but you'll probably return for a visit.

The seclusion, the stunning mountain beauty, the cool clear swimming pools in the river, and the inspiring ridge top trail rides have the most relaxing influence. I'd forgotten the pleasure of natural silence in the wilderness.

How to get there: Request a brochure. Ed sends you directions about how and where to meet him. You request a date and wait to hear if it's available. Recommended fly-in to Petersburg Airport

olive Metcalf

Bavarian Inn & Lodge
Shepherdstown, West Virginia
25443

Innkeepers: Erwin and Carol Asam
Telephone: 304-876-2551
Rooms: 42, all with private bath.
Rates: $53 to $95, double occupancy, EP. Children welcome.
Open: All year. Breakfast, lunch, dinner, bar.
Facilities & Activities: Historic Shepherdstown is the oldest town in
    West Virginia. C & O Towpath located across the river, Harpers
    Ferry, Antietam Battlefield, Charlestown Races, Summit Point
    Raceway, Berkeley Springs, Theatre productions at Old Opera
    House in Charlestown, white-water rafting, and other sports.

The inn is a gray stone mansion that overlooks the tree-
lined bend of the Potomac River. Inside the wooden floors
shine and the white and blue tablecloths are in spotless
order. During the summer the stone veranda with the ☛
lovely view is filled with dinner parties, and during the winter
the scene shifts to in front of the dining room fireplaces. ☛
This is a four-star restaurant and inn.

Impeccably dressed in a suit, Innkeeper Asam personally greets his guests as they arrive. He is himself a chef who
began under a master chef in Munich at the age of thirteen.

At the inn he has a Swiss chef, Thomas Hess; under him are two sous-chefs and two cooks. With all these minds in the kitchen, the specials change often.

The sauerbraten soaks in a pungent marinade that gives a delightfully tangy aroma before it's laid out to dry in preparation for cooking. The Bavarian dishes include Wiener Schnitzel, the Schweinbraten, and Bayriche Bratwurst along with dumplings. Carol Asam's apple strudel has a luscious crust, and her velvety chocolate Black Forest cake is a must for chocoholics. You're in a German settlement and should think German food.

There are three rooms in the stone inn. The other rooms are in new modern chalets. They are large and most have canopied beds. The honeymoon suites in the chalets have 🖝 sunken jacuzzis in the tower rooms and are surrounded by stained glass windows. The other rooms in the chalet have river views and balconies. The hand-painted flowers are by a local artist, and the wallpapers are tasteful subtle flowers chosen by the Asams. The night you arrive a tiny Swiss chocolate is laid at the bedside.

There's a pretty little gift shop with imported mugs.

The main street of Shepherdstown is called German Street and the 🖝 May and October festivals are rousing occasions.

How to get there: From I-81 take Exit 16 East to Martinsburg, then Route 45 to Shepherdstown. In town turn left onto Route 480 to the Potomac River Bridge. The inn is on the left.

⧖

B: *There's nothing like a German innkeeper and his wife and good food to make an inn a destination.*

olive Metcalf

The Wells Inn
Sistersville, West Virginia
26175

Innkeeper: Helene Kurtz
Telephone: 304-652-3111
Rooms: 31, all with private bath; 5 suites.
Rates: $42 to $45, double occupancy; $23 to $34, single; EP. Children welcome.
Open: All year. Breakfast, lunch, dinner, bar.
Facilities & Activities: Guest privileges at 9-hole golf course. Public park, tennis courts, glass factories, and outlet stores, nearby, boating on Ohio River, skiing, historic Mound's sites in Moundsville, Oil and Gas Festival in September.

There's a sprightly quality to this Victorian inn. It might be the slightly gaudy colors, or the pace of life, or the cheerful innkeeper herself. I'll bet it's all three. Coming here puts you in a good mood.

A ☞ memorabilia case in the lobby depicts a lively past. A lady's dance card, invitations to hotel balls, elegant dinner menus, and fascinating newspaper clippings about "The most successful event in the history of the city," the opening of the Wells Hotel during the gas and oil boom days. The year was 1894.

Ephraim Wells, who built the inn, still lives here in ghostly form, explains Helene. He's a friendly ghost, and guests mention his conveniently closing doors and kitchen workers have overheard him in their midst. He has no favorite spot. He prefers to move about the inn in typical innkeeper fashion. Ephraim's portrait hangs in the parlour opposite the grandfather clock that softly chimes the hour.

The opulent dining room has a gold ceiling and red and pink wallpaper with green velvet chairs. The windows are long and narrow, a reminder one came here to be seen, not to see. You can imagine the swish of the elegant gowns that breezed through beside black-coated gentlemen.

In more casual clothing we ordered crunchy fried chicken and pork chops with ☞ home fries, followed by Lee's chocolate surprise, a multilayered affair of chocolate custard and whipped cream.

The rooms have brass beds and plenty of lights. We had the original tin roof and a pretty tiled fireplace.

In the Derrick Room basement bar hang photographs from the early hotel days. The town's past is the story of overnight millionaires and booming success. The Oil and Gas Festival in September is probably a little like those old days. Off season, the pace is peaceful and quiet.

How to get there: From I-70 take Route 2 South along the Ohio to Sistersville. In town turn left on Charles Street and go one block to the inn on the right.

❧

B: *Sometimes we need to slow down and come away to a small-town inn, to leave behind the roar of the city.*

Index

Index

About the author

Brenda Chapin is a mid-Atlantic travel writer whose articles have appeared in the *Washington Post, Ford Magazine, American Way, Chevron, Maryland Magazine,* and others. A resident of Arlington, Virginia, she has traveled extensively in the eastern United States and Europe.

Traveling by car, plane, boat, train, and jeep, Brenda for years has been searching out the old and the new inns in the mid-Atlantic states, from lakeside to mountaintop, from seashore to forest. After staying and eating at inns, talking to innkeepers, and chatting with other guests, Brenda has chosen to recommend here 136 of the 201 inns she has visited.

Other Globe Pequot Books
for your further traveling pleasure

Guide to the Recommended Country Inns of New England,
9th edition
Bed and Breakfast in the Northeast
The Handbook for Beach Strollers from Maine to Cape
Hatteras
Consumer's Guide to Package Travel Around the World
Special Museums of the Northeast
In & Out of Boston with (or without) children
Traveling and Camping in the National Park Areas
• Eastern States • Mid-America • Western States
Guide to Eastern Canada

Daytrips and Budget Vacations in New England
Factory Store Guide to All New York, Pennsylvania, and
New Jersey
Factory Store Guide to All New England
Budget Dining and Lodging in New England

Available at your bookstore or direct from the publisher. For
a free catalogue write: The Globe Pequot Press, Old Chester
Road, Chester, Connecticut 06412.